John Taylor/ **Photography in the Fine Arts**

Volume Eight

The Encyclopedia of

Photography

THE COMPLETE PHOTOGRAPHER:
The Comprehensive Guide and Reference for All Photographers

WILLARD D. MORGAN
General Editor

GREYSTONE PRESS/NEW YORK

Title Page Picture Credits:

Copal Company Limited

Hans Burst/*Zeiss Ikon Photo*

Lou Bernstein

George L. Honeycutt/*Charlotte Observer and News*

The editors wish to express their appreciation for permission to use the color photographs in this volume to the following photographers and organizations:

Jacques Lowe / *Courtesy of De Beers Consolidated Mines, Ltd.*
Fred Lyon / *Sports Illustrated*
Carl Fischer / *RCA Victor Records*
Norman Rothschild
Filippo Accini / *Rollei-Werke*
Barry Hicks / *The British Travel and Holidays Association*
Mort Hecht / *Capitol Records*
Edward Brownrigg / *Popular Photography*
Horn/Griner / *Created for Elizabeth Arden by Trahey/Cadwell*
Ed Hannigan / *U.S. Camera*
Irving Bahrt / *Republic Aviation Corporation*
Sharon Marchant / *Scholastic-Ansco Photography Awards*
A. Kruparz / *Leica Photo*
Hy Peskin / *Sports Illustrated*

Table of Contents | Volume Eight

EXPOSURE

John S. Carroll
Editor, "The Photo-Lab-Index"

[The first step in making a photograph is the exposure of the negative; if this is not correctly done, all the remaining steps will be either difficult or impossible. This article explains the principles of exposing photographic film.]

• *Also see: Copying and Close-up Photography; Exposure (Light) Meters; Exposure with the Zone System; Extension Tubes and Bellows; Films, When and How to Use Them; Filters; Gamma; Incident Light Measurement; Lighting.*

A NEGATIVE IS CORRECTLY EXPOSED when the print from it will correctly reproduce all tones in the scene in their original brightness. However, this ideal is attainable only in a limited number of cases where the scene brightness range lies within the limits of what can be reproduced on the surface of a sheet of white paper.

Thus exposure of a negative for practical purposes always involves some compromise. We are interested in finding not the exact exposure, but the optimum exposure—the exposure which will produce the desired relation of tones in the final print.

Note the use of the word *desired;* it is here that artistry and expressiveness enter into photography, because no two people visualize a picture in quite the same way. The desired relationships of tones will be different for different photographers.

Luckily for the majority of amateurs, the latitude of the photographic process and the limited tone range of many photographic subjects allow a wide variation of exposure; the latitude of the process also provides a margin for error in exposure, development, and printing. Usable negatives will generally result as long as the film is not

A normal exposure preserves the wide range of tones in this photograph of a church in Charleston, S.C. (Photo: F. S. Lincoln)

grossly underexposed nor overexposed.

Underexposure and overexposure are relative terms only. Very often an "incorrectly" exposed negative may produce a print which is more desirable, from the subjective point of view, although all the tones of the subject may not be reproduced in their correct tonal relationships. Such results cannot be obtained by accident, however. These results presuppose a knowledge of the capabilities of the film, careful control of the light reaching it, and a knowledge of the developer to be used.

The first step in making a picture is the exposure of the negative; in order to understand what happens at this stage, we should know something about how films work and how they react to light and the developer.

THE SENSITIVE SILVER HALIDE

It would seem that photographic films should react at once to the tiniest amount of light conceivable and then proceed to add density, step by step for an infinite number of steps, as more and more exposure is given. In theory such an emulsion, if it could be made, would have infinite latitude; it would be impossible to underexpose it or to overexpose it. But you would never be able to take a useful picture on it; it would be incapable of reproducing a pure white or a solid black.

Actual emulsions have a limited range at both ends of the scale. First it takes a certain minimum exposure to produce any effect at all; any amount of light less than this minimum (or "threshold") has no effect on the film. After this point has been reached, increasing exposure produces increased negative density up to a point. This point is reached when all the usable silver in a given area has been exposed. Additional exposure can produce no further result because there is no silver left to expose.

Let us see how practical emulsions work. First, any individual silver grain is either exposed or it is not. There is no such thing as a partly exposed grain. Hence the different tones of a picture are caused not by

light and dark grains, but by areas containing fewer or more grains of completely black silver. Second, any silver grain which has not received its quota of light is normally undevelopable. (Certain developers do affect unexposed grains. The result is called fog; it tends to lower the contrast of the image in an erratic way and is considered undesirable.) Third, the emulsion is a random mixture of grains of various sensitivities. If this were not the case, any exposure above the minimum would blacken the entire film and we could get only black or white tones. Finally, since the mixture of various grains is completely random, it can be studied statistically. There must be a usable and measurable relationship between the light acting on the film and the amount of silver formed in the developer. The study of this relationship is called sensitometry.

ELEMENTARY SENSITOMETRY

To the photographer with little mathematical training, the very sound of the word sensitometry is frightening. It needn't be. We are simply concerned with relationships; $1 + 1 = 2$ expresses a relationship. Four quarts = one gallon expresses a relationship.

More complicated relationships are expressed by plotting a few combinations on paper and then drawing a curve through them which passes the intermediate points. This is known as a graph. In order to understand the exposure-development action of a film, it is necessary to use such a graph.

Suppose we take a piece of film and place it in the developer and hypo without its having been exposed. Assuming we don't have any fog, what we'll get is a perfectly transparent piece of cellulose-ester. The light transmission of this piece of clear plastic is just about 100 percent. Or to look at it another way, it has a transmission of 1.0.

TRANSMISSION MEASUREMENT

Since transmission measurements are relatively easy to make, we could use this method for estimating the amount of silver in the negative image. For instance, if a given area

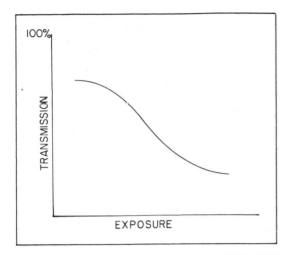

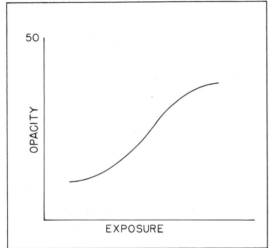

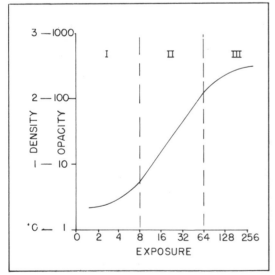

Top: Figure 1. *Graph of negative transmission plotted against exposure.*

Middle: Figure 2. *Graph of negative opacity plotted against exposure. Essentially it is the same curve as in Figure 1, but inverted.*

Bottom: Figure 3. *Graph of density and opacity vs. exposure plotted on logarithmic scales for opacity and exposure.*

transmits only half the light falling on it, we could say it has a transmission of ½ or 50 percent or 0.5. And if it transmits only $^1/_{10}$ of the light, then we could say that it had a transmission of ten percent or 0.1.

Assuming we know how much light was used to expose each area, we could take a piece of film, give it a series of graded exposures, and measure the resulting transmissions. It would be difficult to see any relationship between these numbers, except that more exposure produces less transmission. If a graph is plotted of the whole string of relationships, the result is a curve like that in Figure 1. While such curves are used in the motion-picture industry for certain types of sound tracks, they have little practical value for the still photographer.

OPACITY MEASUREMENT

So we go back to the negative and look for another way to measure the silver deposit. Suppose, instead of transmission, we concern ourselves with the light-stopping power of the silver. This, obviously, is the inverse of transmission, and we use a different scale measuring opacity. On this scale, a transmission of ½ = an opacity of 2, a transmission of $^1/_{10}$ has an opacity of 10, and so on. In plotting the curve again, using opacities instead of transmissions, we get a new curve which looks like that in Figure 2.

Is this really a new curve? Not at all. It is the same curve as in Figure 1, but turned upside down. Transmission is turned upside down to get opacity, that is, ½ became $^2/_1$.

But this curve represents only a relationship (exposure vs. opacity) which is not a linear one. Nor is it a useful one in understanding the process. We are measuring the wrong quantity.

The silver emulsion contains grains of varying sensitivities randomly distributed. Thus a given exposure should produce a given quantity of silver, not a given light-stopping power. Light-stopping power or transmission is easy to measure without damage to the negative, whereas to measure the quantity of silver, we'd have to

resort to chemical analysis and destroy the image in the process.

The work of Hurter and Driffield is useful. They determined that the light-stopping power of a silver deposit is related to the amount of silver in the following way:

Quantity
of silver   1 2 3 4 5 6 7
Opacity   2 4 8 16 32 64 128

This is not difficult to understand if we imagine that silver is present in a number of layers, all alike, each having an opacity of, say 2 (or transmission of ½). Now consider one layer of silver having an opacity of 2; the amount of light coming through it is ½ of what fell upon it. Add a second layer. The second does not know that it is already receiving only half the original light; it simply transmits ½ of what it receives. But ½ × ½ = ¼ and so what appears after two layers is ¼ of the original light—or an opacity of 4. Add a third layer; it transmits ½ of the light falling on it, which in turn is ¼ of the original light. So the light emerging is ¼ × ½ = $^1/_8$ of the original light, and the three layers combined have an opacity of 8.

Suppose we go back to the original example and try plotting a new graph, but this time using a special paper which is laid out in the scale 1,2,4,8,16,32,64, for both exposure and opacity. We get a new curve which looks like the one in Figure 3. This is much better than the others for one major reason: a good part of the curve (region II) is a straight line, and there is a usable, linear relationship between exposure and opacity. But it is hard to work with because of the scale used. It is difficult to determine intermediate values or to see what the relationship really is.

Why not just plot the quantity of silver rather than the opacity? Because we are measuring this only indirectly and don't really know the quantity of silver present. However, there is a relationship between the two, already expressed in the list of numbers.

In this arrangement of numbers,
$A = 0$ 1 2 3 4 5 6 7 8 9
$B = 1$ 2 4 8 16 32 64 128 256 512
the relationship is not obvious at

A short range of tones in this subject is a result of strong sidelight. It would be very difficult to hold detail in the black shadows and still expose for the highlights. (Photo: Massar / Jones & Laughlin Steel Corp.)

first. However, we can see that the numbers in B are successively doubled—that is, each is the preceding one multiplied by two. This is called a geometric progression. But we want to know what the series of numbers called A represents. Without further discussion, we can see that it represents the number of times 1 has been multiplied by 2 to reach the given number in B. That is, if 1 is not multiplied by 2 at all (A=0) it is simply 1. If 1 is multiplied by 2 just once, then A=1 and B=2. If we multiply by 2 twice—$1 \times 2 \times 2 = 4$, A is 2 and B is 4. Multiplying 3 times, that is, $1 \times 2 \times 2 \times 2 = 8$, hence A=3 and B=8.

LOGARITHMS

When two scales of numbers are related in this way—one scale derived by multiplying 1 by a given

factor a certain number of times—then the number of times the multiplication is done is called the logarithm of the final number, and the multiplier itself is called the base of the system of logarithms in question. In the case above, B is a series of numbers, A is the corresponding logarithm scale, and the base of this series is 2, because each number was derived by multiplying the previous one by 2. Expressed symbolically:

$$A = \log_2 B.$$

Different systems use different bases—some use 2, and some use 10. Once we have decided on the base, the relationship is fixed. We use a new term, density, and define it:

$$\text{Density} = \log_{10} \text{Opacity}.$$

Having done this, we build a new meter scaled in densities, and have no further need for logarithms.

Except in the laboratory, it is not necessary to plot the exposure logarithmically. It is just as well to use the geometric scale at the bottom of the paper and continue to plot the actual exposures. It will show a relationship which we are trying to find. At the same time, we are actually plotting the logarithm of the exposure though we aren't using logarithmic numbers.

Now note the density scale in Figure 3. If we examine the middle of the curve, where it is essentially straight, we can find from the graph that exposures of 8,16,32 and 64 seconds produce densities of .5, 1.0, 1.5, and 2.0. If doubled, they show the simple relationship 1,2,3,4. What we have found here is that equal multiples of exposure produce equal differences of density.

The rest of the curve is useful, too, in showing how film actually works. The lower, curved section called the "toe" shows graphically that nothing occurs until the expo-

Exposure in this picture was made to gain some detail in the snow while allowing dark areas to go black. If a straight exposure meter reading were taken from the camera position, it would have indicated a very short exposure that may not have given the best result. (Photo: Rev. B. T. Lukaszewski / Newspaper National Snapshot Awards)

sure has reached a certain minimum level, or threshold. Then a slow rise demonstrates that only a few, very sensitive grains are at first involved and, as exposure increases, more and more silver grains are available to produce density. The middle or straight-line section of the curve represents the area of correct exposure. Finally, there is region III of the curve, where it begins to bend downward again, showing that equal multiples of exposure are no longer producing equal additions of density. This is because most of the silver grains have been used up, and there is not enough left to continue the process.

FILM SPEED MEASUREMENTS

Having exposed a sample of film to an arbitrary but known series of exposures, and having measured the resulting densities, a curve like the one shown can be plotted for any film. From this curve, by various methods, the speed of the film is determined.

The first practical system was devised by Hurter and Driffield. They took the straight-line portion of the curve, extended it down to the base, and read the exposure value at this point. Since faster films will require less exposure, using this number directly would result in a backward scale, where high numbers represent lower speed. So they established the following relationship

$$H\&D \ Speed = \frac{34}{e}$$

which turned the numbers the right way. The factor of 34 was chosen simply to fit the exposure table they were devising. Later users of the system devised different numbers. English film makers used a factor of ten here, and got correspondingly different numbers. The result is that H&D speeds are not of much use unless you know the factor, as one manufacturer's H&D speed will differ from another's by a large and variable amount. The system had one advantage: the base-line point, known as the inertia, varied very little with changes in development, and Hurter and Driffield claimed that the speed of the film was totally unaffected by variation in developing time or gamma.

This, however, is not completely true, especially with modern films developed to low gammas in relatively weak developers. The theory did nonetheless hold up quite well for films of Hurter and Driffield's time, developed in their special pyro developer.

When the Weston meter was introduced, a new method of film-speed rating came with it. This was based on finding a point on the straight line where the density was just equal to the gamma to which the film had been developed. A line was dropped from this point to the base to find the corresponding exposure. The film speed was found from this exposure point by the relationship

$$Weston \ Speed = \frac{4}{e}$$

which had the advantage of taking the development of the film into account. However, it tended to place the exposure high on the curve and did not correspond to practical photography where a good part of the toe is used in portraying shadow details.

When the ASA system was devised, it used a similar method, but the measuring point was taken low on the scale so that some of the toe would be included. Such a system would have resulted in a minimum exposure in all cases, but this was negated by providing a safety factor (from two and one half to four times) in setting the final speed number or exposure index. Many photographers, therefore, established personal exposure indexes based on the ASA scale, but doubled or even quadrupled them. A few manufacturers did the same thing with patent-medicine type developers and claimed the "gain" in speed was due to the use of their secret formula. This was nonsense; they were simply eliminating an unnecessary safety factor.

REVISED ASA SYSTEM

Recently the ASA system was revised to almost eliminate the safety factor, and current ASA Speed Tables give figures that are about twice the old ones for the same films. Obviously n o t h i n g has happened to the films; the change simply reflects a desire for thinner negatives which produce better prints with modern films.

Two other changes were made at the same time. The early ASA exposure indexes offered two values for any film; the higher for daylight, the lower for tungsten. This did not indicate any difference in film speed. Rather it reflected the fact that exposure meters did not match the color sensitivity of the film. Modern meter cells now have sensitivity which closely matches that of a modern panchromatic film, and a single speed rating is adequate.

The second change was a numerical one and consisted in offering two speed values for each film. The first was the familiar Exposure Index on an arithmetic scale—that is, a film with a rating of 100 was twice as fast as one of 50. With modern high-speed films, though, these values ran as high as four figures (Kodak Royal-X Panchromatic Film can be exposed at a rating of 1600). This made for crowding on the dial of the smaller exposure meters, and so a second series of numbers was established on a logarithmic basis, according to the following scale:

Exposure Index	Additive Value
3	0
6	1
12	2
25	3
50	4
100	5
200	6
400	7
800	8
1600	9

By now we should be able to recognize that the scale is a logarithmic one. It is also directly related to the EVS system and the so-called APEX system, explained in

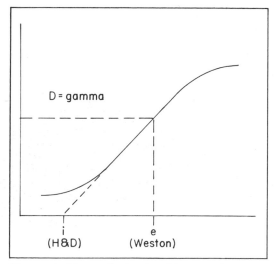

Figure 4. *Two criteria for film speed: the H & D inertia point (i) and the Weston point (e).*

an earlier article of this encyclopedia.

The only other speed system in common use is the German DIN system used in scaling some German exposure meters and cameras. Unfortunately, different manufacturers use somewhat different bases for the DIN measurements, and it is not possible to translate one system directly into the other.

EXPOSURE UNITS

Exposure depends on two factors —the strength of the light and the length of time it is permitted to act on the film. In a camera, each of these factors can be controlled, either separately or in combination.

The strength of the light reaching the film is determined by the lens aperture. The diaphragm scale is marked in a series of numbers: 1, 1.4, 2, 2.8, 4, 5.6, 8, 11, 16, 22, 32. While it may not at first be obvious, this is logarithmic scale again, only this time the multiplying factor is not 2 but $\sqrt{2} = 1.4$. The reason is that the light transmitted by a circular aperture varies with the area of the opening, which in turn is proportional to the square of its diameter. That is, a two-inch diameter lens passes not twice as much light as a one-inch diameter, but four times as much. By using the square-root steps, we have a series of apertures in which each passes just half the amount of light as the preceding one (or double, going the other way). Note, though, that shutter-size restrictions, and

other mechanical reasons sometimes make it necessary to use an odd aperture as the maximum for a given lens. However all succeeding apertures are marked in the standard scale. Thus on an $f/4.7$ lens, the next aperture would still be $f/5.6$ but $f/4.7$ does not transmit twice the light of $f/5.6$. So we must be careful to watch this first step.

A few older European lenses are marked in a different scale: 1.1, 1.6, 2.2, 3.2, 4.5, 6.3, 9, 12.5, 18, 25. Again, each succeeding step is double or half, depending on which way we are going. Again, remember to watch the first step— from $f/3.5$ to $f/4.5$ is not a full stop.

Shutter speeds are usually marked directly in fractional seconds, the mark 25 indicating $1/25$ of a second, 100 representing $1/100$ of a second. Modern shutters also follow a practically logarithmic scale: 1, $\frac{1}{2}$, $1/5$, $1/10$, $1/25$, $1/50$, $1/100$, $1/200$, $1/500$, $1/1000$.

While there are some discrepancies here, it must be remembered that shutter speeds are seldom very accurate, and the latitude of the film is wide enough to take care of small errors. However, this is why it was stressed that we must not waste latitude in carelessness.

Now that we have noted a method for specifying the speed of film, and have a set of numbers for lens apertures and shutter speeds, we are left with only the mechanical problem of measuring the brightness of the subject. It would probably be better if we could measure the actual brightness of the image inside the camera but, except for a few 8 mm home-movie cameras, this has not yet been done on a practical basis. So we measure subject brightness. The meter calculator then registers what lens stop and shutter speed to use to get the right quantity of light on the film. This particular relationship does not concern the photographer at all; it has been worked out by the designer of the meter

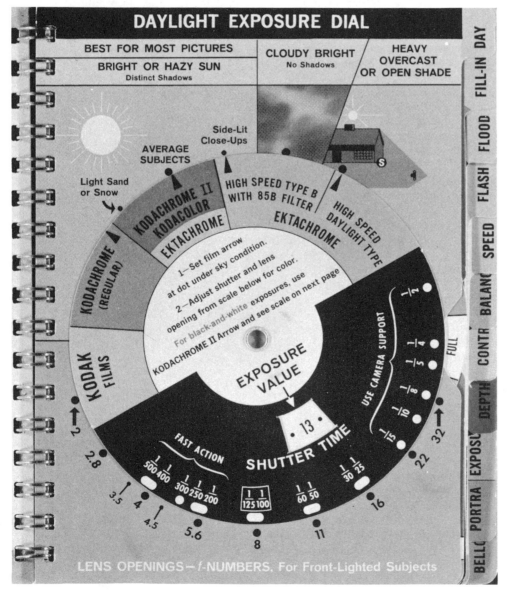

The Kodak Master Photoguide has various calculator dials for determining exposure for daylight, flash, photofloods, filters, copying, close-up, lenses, and other situations. (Copyrighted Kodak booklet, reproduced by permission)

and built into the calculator.

THE EXPOSURE VALUE SYSTEM

For many years photographers have been using the familiar f/stop- and shutter-speed system for translating exposure readings into camera settings. And every beginner has to learn that $1/200$ of a second at $f/5.6$, $1/100$ of a second at $f/8$, $1/50$ of a second at $f/11$, $1/25$ of a second at $f/16$ all represent the same total exposure.

Recently a new system has come into use in which lens apertures and shutter speeds are represented by what seem to be arbitrary numbers. For each shutter speed and for each aperture a number is assigned from the following table:

EV number	Seconds	f-stop
0	1	1
1	½	1.4
2	¼	2
3	$1/8$	2.8
4	$1/15$	4
5	$1/30$	5.6
6	$1/60$	8
7	$1/125$	11
8	$1/250$	16
9	$1/500$	22
10	$1/1000$	32

And as we can see, any shutter speed-aperture combination having the same total, for example 10, produces the same exposure:

Seconds		f-stop	Exposure	
1	+	9	½	at f/22
2	+	8	¼	at f/16
3	+	7	$1/8$	at f/11
4	+	6	$1/15$	at f/8
5	+	5	$1/30$	at f/5.6
6	+	4	$1/60$	at f/4
7	+	3	$1/125$	at f/2.8
8	+	2	$1/250$	at f/2
9	+	1	$1/500$	at f/1.4
10	+	0	$1/1000$	at f/1.0

There are several uses for these number values. Many exposure meters have scales which have EVS (or LVS) numbers. Some cameras have the shutter-speed dial and diaphragm lever interlocked, so once a given aperture-shutter speed combination is set, changing one automatically changes the other to produce a constant exposure.

There are more possibilities in the EV system which will come into being as film manufacturers assign the newer Additive Speed Values to

film. The Additive Speed Value is derived from the ASA speed according to the following table:

Exposure Index	Additive Speed
3	0
6	1
12	2
25	3
50	4
100	5
200	6
400	7
800	8
1600	9
3200	10

These numbers are distinguished from the older values by being printed with a degree mark thus, 4°. They have the advantage of being smaller and easier to handle than the big numbers now coming into use with the faster films, but their major value will be in connection with exposure meters calibrated in light values. For instance, the following scale could be used on an exposure meter calibrated in foot-candles (that is, an incident light meter; by taking the 18 percent scene reflectance into account, a reflected light meter could be given the same scale).

Foot-candles	Light Value
6	0
12	1
25	2
50	3
100	4
200	5
400	6
800	7
1600	8
3200	9
6400	10

If we had a meter calibrated like this, we would need no calculator dial at all. Instead, if we know the speed of the film in additive numbers, we simply add it to the meter reading and the result is the EVS setting for the camera. For instance, suppose we have a film of ASA 100 speed; its Additive Speed is 5. If we get a meter reading of 4, we just add $4+5$ and the exposure is EVS 9. So any lens and shutter setting totaling 9 will produce the required exposure.

This system is a little too widely

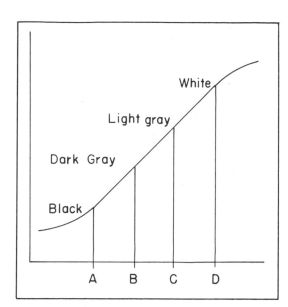

Figure 5. *Latitude of film.*

spaced for color films, but fractional EVS numbers may be used. Thus a film of ASA 80 would have an Additive Speed of 3.5, and the light meter could show half steps between the main ones.

Obviously this system will not be of maximum value until meters are calibrated in Light Values, but it does open the possibility of very small, yet easily readable light meters. They would require nothing but the meter needle itself, running over a 1 to 10 scale. All the user would have to do is take a reading, add the film speed value to the meter reading, and he would have his camera setting.

LATITUDE AND SCENE BRIGHTNESS

So far it has been assumed that the exposure meter is simply used to determine a camera setting for making a picture. But in more advanced work, it has other uses. One is to measure and control the range of the scene so that the negative will print on the desired contrast paper. In addition, you have to realize that there is not necessarily just one correct exposure for any given subject. Usually a number of exposures can be given which will produce negatives that are quite different in appearance; but from which prints can be made that are substantially alike.

To understand this, go back to the curve which was studied at the beginning of this article. Assuming that the correct exposure has been given to a subject which consists of four tones, solid black, dark gray, light gray, and white, it is possible that all of these tones can be accommodated on the straight line of the curve, as in Figure 5. Such a wide range of tones, though, is seldom found in nature. Most likely the average subject would extend only from B to C in the diagram. If the exposure were doubled, the tonal range of the negative would move to the area from C to D. If the exposure were halved, it would move to the area from A to B. In each case, the negative would look quite different, but, since they are all on the straight-line section, the prints would be identical. Thus it could be said that for this film and subject there is an available exposure latitude of four to one.

Obviously then, latitude is dependent to a large extent on subject matter. It is perfectly possible that one photographer would place a given subject in the range from C to D, while another could underexpose four times and get a final print that is exactly the same as the first. There are many cases of subject matter of even narrower range, and some of it would permit an underexposure of as much as ten times. This is equivalent to rating Tri-X Pan at 2500 rather than a more normal 250.

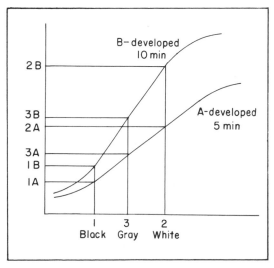

Figure 6. *Effect of development on image contrast and exposure latitude.*

Some unscrupulous persons take advantage of such latitude to make outlandish claims for developers of secret composition. As we have demonstrated, the latitude here is the result of film latitude plus a restricted range of subject brightness. No known developer can produce much more emulsion speed than the basic D-76, and those few which do usually also produce bigger grain and a good deal of fog. In any case, the true gain is usually less than half a stop, and far from the ten times and more claimed for the "wonder" developers.

LATITUDE AND DEVELOPMENT

Development does have some effect on latitude, but it decreases rather than increases it. That is, the higher the gamma, the less the latitude in negative exposure. Increasing development time increases development contrast or gamma (see Gamma). This is represented by the angle of the straight-line part of the curve. The longer we develop, the steeper this angle becomes and this in turn shortens its projection onto the base line.

The practical effect of this is shown in Figure 6. Take a subject which extends from black (1) to white (2) along the baseline. If two negatives are exposed in the same manner, and one is developed for five minutes, the other for ten minutes, we will get curves which appear as in Figure 6. It can be seen that exposures 1 and 2, representing extreme black and extreme white, have resulted in densities 1A and 2A in the five-minute negative, and densities 1B and 2B in the negative developed for ten minutes.

Note the greatly increased distance along the vertical axis, between 1B and 2B, as compared with 1A and 2A. That is, negative B has more contrast than negative A.

But what is of interest here is that curve A has a considerable part of the straight line unused, whereas curve B has almost all the straight-line portion used. Yet both curves are from the same film, the same subject, and had the same exposure. In short, increased development has definitely reduced the latitude of the

film. We cannot overexpose negative B without running into the upper curve.

USE OF GAMMA

"Blocking up" of highlights, in what appeared to be correctly exposed negatives, is a result of overdevelopment. If it is known that development will be very full, the exposure must be kept short, although this will cause some loss of shadow detail.

This effect is useful in practical work. We can, for instance, fit a given negative to a certain contrast paper by choice of the gamma to which we develop. To do this, we must know the brightness range of the subject and the negative density range which can be accommodated on the paper. Then we can determine the gamma to which the negative must be developed so that its scale will just match that of the paper, and the resulting print will have a complete range of tones from black to white.

A practical, nonmathematical way of doing this is described by Ansel Adams in the article Exposure with the Zone System.

Examine what happens to the middle tones during development. Consider point 3, representing a gray tone in the subject. In the two negatives in Figure 6, 3 is represented in the five-minute negative by 3A and in the ten-minute negative by 3B. But note that 3 is just halfway between 1 and 2; 3A is halfway between 1A and 2A; and 3B halfway between 1B and 2B.

Thus the relationship between tones is not changed by variation in development, as long as exposure is correct. If the exposure is wrong, putting negative 1 down on the toe, or 2 on the shoulder, then 3 will be closer to one end than to the other, which will represent a distorted tone rendition. It is, in any case, entirely impossible to transpose tones by development manipulation —that is, to make 3 lighter than 2, or darker than 1 in the final print.

EXPOSURE OF COLOR FILMS

Color-reversal films, like all reversal films, have a somewhat limited latitude compared with

Intentional highlight overexposure brings out the texture of the hair and beard in this photo. Note that the book is used as a reflecting surface to fill in the shadows of the face. Super Ikonta I 6×6 camera with Tessar f/2.8 lens. Agfa F Isopan film exposed for one second at f/3.5. (Photo: Baumeister / Zeiss Ikon)

and rich in the highlights with ample detail. Shadow detail can be augmented by the use of fill lighting or a reflector.

Some confusion seems to exist with the lighting ratio recommended for color films. It is usually stated that portraits should be lighted with a 3:1 ratio of highlight to shadow illumination. This is sometimes erroneously taken to mean that the highest light in the scene, as measured with a reflected-light meter, should not be more than three times as bright as the deepest shadow. This is true only if highlight and shadow are both measured on a surface with uniform reflectance, such as the face. Attempting to secure a 3:1 ratio between the highlight on the face and the shadow on a blue serge suit will result in a hopelessly flat picture, if the ratio can be secured at all with the available lighting equipment.

Actually the 3:1 lighting ratio refers to an incident-light reading, in which we measure the ratio between key light and fill light. The scale of tones which a color film can reproduce is more nearly 30:1, which is about one third the range of most black-and-white films. The purpose of the 3:1 illumination limit, therefore, is merely to avoid having a reflected light ratio greater than 30:1. If, then, an incident-light meter is used correctly, and the lighting ratio is kept at 3:1, no difficulty should be experienced with the average portrait.

Because exposure of color films, particularly reversal films, is more critical than that of black-and-white films, it is best for the photographer to take nothing for granted and to calibrate his own meter, lens, and shutter. A series of test exposures is given, from one full stop over to one full stop under the meter reading, and the finished transparencies are checked. If the best transparency is one which has received more or less exposure than the meter reading, and this occurs consistently, it may be best to adopt a new Film Speed setting for that particular film, when used with that meter, lens, and shutter. This does not mean that the published speed rating is wrong; it simply indicates

black-and-white negative materials. Color negative materials, such as Kodacolor, Agfacolor, FR color, and Ektacolor are somewhat better in this respect, but their latitude is mainly on the overexposure side. In Kodacolor film, particularly, the latitude is limited also by the use of a single color emulsion for both daylight and flash. What is happening in this film is that a good deal of the latitude of the blue-sensitive layer is being used up to permit exposure under both conditions without a filter. The same thing happens with the red-sensitive layer, and only the middle, or green-

sensitive layer, can be considered to have a more or less constant exposure in both light types. However, if Kodacolor is exposed with flash and no filter and with daylight and a number 85C conversion filter, somewhat more latitude is available in exposure because the same part of the curve is being used by all three layers.

In the case of transparency films the error, if any, should be on the underexposure side, since highlight color is usually more important than shadow rendition. The resulting transparency, if underexposed by no more than a half stop, will be full a combined variation in the meter, lens, and shutter which is greater than normal tolerance.

If the best exposure is one-third stop more than recommended, then use the next lower emulsion speed (say 24 instead of 32). If the best exposure is one-third stop less than recommended, then use the next higher emulsion speed (say 40 instead of 32). If the variation is much greater than this, it may be better to have the lens, shutter or exposure meter checked and, if necessary, repaired.

EFFECTIVE APERTURE CORRECTION

The f-stop of any lens is measured by dividing the focal length by the diameter of the lens. The focal length and the lens extension are the same at infinity. At closer distances the extension is always greater than the focal length,

and the resulting f-stop is a higher number, or effectively smaller aperture. This can result in underexposure if not compensated. In 1:1 copying, for example, the bellows is extended to twice its normal length and the resulting effective aperture for a marked f/8 would actually be f/16, an underexposure of two full stops.

A simple calculator is available in the Kodak Master Photoguide, or the following formula can be used to calculate the true f-stop:

$$\text{Effective aperture} = \frac{\text{Marked } f\text{-number} \times \text{Lens-to-Film distance}}{\text{Focal length of lens}}$$

Thus for a 14-inch lens used at a focal distance of 19 inches, the effective aperture at f/16 is:

$$\frac{16 \times 19}{14} = f/22$$

Therefore there is a full stop difference when the bellows is extended from its normal 14 inches to 19 inches. Exposure must be figured on the basis of f/22 when the lens is set at f/16, and the same full stop increase must be used with other marked apertures.

It is not always easy to measure the distance from the lens to the film. However, most cameras have a definite infinity position, and it is easy enough to measure how far the lens has been moved from this setting. Simply add this extension

Sometimes it is impossible to capture details in both highlights and shadows. Here the kitten's face was more important, so the photographer permitted the highlights to be overexposed. Tri-X film exposed at f/2.8 for 1/1000 of a second. (Photo: William Ing / Kodak High School Photo Awards)

to the marked focal length of the lens to get the total extension.

On cameras having rotating focusing mounts, this measurement is more difficult; however, these mounts seldom move far enough to cause difficulty from aperture change. The two-inch lens on a miniature camera, focused at three feet, which is its usual closest point, is still 18 times the focal length away from the subject and will not have any great change of aperture. If extension tubes are used, it is sufficient to add the length of the tube to the marked focal length of the lens to use the above formula.

EXPOSURE IN COPYING

The most important thing in copying is to remember that in most cases the bellows is greatly extended and the effective aperture correction just mentioned must be made. This does not hold true if a supplementary lens is used; here the lens remains at its infinity setting and the marked *f*-stops are unaltered.

Since the usual exposure meter is calibrated for a scene having an average reflectance of 18 percent, it may be used to find proper exposure for copying materials such as photographs, oil paintings, and wash drawings. For line work, where the major part of the original is white paper, the reading will be far too high and underexposure will result. In such cases we may do one of three things:

1) Place a Kodak Gray Card over the copy material before taking the exposure reading. This has a reflectance of 18 percent and will effectively place the exposure at the optimum point for proper rendition of the extreme black-and-white tones of the line original.

2) Use an incident-light meter rather than the reflected-light meter. This will automatically accomplish the same thing as method 1.

3) Take the reading of a sheet of white paper at the subject position and give five times the resulting exposure reading. Or, set the meter to one fifth the normal Exposure Index of the film in question and it will calculate the exposure automatically.

EXPOSURE (LIGHT) METERS

JOHN S. CARROLL
Editor, The "Photo-Lab-Index"
[Supplementing Mr. Carroll's article on Exposure, this article explains the history and operation of the exposure meter. A clear distinction is made between illumination meters and brightness (or "luminance") meters. The component parts of meters are also discussed.]
• *Also see: ASA Speeds, ASA Exposure Indexes, and ASA Additive Speed Values; Exposure; Lighting; Sensitometry.*

FROM THE CAMERA'S EARLIEST DAYS, one of the photographer's major problems has been determining the correct exposure. Prior to the pioneer work of Hurter and Driffield, there was no scientific basis on which a really practical exposure could be devised. This had to wait until they determined that there was a definite speed rating for each emulsion and that a definite amount of light was required to produce a properly exposed negative. Today there is a variety of exposure meters, almost all of which are based on some sort of photoelectric measuring device which actually meters the light and indicates its strength.

TYPES OF EXPOSURE (LIGHT) METERS

Through the years there have been, basically, five ways of measuring the intensity of light, by using:

1. An actinometer
2. An exposure table
3. An extinction meter
4. A photometer
5. A photoelectric exposure meter.

Of these types, the second, fourth, and fifth still survive, but for ease of use the fifth group (photoelectric exposure meters) is the most preferred and widely used. Let us look at each type of measuring device in turn.

Actinometer. This is a device that measures the actinic value or strength of the light for photographic purposes. Visible light may be made up of many colors, but if the film is sensitive only to blue, the photographer is interested in the blue-light component of the light source. One of the earliest actinometers was the gas thermometer

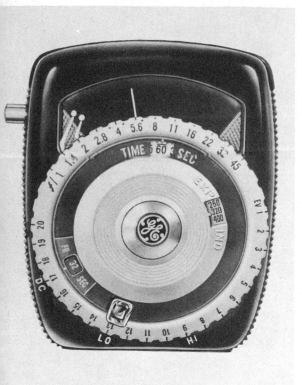

Above: *General Electric Golden Crown PR-3 meter. This photoelectric meter is calibrated in ASA speeds from 0.1 to 20,000 and shows a shutter speed range from 120 to 1/32,000 seconds. Exposure Value settings from 1 to 20; Polaroid Land settings 1 to 9; movie settings 8 to 128 fps.*

Below: *Weston Master IV photoelectric meter. Calibrated in ASA exposure ratings from 0.1 to 16,000. Measures reflected and incident light; movie and Polaroid settings; built-in booster; low and high scale.*

used by Hurter and Driffield, arranged so that when it was exposed to sunlight it would indicate the amount of light present by the heat produced. The disadvantages of this instrument were its bulk and its extreme delicacy.

From a purely photographic standpoint, the actinometer had a major defect, particularly at that period. Since it was actually measuring heat, which is mainly the infrared component of light (to which the emulsions of that period were insensitive), the actinometer could be accurate only when the ratio of infrared rays to visible light was constant. This limited its use to one type of light.

However, the most common actinometer operated somewhat differently. It had a small piece of printing-out paper placed behind a window, alongside of which was placed a printed, constant tint. The paper was exposed to light until it matched the reference tint, and the time taken to darken was noted. The length of time of this reaction was coordinated with a table on the meter which provided the exposure information for the film or plate being used.

This device worked fairly well outdoors, but gave poor readings, or none at all, in tungsten light. It was most accurate with color-blind films that were sensitive only to blue since the printing-out paper was similarly color blind. A serious failing was the length of time necessary to obtain a reading. Its use was obviously out of the question for fast-moving subject matter.

Exposure table. Properly used, exposure tables can be very helpful for the scenes that snapshooters usually photograph. Present exposure tables still use much of the extensive research information propounded during the last century by Hurter and Driffield who laboriously determined the intensity of natural illumination for each hour of the day. This study enabled them to predict the amount of illumination one could expect for any hour of the day and for any month of the year. In addition, they were able to compensate for variations in weather conditions, such as atmospheric haze and clouds.

An exposure table of this kind is economical and compact. It does, however, have the disadvantage of depending upon human judgment in selecting the correct type of scene. In addition, it takes time to adjust and is less useful in artificial light because of the wide variations in indoor lighting.

Extinction meter. The drawback of the two preceding types of exposure-determining devices was that they considered only the light falling on the scene rather than the light which was reflected to the camera. This is an important distinction be-

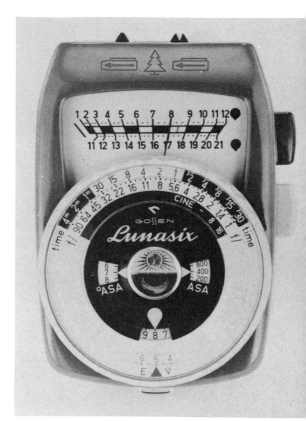

Above: *Sometimes the brightness range of the scene exceeds that of the film. The photographer must decide where there should be detail—in the highlights or shadows. Here the cameraman wanted to record the detail of the construction workmen and was forced to overexpose the sky.* (Photo: Du Pont)

cause a picture consists of a series of tone values which represent different objects in the original scene. Some of these objects are bright and therefore reflect more light, whereas others are dark and reflect less light. Also, the range of reflection of any two scenes may be different.

In an effort to solve this problem, photographers whose cameras were equipped with a groundglass would focus the image on the

Right top: *The Gossen Lunasix cadmium sulfide exposure meter, powered by tiny mercury battery, gives wide range of exposure times from 1/4000 of a second to eight hours. Adjustable for any film speed from ASA 6 to 12,000; thirty-degree acceptance angle; f-stops from 1 to 90; EVS and movie settings.*

Right center: *Honeywell Pentax clip-on photoelectric cadmium sulfide-type meter. ASA speeds 6 to 1600; f-stops, f/1.4 to f/22; couples to shutter speed dial of Pentax cameras.*

Right bottom: *Polaroid Model 625 photoelectric meter. EV settings; ASA equivalent speeds from 12 to 12,000; reads shutter settings directly; clips to camera.*

groundglass and then stop down until they were no longer able to distinguish detail in the shadows of the scene. With a given film and shutter speed, the stopping down indicated what exposure would be necessary to record the shadow detail. This method of determining exposure by extinguishing the image was practical only with groundglass cameras.

A number of devices were marketed at one time or another, based on this principle. These "meters" had an eyepiece through which one viewed, variously, the scene itself, a reduced image of the scene, or some kind of target. While looking at the scene or target, the meter aperture was gradually closed down, much like a lens, until the shadows of the scene, or a marked section of the target, became almost indistinguishable. The required exposure was then read off a scale on the diaphragm ring.

These devices had the advantages of being compact and inexpensive and of reading the light from the scene itself. Their disadvantage was that the fallible human eye had to be used for the final decision. At night, for instance, it takes a greater brightness difference than during the day to be noticed by the eye. And since the eye is being used as a measuring device, the time of day may make a considerable difference in the reading. In addition, individual eye differences will result in different readings. Many of these meters had, instead of a clear glass, a groundglass which would not show detail in the subject to be photographed. Again, under tungsten

light, the eye proves less useful because it is relatively insensitive to red rays which make up the greater part of tungsten illumination.

Photometer. When the advantages of measuring the brightness reflected from the subject were fully recognized, the photometer type of exposure meter came into use. The photometer principle involves a comparison of the brightness reflected from the subject with the known brightness of a controllable light source in the meter.

Basically these instruments consist of a barrel containing an eyepiece through which the photographer observes the subject being photographed. In addition it features a small transparent mirror which reflects the image of a small electric lamp into the scene being viewed. The brightness of the lamp is controlled by a rheostat, the dial of which is calibrated in terms of scene brightness.

In use the photographer sights the instrument at the scene and increases the brightness of the lamp filament until it appears brighter than the object being measured. Gradually the brightness of the filament is reduced until it just blends into the object being measured. At this point the shutter speed, diaphragm setting, or both, can be read from the calibrated dial of the rheostat.

The photometer has the distinct advantage of being able to read the brightness of individual objects in the scene, provided they are not too small. When used correctly this type of meter is accurate for all neutral objects.

It has a disadvantage in that the user must acquire a reasonable skill in balancing the brightness of the scene against the brightness of the filament. Furthermore the photographer must recognize the possibility of error, because the color

The brightness of the photographer's hand is similar to that of the subject in indoor photography. This illustration shows the substitute method of exposure reading, when it is more convenient to check with the hand instead of walking to the subject and making a similar reading.

sensitivity of the eye varies with the brightness level being measured.

A serious difficulty with earlier meters of this type was due to the instability of the measuring medium itself. The lamp was operated by batteries and, as the batteries weakened, the rheostat had to be advanced to obtain the same brightness setting or a false reading would result.

In the earlier instruments, calibration was accomplished by a "zero-setting" method. Before using the meter, the operator sighted through it with the objective covered, so no light from the scene could enter. Then the lamp was dimmed down until it was just extinguished. At this point, the "zero" setting of the scale was made. This method had the disadvantage of depending on the sensitivity of the user's eye to determine when the lamp was just extinguished.

One currently available meter of this type, the SEI Photometer, is a combination of photometer and photoelectric meter. It features the same arrangement of matching lamp and mirrors as the older meters but, in addition, contains a small photocell and meter. These are used only to set the basic lamp brightness calibration and are not used in the actual exposure reading. For calibration, it is only necessary to turn on the lamp and rotate a calibrating knob until the meter needle reaches a single mark on the scale. The device then can be sighted much like older types and the result read.

THE PHOTOELECTRIC METER

When the photoelectric cell was made practical, it was realized that by combining the cell with a sensitive indicating instrument, the result would be a means of measuring light with an accuracy heretofore impossible.

There are two schools of thought concerning the proper method of using a photoelectric exposure meter. Some favor measuring incident illumination (foot-candles) and others prefer measuring reflected brightness (candles per square foot).

Beach scenes are similar to snow scenes in that it is easy to miscalculate their exposure. It is advisable to take close or substitute readings instead of over-all ones. Panatomic-X exposed for 1/100 of a second at f/4. (Photo: Edward Lettau)

Illumination meter. The illumination meter enables the photographer to measure the light falling on the subject. This type of meter consists simply of a photoelectric cell connected directly to an indicating instrument which has been calibrated in foot-candles. In general, devices of this kind enable the photographer to point the instrument from the subject position toward the main source of illumination of the scene and arrive at camera settings.

This system of incident-light measurement was used mainly by motion-picture cameramen. Later Don Norwood devised a modified illumination meter in which the light collector was hemispherical, thus picking up light through a 180-degree angle. In use this meter is aimed not at the light sources, but at the camera from the subject position; it thus collects light from all the sources in proportion to the strength of each.

Another incident-light method is the Smethurst highlight method. The photographer measures the light reflected from an artificial highlight (a piece of white paper), assumes this will be the brightest part of the scene, and determines the exposure for this reading.

While there are a number of photographers using this system, it is most successful where the range of illumination of the scene being photographed is kept relatively short. The system cannot be used when photographing a translucent or transparent object such as a stained-glass window or the like.

Brightness meter. The vast majority of exposure meters depend for their operation on the measurement of brightness reflected from the scene. Even though the illumination falling on the scene may be constant, the light reflected to the camera will depend not only on the reflection coefficient of the objects in the scene, but also on whether or not the object is in shadow or in direct light.

To build a brightness meter, it is necessary to limit the angle of view of the photoelectric cell to some value predetermined before calibration. In practice this value should be at least as small as the average camera lens, and preferably slightly smaller.

Most amateurs have a tendency to expose snow scenes incorrectly because they forget to compensate for the bright snow reflections. Under these conditions, it is best to take close readings rather than over-all ones. Plus-X exposed 1/1000 of a second at f/8. (Photo: Jan Brunner)

USING THE BRIGHTNESS METER

There are several ways to use the brightness meter. If it sees the same area as does the camera, the simplest method is to hold it at the camera position and measure the average light reflected from the scene. As long as the scene is not excessively contrasty, the exposure can be determined by the camera-position reading with a high degree of accuracy. This method is used when the meter is built into the camera, especially when the meter operates the lens diaphragm directly.

Another and more accurate method of exposure determination is to take a close-up reading of the darkest object in the scene. Once this reading is known, the photographer can adjust his exposure to give a definite density value on the negative to the darkest object. All of the brighter objects in the scene will be correctly exposed, provided the scene does not exceed the limitations of the film.

Still another way is the substitution method by which the photographer takes a reading of his own hand. In outdoor photography the brightness of the photographer's hand is very similar to that of the subject's face, and all that he is doing is substituting one for the other. This method is not quite accurate for all subject matter. The usual exposure meter is calibrated for a scene having an average reflectance of 18 percent, and the photographer's hand (and in fact most flesh tones) reflects nearly 35 percent of the light. This can cause an error of nearly one full stop. This error can be compensated for by doubling the indicated exposure or by substituting some object other than the photographer's hand. The Kodak Gray Card reflects almost 18 percent of the light and can be considered an accurate substitute for an average scene. A white card also can be used to gain

a reading. It has a reflectance of approximately 90 percent so that the exposure must be lessened by a factor of five. This method of reading is useful in very dim light when the meter needle hardly budges.

Sometimes the effectiveness of the substitution method is questioned, since the distances from the camera, substitute, and object to be photographed are not the same. In theory, as well as in practice, the substitution method is perfectly sound and may be checked by a very simple test. Take a reading from a reasonably large uniform surface, such as the door of an automobile, and then photograph this object close up and from several times that distance with the same camera settings. When the negatives are processed identically, the measured density values on the door panel will be the same.

Because the measurement is one

of brightness, rather than illumination, the results are the same. As long as the area being measured in the scene will result in a discernible area on the negative (as distinguished from a point), its resulting density will be independent of the distance to the camera. This is because the light from any area measured is concentrated on a smaller area of the negative which varies proportionately as the distance between the object and the camera is increased. Thus the camera lens gathers proportionately the same amount of light either close to the door of the car or at a distance.

A little thought will make it quite clear that the practical effect of substitution readings, especially where a calibrated gray card is used, is simply to convert a reflection-type reading into a type of incident-light reading. The gray card acts as a light collector of constant absorption and merely redirects the light, or a fixed percentage of it, into the meter.

HOLDING DISTANCE

In designing exposure meters, it is not always possible to make each instrument see the same area as that viewed by the camera. In order to obtain accurate results, it is sometimes necessary to compensate for difference in view by holding the meter at a distance closer to the object than the camera distance in order to measure the same area that the camera views.

While on the subject of the angle of view of an exposure meter, it might be pointed out that it is difficult to compare exposure meters in the field unless such comparison is made on a relatively large and uniformly illuminated surface, such as a motion-picture screen indoors, an evenly illuminated wall, or a clear north sky.

High and low range. If this type of subject is not used for comparison measurement, it is extremely difficult to get instruments to agree, even in the case of instruments that have two different ranges, the high range and the low range made for high- or low-intensity illumination.

In some cases where the high range is obtained by a baffle placed over the photoelectric cell, the angles of view of the two ranges differ. Suppose you were trying to compare these two ranges using an ordinary light bulb as a source of illumination. With the exposure meter held at a given distance from the light bulb, the bulb itself would include a relatively small percentage of the area as viewed by the broader angle of the low range. On the other hand, with the narrow angle or high range, the bulb would constitute a relatively large percentage of the area and therefore give a relatively higher reading, even though the two ranges read alike on a uniformly illuminated surface.

Another thing to remember is that the low range is there to increase the accuracy in reading the low values at the bottom of the high range. It has the same purpose as the second hand on a watch—to make possible more accurate calculation.

In comparing two ranges, one should set the instrument on a rigid support in front of a uniformly illuminated surface so that it reads at the top mark or full-scale value on the low range. Then close the baffle and it will undoubtedly read the same value on the high range, although at a different position on the scale.

COLOR SENSITIVITY

The photocells used in earlier exposure meters had an excessive sensitivity to the red part of the spectrum. As a result, these meters tended to read too high in tungsten light, and the readings would result in underexposed film. For this reason it was customary to assign two speeds to all films, one for Daylight, and a lower one for Tungsten.

Currently all exposure meters have photocells whose color sensitivity is practically the same as that of a Type B panchromatic film. Their readings are quite accurate in any normal kind of tungsten light as well as in daylight, and for this reason, only a single speed value is

Making a direct reading with the photoelectric meter held near the subject.

being assigned to panchromatic films. However, where a film is lacking in red sensitivity (as in the case of color-blind and ortho films) separate ratings are still being assigned for Tungsten and Daylight.

In the case of color films, the meter will indicate accurately for practically every film on the market. Separate Daylight and Tungsten ratings are still necessary for color films, due to the need for conversion filters in various kinds of light; these filters alter the film speed in many cases.

CHOOSING AN EXPOSURE METER

The best way to decide on a meter to suit your specific needs is to compare basic features of several.

Photocells: The most important part of the exposure meter is the photocell. It is basically a simple device that takes in a certain amount of light and emits (or passes, depending on type) a current in proportion to the amount of light falling on it.

Early attempts at making photoelectric exposure meters were unsuccessful because early photocells were large, fragile, and usually required an outside source of current, such as a battery, for operation.

The first practical exposure meter came about as a result of the invention of the selenium barrier-layer photocell, which was incorporated in the earliest Weston meters and in all others until very recently. The barrier-layer cell is self-generating—that is, it emits current in proportion to the light falling on it and does not require batteries or other outside sources of current. Some meters today have two cells—a normal one for average illumination and an attachable "booster" cell for making readings

Left: *Gossen Pilot photoelectric meter. Exposure range from 1/1000 of a second to one minute. Exposure indexes from ASA 6 to 6400; f-stops from 1.4 to 22; reflected- and incident-light readings.* Right: *Bower Model 31 photoelectric meter. ASA speeds from 6 to 12,000; f-stops, 1 to 32; shutter speeds, 1 to 1/1000 of a second; LVS and Polaroid settings; movie settings.*

in dim light.

A breakthrough in sensitivity came with the introduction of the cadmium sulfide photoconductive cell. As the name implies, this cell does not generate any current at all; it merely changes its resistance according to the light falling upon it. The more light it receives, the more current will pass through it. But the current must be provided from an outside battery, a new type which is very small, has a long life under small loads, and whose voltage is quite constant until it finally is exhausted.

Some new meters incorporate a cadmium sulfide cell and a small mercury battery as their basic elements. Generally a push-button switch is provided so that current is drawn from the battery only when a reading is being taken. Under these circumstances a single battery will last up to a year and, in some cases, longer.

There are a great many cases where the tremendous sensitivity of the cadmium sulfide cell is not needed and for much general photography, the older type of barrier-layer cell is sufficiently sensitive. Some meters incorporate both features in one unit; a push button connects the battery and transfers the meter movement from one cell to the other.

Calculators: The meter dial is usually calibrated in some kind of number series. The Weston meters read directly in candles-per-square-foot. Other meters read in an arbitrary scale of numbers. In either case a reading is taken from the meter needle, then the same number is found on the calculator. The calculator is set according to the manufacturer's instructions to determine the actual exposure.

Another group of meters has no numbers on the dial. Instead there is a pointer attached to the calculator dial, and this pointer is matched to the position of the meter needle, usually in a series of white-and-black-striped fields. This eliminates any number reading at all and makes the meter essentially direct-reading.

Now and then there has been an attempt to make a meter read directly in exposure from the pointer. Since there are a great many combinations of f-stop and shutter speed which produce the same exposure, such meters either have to be built for an arbitrary shutter speed, or some kind of movable dial has to be supplied which can be set in advance for the shutter speed desired. Such meters were most successful for movie use, since most movie cameras are used at a single shutter speed.

INCIDENT-LIGHT ATTACHMENTS

The old meter-reading method, used by many Hollywood cameramen, was to use an illumination meter, not a brightness meter, to measure the strength of each light source separately. Having many controllable light sources, it was the custom of the movie cameraman to adjust each to a desired strength to secure a certain lighting balance. The cameraman knew that for a given key-light strength he would have to use a given lens stop. All the other lights on the set were simply balanced in proportion to the key light for a visual effect.

With a single, simple innovation, Don Norwood picked up this method and made it possible to read an exposure of an entire set from the effect of the various lights on it. This was done by placing a translucent hemisphere over the photocell of the meter and using the meter from the subject position, aimed at the camera. It is evident that a full frontlight will illuminate the entire hemisphere, a sidelight will illuminate only half of it, a backlight will not illuminate it at all. The result is a proportionate exposure reading, taking into account not only the strength of the lights but also their position.

The attachment need not, of course, be hemispherical; the Weston Invercone produces much the same result with a device of very different shape. Other meters have incident-light attachments in shapes all the way to perfectly flat, but these are really illumination meters and in using them several readings may have to be taken and averaged to produce an accurate incident-light reading.

ACCEPTANCE ANGLE

A brightness meter, rather than an illumination meter, is produced by restricting the angle of view of the photocell so it picks up the light from a specific area. But with this restricted angle of view, the meter will not be very sensitive.

If the angle is broadened, the meter will have a greater sensitivity, but it also may pick up unwanted light from areas outside that of the subject field (such as the sky in landscapes) and can give false readings.

A workable compromise has been arrived at. The angle of acceptance of the usual meter is about 45 degrees to 55 degrees, which is about the same as that of the average camera lens. Thus a reading from camera position will cover about the same area as the camera sees.

The Weston meter, and others using a perforated baffle for the high range, have a narrower angle when used in bright light. With the baffle open, the angle of acceptance is wider for use mainly in very dim light, when the meter is used as a "search" instrument and readings are taken close to the brightest parts of the subjects.

A similar idea is found in several meters which use the new cadmium sulfide cell and limit the acceptance angle to between two and four degrees. Such meters are used for "spot" readings on specific parts of

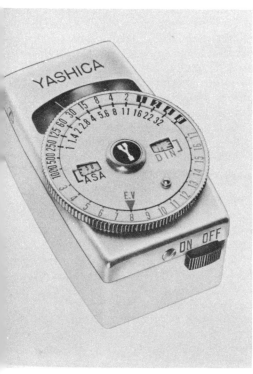

Yashica Model YEM-35 meter, powered by mercury cell. Measures ¾×1×2 inches, clips onto any camera. ASA speeds from 6 to 12,000; EVS scale; shutter speeds, eight seconds to 1/1000.

the object, usually the principal highlight. Because of the narrow angle of view, a finder is essential, and most of these meters have an eyepiece showing a fairly broad angle of view, with a spot or circle in the center indicating the exact part of the scene being read by the meter. This feature is found in the Elwood, Honeywell, and some other meters.

CARE OF EXPOSURE METER

An exposure meter should be given careful handling to insure a long, useful life. Sometimes slight jars will cause the instrument to come to rest at a position off zero. Correction can be made on some meters by means of the zero corrector on the meter. The instrument should be held in the position normally used, with the cell covered by an opaque object, and the zero adjusting screw should be turned until the pointer returns to zero.

It is desirable to clean the glass covering the photoelectric cell from time to time, although in dry weather it may be found that rubbing the glass with a piece of cloth may generate a static electricity charge, so that the instrument pointer will rest at some place other than zero. The charge may be dissipated by simply breathing on the scale glass.

The photoelectric cell in an exposure meter should not be subjected to temperatures above 125 F, and it is advisable to keep the instrument in its carrying case in relatively high temperatures or hot direct sun.

The question is sometimes asked. How long will an exposure meter last? We must assume, of course, that it is not dropped or damaged, and then we can only say, we don't know. The barrier-layer cell transforms the light into current; nothing in the cell itself is used up. Meter movement is subject to very little wear from the swinging of the needle. The writer of this article has in his kit an early Weston Master I meter which is at least 20 years old; it reads as accurately today as it did when it was purchased. How much longer will it last? Who knows?

EXPOSURE METERS: HOW TO USE THEM

ANSEL ADAMS
[Here Ansel Adams supplements the previous article on exposure meters. He discusses the practical use of the meter, warns of pitfalls to be avoided, and shows how the lessons of the Zone System can be applied to meter reading to produce correct as well as expressive exposures.]
• *Also See: Exposure; Exposure (Light) Meters; Exposure with the Zone System.*

IN THE COURSE OF TEACHING PHOtography and working with various exposure meters and exposure photometers, I became painfully aware that few instruments give equivalent exposure indications for the same subject and same lighting conditions. At first, I used to accuse the meters of poor construction, poor adjustment, or inadequate design. Considerable practical study and experience have convinced me that different manufacturers calibrate their meters differently for various reasons, some of which may be valid. The purpose of this article is to review the basic types of meters and their functions in the domain of creative photography. Meter calibrations, etc., as discussed herein, are those in use at the date of writing; changes may be made at any time, but they can be evaluated by the suggested test procedures.

MEASURING LIGHT

For our purposes, there are two basic types of light: *incident light* (illumination), which is the light falling upon the subject; and *reflected light* (luminance), which is the light reflected from the subject to our eyes and to the camera lens.

Incident light is usually measured in foot-candles (fc). A foot-candle ideally represents the amount of light falling upon a surface placed one foot away from one candle. Of course, this "candle" has been given a very precise value and is a basic unit of measurement for illumination engineers.

Now, if 100 foot-candles fall

upon a surface of 100 percent diffuse reflectivity (an unapproachable ideal), the diffuse reflected light could be measured as 100 foot-lamberts (ftl). If the reflecting surface reflected 36 percent of the light we would have 36 foot-lamberts; if it reflected 18 percent we would have the equivalent of the standard gray card, and so on. This is a unit of measurement used extensively in technological fields.

When we divide foot-lamberts by Pi ($\pi = 3.1416$), we get candles-per-square-foot (c/ft²), which is the unit of measurement of reflected light used with many exposure meters, including the Weston Master Meter. We call this reflected light value the "luminance" of the scene.

For those who are inclined to experiment and who have meters of various types, the following procedure will be interesting and rewarding. Place a Kodak Neutral Test Card, commonly known as a standard gray card, of 18 percent reflectance (it diffusely reflects 18 percent of the incident light falling upon it) on a table and direct toward it a light source at a nonglare angle to the observer. Lay the cell of an incident-light meter (Photovolt, G.E., etc.) on the card, and take a reading of the strength of the illumination in terms of foot-candles. Suppose we had a reading of 100 foot-candles. From an ideal 100 percent reflective surface, this would show 100 foot-lamberts of reflected light. From the 18 percent gray card, we would get a reflectance of 18 foot-lamberts. Dividing this by Pi would give us, in round figures, about six candles per square foot. This is also the reading we would get from the Weston Meter directed to the gray card. We say, then, that the luminance of the card is about six c/ft².

So much for the common units of light measurement. No matter what we call them, they relate to specific quantities of illumination and reflectance (luminance) which affect sensitive photographic materials in very predictable ways. Some meters are calibrated to give EV (Exposure Value) numbers alone; some give actual lens and stop settings alone; some directly activate the lens and shutter settings, as with the Polaroid Land automatic cameras.

VARIATIONS IN METERS

All of the above is informative, but it does not explain why different meters indicate different exposures for the same subject under the same lighting conditions. (We of course assume that the same film speed settings are used when we are making comparisons of various meters.) Before we discuss the reasons for these differences, we should mention the direct relationship between candles-per-square-foot, ASA film speeds, and the lens-stop and shutter-speed values.

For some reason this very rewarding relationship is not mentioned by manufacturers, nor is it found in film and camera instruction sheets. Perhaps the average camera user is considered incapable of comprehending simple arithmetical relationship, but I encounter little difficulty in getting people to grasp these basic relationships. It is true that the calculations on which all our technical facilities depend are very precise and complex. But we, as photographers, need only to know the basic operational principles. A good pianist does not have to know how to construct a piano. But he does have to know how to use it.

Let us take the standard Weston Master III or IV Meter in hand. If we point the meter at a large single-value surface, such as a wall, the smooth side of a house, or a smooth card, we will note that the needle of the meter moves to a given number; the number depends upon the strength of the incident light and the reflectance of the substance of the wall, house, or card.

At any event, let us assume the needle moves to the 100 mark, signifying that the subject reflects 100 c/ft². Now let us set the ASA film-speed dial at 64 and then set the figure of 100 on the main dial opposite the arrow (this represents Zone V of the exposure scale, which will be discussed later). Then, looking at the lens-stop and shutter-speed scales, we note that the exposure indicated is $^1/_{100}$ of a second at $f/8$. This relates to the 100 c/ft² reading ($^1/_{100}$ is the reciprocal of 100) and to $f/8$ as the square root of 64 (or, 64 is the square of 8). This relationship can be expressed as follows: THE INDICATED BASIC EXPOSURE IS BASED ON THE SHUTTER SPEED AS THE RECIPROCAL (in fractions of a second) OF THE LUMINANCE (in c/ft²) SET OPPOSITE THE LENS STOP WHICH IS THE SQUARE ROOT OF THE ASA FILM SPEED.

Read this several times until you understand it. It may sound complex at first but it is really simple. Try it with various combinations: with a luminance reading of 200 and an ASA film speed of 250, the indicated exposure will be $^1/_{200}$ of a second at $f/16$ (16 is the approximate square root of 250). Of course, this is the basic exposure; any equivalent exposure can be given—$^1/_{50}$ at $f/32$, $^1/_{400}$ at $f/11$, etc. It is perfectly obvious that there is a simple and definite connection between film speeds, luminance values, lens stops, and shutter speeds.

To digress for a moment: the incident-light meter is calibrated to indicate lens stop and shutter speed to give the same exposure indicated by the standard reflected-light (reflectance) meter with direct gray-card readings. Provided they are all related to the same lighting conditions, the reflectances of the subject would then fall on their appropriate zones of the exposure scale. With complex lighting conditions (sun and shadow, for instance) the incident-light meters do not function efficiently; too much computation and adjustment are required to get a reasonably well-balanced exposure. In my opinion, "averaging" light values is a rather uncertain way to solve exposure problems. (More about this later.)

I am frank to say I very seldom use an exposure meter as such; I use it as a photometer. Evaluating the important luminances of the subject and placing them on the appropriate Zones of the exposure scale of the film is the most satisfactory and consistent system. Contrary to common opinion, this does not involve time-consuming calcula-

The SEI Exposure Photometer. This instrument enables the photographer to measure subject luminance of small areas (acceptance angle of one degree) over a wide range of luminances (1:1,000,000). Such a range includes twilight scenes with street lights; very dark areas of architectural interiors; brilliant clouds near the sun. It is especially helpful in color photography, where a critical evaluation of highlight and shadow values is of decisive importance.

tions; the entire process becomes almost automatic after a little experience.

CALIBRATING VARIOUS METERS

The first step is, of course, to calibrate various meters to read as much the same as possible. Different meters do have some variation in color sensitivity, but as most of the colors of nature, skin, and of manufactured things are relatively low in saturation, this difference has little practical effect.

First, we should discuss the different kinds of reflected-light meters. (I shall mention only a few typical meters here.) The Weston Master

Meter has a rather wide field of view (30 to 45 degrees). It is commonly used as an averaging or "integrating" meter, but can be used as a "spot" meter if the area read is sufficiently large to be encompassed in its angle of view. By "spot" readings we mean the readings of specific areas of consistent value in the subject.

With the Heiland 3°/21 Meter, we can read the luminance within an angle of three degrees, and with the SEI Exposure Photometer, our angle of view is one degree (with a range of luminances of 1:1,000,000). Obviously, with the latter two meters, we cannot take "integrated"

readings; hence these are termed "spot" meters.

With a photometer, we are concerned with precise measurements of small areas of the subject as seen from the camera position. With an integrating reflectance meter, we either scan the general field of view from the camera position or closely approach the subject for "spot" readings of sufficiently large areas. With incident-light meters we take our reading at the subject, pointing the meter toward the camera.

If we have a variety of reflectance meters at hand we should adjust them so they all yield the same exposure when directed to the subject in the same way. As stated before, various meters are calibrated in various ways according to the opinions or theories of the manufacturers. Experience with teaching groups shows that the first important technical hurdle is the adjustment of all the meters to read the same exposure on the same object. A large card is set up, and, under sunlight or shadowed light (always even), exposure readings are taken. The basic readings are made with an accurately adjusted Weston and one or two SEI Meters (which have been calibrated with a laboratory photometer). Assuming the meters are clean, the grids free from dust, and the needle set to zero position, we can proceed to check them with the "standard" meters. If they read high, we set the film-speed dial to a lower speed; if they read low, we raise the film-speed setting.

The object of these tests is to get consistent exposure readings at, say, $f/8$ and a film speed of ASA 64, or $f/11$ and a speed of ASA 125, etc. We make these tests on both bright- and low-luminance surfaces, and if any discrepancy shows, we can at least compensate for it.

Once all meters are set for the same exposure indications, we have a rewarding mutual consistency and—what is very important—we also have a group of practical photometers. They are wide-field photometers, it is true, but if the areas read are large enough, "spot" readings can be made.

To study the principles involved it is not important that we set the ASA film speed to any particular value. Select a speed which has an easy-to-remember approximate square root, such as:

ASA 64 = f/8
ASA 125 = f/11
ASA 250 = f/16
ASA 500 = f/22

If we are using only one film we would naturally set the ASA film speed for that film. But if the speed were, for example, ASA 160, our key stop would be approximately f/12.5. Since lenses are seldom marked with this number we will have to do some extra computing or interpolation.

Now, suppose we approach an important (and adequately large) area of the subject and take a reading with a meter other than a Weston. Say the exposure reads $1/80$ of a second at f/8 (with the ASA speed set at 64). By interpolation we see that the luminance is 80 c/ft². If the film speed were set at 125, the exposure would be $1/80$ of a second at f/11, and the interpolation would be the same, 80 c/ft² luminance value for the area measured. If we measure the luminance of the standard gray card (set about 45 degrees to the sun and viewed from a nonglare angle) the indicated exposure would be "basic," that is, it would relate to "middle gray" or 18 percent standard-gray-card value.

However, we must always bear in mind this very important fact: WHATEVER LUMINANCE VALUE IS PLACED ON ZONE V OF THE EXPOSURE SCALE, THE NEGATIVE (OR THE COLOR TRANSPARENCY) WILL HAVE DENSITY VALUE V, AND WITH NORMAL PRINTING, PRINT VALUE V WILL BE OBTAINED.

Hence, while the Weston Meter has the exposure scale on its dial and Zone V is easy to see (the arrow of this scale) other meters, calibrated to read in the same way as the Weston, will automatically show a Zone V exposure for any single-subject luminance (although there may be no "dial point" to prove it).

Suppose we are photographing a light-toned building with a stucco wall in which we want to preserve texture, while retaining a feeling of high value and light. Let us say this subject value (luminance) should fall on Zone VII. With the Weston Meter we find that the wall measures 800 c/ft² in sunlight. We can place this directly on Zone VII of the scale (the point between C and O). We will then note that 200 falls opposite the arrow; at ASA 64 speed, the exposure is $1/200$ of a second at f/8 (or equivalent at different stops or shutter speeds).

Now, suppose we are using Meter X, which shows only direct exposure values. If calibrated properly it will indicate an exposure of $1/800$ of a second at f/8 (at ASA 64 film speed). Remember, if this exposure is given we will get a Zone V exposure, and a Density Value V

Ansel Adams with the SEI Exposure Photometer.

in the negative. This would, of course, be too little exposure for the bright wall. To "place" this value on Zone VII we multiply the exposure four times. Or, if we wished to think in terms of luminance values alone (c/ft²) we would write (on the Exposure Record sheet) 800 in the Zone VII column. This would indicate 400 on Zone VI, and 200 on Zone V. The exposure is then $1/200$ of a second at f/8 with film of ASA 64 speed (or f/16 with film of 250 ASA, or f/5 with film of 25 ASA speed).

Another example: we are working in a grove of trees, and wish to hold the luminance of the shadowed tree trunks on Zone III to get ample textural value. The Weston reads 6.5 c/ft². Placing this on Zone III we find that 25 falls opposite the arrow; hence, with ASA 64 film speed, the exposure would be $^1/_{25}$ of a second at $f/8$.

Now, with Meter X, the exposure for this part of the scene would show about $^1/_6$ of a second at $f/8$. If we give this exposure, the shadowed tree trunks would have a Zone V exposure and have Density Value V in the negative. We can get Zone III exposure by dividing $^1/_6$ by 4—about $^1/_{25}$ of a second. Or, we can write 6.5 in the Zone III column and, doubling for Zone IV, and doubling again for Zone V, we will see that 25 lies in the Zone V column. Therefore, the exposure is $^1/_{25}$ of a second at $f/8$ (or at $f/11$, if the ASA speed were 125).

THE SEI METER

With the SEI Meter, I set the black dot opposite ASA 6 and note the exposure indicated opposite $f/8$ on the lens-stop ring. The reciprocal of the exposure time is the c/ft^2 value. If I point the meter to a very dark area of the subject and get ½ of a second opposite $f/8$, I know that the luminance of this area is 2 c/ft^2. (If the exposure were two seconds, the luminance would be ½ c/ft^2.)

With the SEI Meter we can "explore" the subject thoroughly from the camera position. Conventionally, we place the low-value luminances (shadows) on the desired Zone, and then develop for the high values (which may fall on, above, or below the desired visualized exposure Zone). With positive color film we expose for the proper placement of the high values. And this procedure is also followed for Polaroid Land materials (since the Polaroid Land process is a positive process).

HEILAND 3°/21 METER

With the Heiland 3°/21 Meter, we set the outer ring to the number at which the needle points. We may find that this meter is so calibrated that we have to set the ASA film-speed ring two or three points higher than the engraved numbers to get the true c/ft^2 values. This does not signify anything is wrong with the meter as such; it has just been calibrated differently, perhaps on the basis of getting the right placement of skin luminance on or near Zone VI. By this I mean that a direct reading with the Heiland Meter on skin (not including highlights on forehead, etc.) would automatically place its value of Zone VI where it belongs (skin reflects about 36 percent of the incident light). But this means that every single subject-luminance value as seen by the meter would result in a Zone VI exposure, too. However, adjusting the calibration to give Zone V value with this meter makes it an excellent device for photometer evaluation of luminances. Suppose, with the meter properly adjusted, we find that the skin value in sunlight reads 400 c/ft^2. Placing 400 on Zone VI (an easy thing to do in the mind) would give us 200 on Zone V; the basic exposure would then be $^1/_{200}$ of a second at $f/5$ with a film speed of ASA 25, $^1/_{40}$ of a second at $f/11$, or $^1/_{10}$ of a second at $f/22$.

Now, suppose we use the Weston Meter as an averaging or "integrating" meter. This means that it collects all the reflected light within a scan of about 30 degrees and indicates an exposure which, if all the subject details could be scrambled and merged into one smooth continuous tone, would simply be equivalent to a Zone V exposure of an 18 percent standard gray card. A useful simile is this: suppose we want to fill a container with material enough to total one pound in weight. We add all kinds of things—feathers, lead shot, wood shavings, sand, etc. At a certain point the scales will tip and our container can be said to weigh one pound. But we do not know the particular weights of the feathers, the shot, the sand, or the wood shavings.

So it is with averaged light reflected from the subject; we can measure the total amount of light, but not the luminances of the particular parts. But with the spot-luminance approach all values of the subject come under scrutiny and can be placed as desired on the exposure scale of the film, or as they "fall" in geometrical ratio after the dominant value is placed on the desired Zone.

AVERAGING LUMINANCE VALUES

The problem of "averaging" different luminance values, with the object of setting the meter "between" these values, is perplexing to many. First, we have the arithmetic "average" of two or more actual luminance values. Say that a light-toned wall registers 800 c/ft^2 and the deepest shadow registers 50 c/ft^2; the "average" of 50 and 800 would be 425. A setting of 425 c/ft^2 at the arrow of the Weston Meter (Zone V) would place the high value on about Zone VI (much too low) and 50 would fall on about Zone II (probably too low). Suppose that we had luminances of 50, 100, 200, 300, and 800 to "average;" we would get 290. This would be a more favorable situation; 800 would fall on about Zone VI-VII, and 50 on about Zone II-III. In such cases, we will find that we should usually double the exposure indicated.

The Honeywell Pentax 3°/21° Exposure Meter. Measures reflected light for ASA speeds of three to 6400. The viewing screen covers an included angle of 21 degrees; in the center of the screen is a circle defining the three-degree included angle in which the meter's light-sensitive element functions.

Fotomatic Model Z-4 Foto-Meter. Gives spot readings covering a two-degree angle of the reflected light from a subject. ASA indexes from 0.2 to 6400.

However, if we think of visually approximating the "average" on the *geometric* scale of the Weston Meter, we will find that the luminance values fall much more agreeably into place on the appropriate Zones. Let us take luminance values of 50 and 800 c/ft². Place the 50 the same number of steps (blocks) below the arrow as the 800 above (in this case they fall two Zones on either side of the arrow). The value which appears opposite the arrow is 200; this places the 800 on Zone VII, which is approximately correct. If the range were 25 to 800, we would see that 25 would fall 2½ Zones below the arrow and 800, 2½ Zones above. With a very flat subject of 25 to 100 c/ft² luminance values, the "visual" average on the Weston scale would "place" 25 on IV and 100 on VI, with 50 c/ft² opposite Zone V. This approach will yield a rather high order of "correct" exposures; if the low values fall approximately where they should, we can then indicate the optimum development in rela-

tion to the placement of the high values.

We find (and I can corroborate this by much direct experience) that in about 75 percent of cases tested, the Weston Meter, pointed along the axis of the lens, indicates about one half the optimum exposure. This is no fault of the meter. Rather, it represents random-distribution situations of the luminance values of the subject. We can resort to various intuitive "tricks" to adjust these integrated readings to the optimum. In about 25 percent of the cases the integrated reading is correct. Again, the spot-luminance approach overcomes this operational difficulty.

Many meters are calibrated to take into consideration this statistical subject-luminance variance, and they yield about twice the normal exposure which the Weston Meter gives with its integrated readings. This applies to many meters built into the camera. Using my Zeiss Contarex I get very good results with integrated readings of general subjects, but when I wish to use it as a "spot" meter I must double the ASA speed values of the film I am using.

With the Polaroid 900 camera, pointing the electric eye to a single luminance value will result in a Value VI in the print. To get Value V, I must double the film-speed value. This excellent instrument offers a very wide range of control with small changes in the film-speed settings. Suppose I want to "place" the aforementioned light wall on Zone VII with the 900 camera and Polaroid Land type 47 film (which I use at ASA 4000 daylight). I determine my position and composition, set the film speed at 2000, then come close to the wall and depress the shutter release *part way;* this activates the electric eye and sets the shutter system. Holding the shutter release in the halfway position, I return to the taking position, compose through the finder, and complete operation of the shutter release. The important point is: to get a Zone VII exposure which gives Value VII in the print, I must set the film speed at ASA 2000 instead of 4000 (4000 would give me Value IV for the light wall).

EXPOSURE WITH THE ZONE SYSTEM

Ansel Adams
Photographer, Author of "Camera and Lens"; "The Negative, Exposure and Development," "The Print, Contact Printing and Enlarging"; "Exposure Record"; "Polaroid Land Photography Manual."

[After many years of practical experience in photography, Ansel Adams has evolved a technique which constitutes an important contribution to the general practice of the art. It simplifies the relationship between exposure and development of the negative. This system of exposure is designed to clarify the practical relationship of exposure, negative density, and print values.]

• *Also see: Contrast; Exposure; Exposure (Light) Meters.*

Controlled experimentation, trial-and-error methods, and downright luck have given us a good working knowledge of photography. But I have always believed that, for the creative photographer, there must be a meeting point somewhere between the rigors of pure sensitometry and the slap-happy procedures of amateur work.

I have developed my approach over 30 years of constant photographic activity and feel that it is of value in all phases of practical and expressive photography. This article will contain a brief outline of my approach to exposure and development of the negative and of the importance of visualization in terms of the final print.

COMMON PHOTOGRAPHIC TERMS

To avoid confusion in the reading of this article, the following description of photographic terms will be of help to the reader.

Intensity. Relates to the light source, as intensity of illumination.

Luminance. Refers to light reflected from the subject, as the luminance of the white dress; the luminance of the deepest shadow. It is this reflected light with which we photograph. (Unit of measurement: candles-per-square-foot or c/ft².)

Flare. The scattering of light by reflection from the air-glass surfaces of the lens and from the interior of the camera. Optical coating removes much of this flare from the lens, but camera flare is always present to some degree, except with carefully baffled camera interiors. Flare produces an all-over haze of light on the negative, reducing the contrast of the image. Sometimes flarespots (ghost images) are produced. Uncoated lenses transmit less light than coated lenses, due to the reflection of light (about four to five percent from each uncoated surface). Hence a coated lens transmits more light and gives images of greater contrast than an uncoated lens.

Image brightness. The brightness of the image on the groundglass or on the negative. This depends upon transmission capabilities of the lens, aperture of the lens, and lens and camera flare.

Image-brightness range. The difference between the darkest and brightest parts of the subject and of the image. Due to flare and transmission effects, the image-brightness range will always be less than subject-luminance range. For precise work, we should always make careful tests to determine the relation of subject-luminance range to the image-brightness range of any particular lens and camera combination. It can be safely assumed that all good, coated lenses have practically the same transmission and contrast effects, but that flare may vary considerably in different cameras.

Exposure. The amount of light permitted to fall upon the sensitive emulsion. The classic formula is Exposure = Intensity × Time. In practical photography Luminance should be used instead of Intensity, as the photograph is made with light reflected from the subject. In general terms, one unit of light and ten units of exposure will give the same effect as ten units of light and one unit of exposure.

Development. The reduction of the exposed light-sensitive halides of the emulsion to visible metallic silver.

Fixation. The removal by chemical means of the unexposed silver halides from the developed film, which renders permanent the negative image composed of varying deposits of metallic silver.

The negative. The "reverse" or negative image of the subject photographed. In the ideal negative the values are proportionately related to the luminances of the subject. This relationship is modified by the degree of exposure, the amount of development, and by the inherent character of the emulsion. Negative values are described by three terms —transparency, opacity and density.

Transparency. If 100 units of light are incident on any one part of the negative, and 25 units pass through it, we can say that the transparency is 25 percent. Transparency can never be 100 percent— the film base and minimum emulsion fog will always hold back a small amount of light. If the lightest part of the image has a transparency of 90 percent, and the darkest part 1 percent, the transparency range would be 1 to 90.

Opacity. The reciprocal of transparency is opacity. Twenty-five percent transparency is opacity 4; 10 percent transparency is opacity 10; 1 percent transparency is opacity 100. The opacity range is 0 max/0 min. If the highest opacity is 200 and the lowest 4, the opacity range is 1 to 50, or just 50.

Density. This is the logarithm of the opacity. For those who are acquainted with logs, the term is readily understood. As mathematical shorthand it has great value in sensitometric computations and the plotting of characteristic curves (see below). But for the average photographer, I feel that the arithmetic equivalent of log density—the opacity—is more readily understood. In approximate round figures, the relationship of transparency, opacity, and density is shown in the following table:

Transparency	Opacity	Density
100%	1	0.00
80%	1.26	0.10
63%	1.59	0.20
50%	2.00	0.30
40%	2.50	0.40
32%	3.20	0.50
25%	4.00	0.60
20%	5.00	0.70
16%	6.30	0.80
12.5%	7.90	0.90
10%	10.00	1.00

The table can be extended auto-

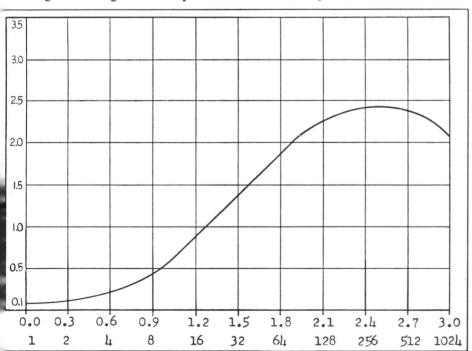

Figure 1. *A typical sensitometric characteristic curve. The curve shows reversal with extreme exposure. The log exposure values are merely proportional.*

matically by relating the above values to a factor of 1/10 and 10 for every unit increase of the characteristic (the number to the left of the decimal) of the log. For example:

4%	25.00	1.40
2%	50.00	1.70
.4%	250.00	2.40
.2%	500.00	2.70
.1%	1000.00	3.00
.063%	1590.00	3.20

The density range is computed by subtracting D min from D max. It should be remembered that when we subtract logs we divide; when we add logs we multiply. If the lowest density is 0.20, and the highest density 1.80, the density range is 1.60 and the opacity range is about 40.

The characteristic curve. In 1890 Hurter and Driffield propounded the classic theory of the exposure-density relationship of light-sensitive materials. This relationship is plotted on what is called the D log E curve, the H & D curve, or the characteristic curve—as it graphically defines the exposure-density characteristics of the light-sensitive emulsion. It will be noted that as exposure increases, the curve alters its shape.

At the threshold the first effect of light is noticed. As exposure increases the curve rises through the "toe," signifying increasing density for equal increases of exposure. Then comes the straight-line section, in which the increase in density is proportionate to the increase in exposure. Then follows the "shoulder" where equal increase of exposure results in reduced density increase. The curve finally flattens out—increase in exposure produces no increase in density—and then actually reverses.

The high values of exposure required to produce true flattening or reversal are far beyond the values used in ordinary practical photography. The proportionate relation of density to subject luminance (actually image-brightness) is sustained in the straight-line section of the curve, although frequently subject values are represented in the toe and near the shoulder of the curve.

The steepness of the curve is determined by the characteristics of the emulsion and the degree of development. Steepness represents image contrast, and this is termed gamma—a term valuable in sensitometry, but confusing to the practical photographer. Gamma is the angle of the straight-line section of the curve in relation to the base; gamma 1 represents an angle of 45 degrees. The accurate evaluation of gamma is far beyond the capacities of the average nontechnical photographer. The practical evaluation of contrast can be determined by much simpler means. Figure 6 shows symbolically the different shapes of the curve produced by different degrees of development.

The print. The print is the reverse of the negative—it is the negative of the negative or the positive image. Ideally if the negative emulsion had a perfect proportional density scale, and if the paper emulsion likewise had a perfect scale, the image would contain values directly proportionate to the luminances of the subject. Neither negatives nor papers have perfect scales, and the limited reflectivity of the print prevents a true literal representation of the subject. The values of the print are chiefly subjective, and it is here that the photographer's expressive controls may be applied with maximum effect. The negative is only a step toward the ultimate statement, which is the print. The print is the realization of the visualization of the photograph made before the negative is exposed.

Brilliancy. As the print is seen by reflected light, no part of it can reflect quite as much light as falls upon it. Even the pure white paper base cannot reflect more than 90 or 95 percent of the incident light falling upon it. If the heaviest deposit of silver of the image reflects 2 percent and the white paper base reflects 90 percent, the reflection range is about 1 to 45. In terms of reflection density, this would be about (log) 1.66. The usual glossy print does not exceed a reflection density range of 1.70—or a brilliancy range of 1 to 50. Matte and rough surfaces have much lower

brilliancy ranges—sometimes as low as 1 to 15.

Paper-exposure scales. Do not confuse paper-exposure scales with the brilliancy range of the completed print. For the sake of image quality, the print should always be fully developed so it has a full range, from black to white. But the various paper "grades" or "contrasts" will respond to different opacity ranges of the negative: for example, an opacity range of 10 for a "hard" or contrasty paper (used for "soft" negatives) or an opacity range of 100 for "soft" paper (used for "contrasty" negatives). It is unfortunate that manufacturers do not consistently grade their papers with a single specific term or number for each contrast grade. A No. 2 paper of one firm may have very different characteristics from a No. 2 paper of another firm. In this article I refer to a "No. 2" paper as having a full exposure scale of about 1 to 50. It must be remembered that the characteristics of any paper are somewhat modified by changes in the composition, dilution, and application of the developer.

THE GRAY SCALE

The full scale of values in nature, or in the photographic print, can be expressed as a continuous or intermittent scale of gray values.

These values do not coincide, but both subject and print values can be expressively related. While the subject-luminance range may be far greater than the print-brilliancy range, we may assume that the darkest-to-lightest luminances of the subject may be expressively interpreted by the blackest-to-whitest range of the print.

If we divide a continuous black-to-white gray scale into ten steps, we will have "pivot points" from which we can evaluate the approximate relative values of subject-luminances or print-brilliancies. We do not go around with a gray scale making comparisons to the luminance scale of nature; the relationship is far too approximate. But we can use a gray scale in direct relation to our print.

The aforementioned ten steps,

EL. LENS STOP F/	64	45	32	22	16	11	8	5.6	4	2.8
REL. EXP. FOR V	1/32	1/16	1/8	1/4	1/2	1	2	4	8	16
REL. EXP. FOR I	1/2	1	2	4	8	16	32	64	128	256
WESTON SCALE	—	U	—	—	A	↓	C	—	□	—
ZONES	0	I	II	III	IV	V	VI	VII	VIII	IX
GRAY SCALE										

Figure 2. *The gray scale.*

from black to white including eight intermediary steps of grays, may be related to the scale of the Weston Meter and to the sequence of zones of my exposure system. In Figure 2 we see this relationship, including relative exposure units, and relative lens apertures. Zone O represents total (maximum) black, and Zone IX represents maximum white. Zone V represents "middle gray" (about 18 percent reflectance) and Zone VI represents the average monochromatic values of Caucasian skin. Do not take the values in this reproduction literally—the average printing process cannot be expected to preserve subtle tone values. It is advised that the reader become familiar with zone tones by looking at a variety of photographs and mentally placing various values on their appropriate gray-scale zones.

AWARENESS OF SUBJECT VALUES

It is extremely important that the photographer learn to evaluate the various luminances of his subject, and to think of them in terms of relative zones. Be sure you recognize the objects of maximum blackness and maximum whiteness. This is not always as simple as it sounds.

For example, we are sitting in a room containing a blackboard, light gray walls on which white papers are attached, and an aluminum photoflood reflector. High up on the wall is a ventilator grille. A man in the room is wearing a dark gray suit. Most people, after a look about the room, would say the blackboard was the blackest object.

But what of the intensely black depths of the ventilator grille? It might seem at first glance that the white papers on the wall would surely be the whitest objects. But how about the reflections of the light source (the window) in the polished aluminum reflector? With the depths of the ventilator placed on Zone O, and the reflection from the polished aluminum placed on Zone IX, we have encompassed the extreme range of the scale. Remember, this is the "awareness" scale—not the visualization or exposure scale.

In relation to the extremes of values, the luminances in the room might fall as follows: highlight on aluminum reflector, Zone IX or above (maximum white); white paper, Zone VIII; light gray walls, Zone VII; skin of occupant's face, Zone VI; dark gray suit, Zone IV; blackboard, Zone III; depths of ventilator, Zone O (maximum black).

Figure 3 shows how these various values would be placed on the chart. There would probably be values relating to Zones I, II, and V, but it is seldom that all important luminances need be designated as zones. The extremes must first be established, then the values within placed on the appropriate related zones of the gray scale.

VISUALIZATION

After we have become used to thinking of subject luminances in relation to the ten steps of the gray scale, we can begin to think of ten actual steps of tone in the

print, and relate them to subject luminances. We are not thinking of exposure values yet but of relative steps of tone in the print representing our concept of the subject luminances.

For example, we are on a city street one side of which is in shade and the other in sunlight. The sky is a clear blue. A building of white stone stands in the sun, another building of the same material is on the shaded side of the street. Several dark automobiles are parked along the gray curb. A door is open into a dark vestibule; white marble steps shine in the sun before it. Both sunlit and shaded houses have green hedges enclosing their yards. A bald-headed man talks to a dark-uniformed policeman in the sun.

Let us visualize the print of this scene. The whitest objects in the field are the marble steps glaring in the sun. We will consider them on Zone IX (they are too small in the image to need preservation of texture, otherwise they should fall on Zone VIII). Directly above them is the open door and the very dark vestibule. These we will think of as on Zones O and I. We find the two extremes of light and dark are close together in the picture. The white building in the sunlight we will place on Zone VIII. The white building in shade will fall on Zone V/VI. The green hedge in sun will fall on Zone VI; in shade the hedge falls on Zone III/IV. The uniform of the policeman in sun falls approximately on Zone IV; the bald head of the man on Zone VI/VII. The automobiles in sun fall approximately on Zone III; in shade they are approximately on Zone I. (Their chromium trim shines brightly—on Zone IX in both sun and shade.) The blue sky falls on Zone V/VI.

Note that all values in relation to their disposition in the field of view are well separated, except the blue sky and the shaded white building. In a photograph these values would merge, unless the sky were made lighter (in which case it might merge with the sunlit building) or darker. Sometimes little or nothing can be done to avoid such mergers and visualization is helpful in enabling us to reject impossible

REL. EXP. FOR I	1/2	1	2	4	8	16	32	64	128	256
WESTON SCALE	–	U	–	–	A	↓	C	–	D	–
ZONES	0	I	II	III	IV	V	VI	VII	VIII	IX
Highlight on Aluminum Ref										X
White Paper									X	
Light Gray Walls								X		
Skin of Occupant							X			
Dark gray Suit					X					
Blackboard			X							
Depths of Ventilator	X									

Figure 3. *Awareness scale.*

REL. EXP. FOR I	1/2	1	2	4	8	16	32	64	128	256
WESTON SCALE	–	U	–	–	A	↓	C	–	D	–
ZONES	0	I	II	III	IV	V	VI	VII	VIII	IX
Marble Steps										X
Vestibule	X	X								
White Build. in sun								X		
White Build. in shade						X	X			
Uniform					X					
Autos in sun					X					
Autos, shade		X								
Blue Sky			.			X	X			

Figure 4. *Visualization scale.*

REL. EXP. FOR I	1/2	1	2	4	8	16	32	64	128	256
WESTON SCALE	–	U	–	–	A	↓	C	–	D	–
ZONES	0	I	II	III	IV	V	VI	VII	VIII	IX
Shadows und. Rocks	X	X								
Tree Trunks				X	X					
Brightest Rocks								X		
Average Rock						X	X	X		
Rock, shade					X	X	X			

Figure 5. *Visualization scale.*

combinations before we try to photograph them. The above example would certainly be termed a full-scale scene.

As most subjects have complex textures and values, it is quite hard to assign a single zone to them. A face may represent, on the average, Zone VI value, but may be made up of Zones V, VI, and VII values, exclusive of deep shadows and shining highlights.

Now let us take a very "quiet" scene—a group of rocks and trees in soft gray light. Obviously the luminance scale here is very much shorter than in the example above, but our print must have a strong sequence of tones. We must achieve a certain departure from reality.

First, the shadows under the rocks are obviously on Zones O and I. The whitest objects are the planes of the rocks catching most of the light from the sky. We will think of them as on Zone VIII (we must preserve texture; there is no true Zone IX value in the scene). The general surfaces of the rocks represent Zones V, VI, and VII, and the slight shadows on the rocks represent Zones IV, V, and VI. The trees show values from Zone III to Zone VI. Here we have an emotional interpretation which, if translated directly to print-brilliancy values, would imply a luminance scale of 1 to 128. Actually the luminance scale might be only 1 to 8 or 1 to 16.

By proper exposure and development we can expand this relatively short scale in the negative so it produces a print of the desired tonal range on No. 2 paper. Figures 4 and 5 show the placements of the values of these subjects on the visualization scale.

EXPOSURE

Before we discuss exposure, a few basic characteristics of exposure meters, film speeds, and developers should be defined.

Exposure meters. My zone system of exposure determination is based on the Weston Master Meter which, to my knowledge, is the only meter indicating the exposure scale of the negative on its dials. (Refer to Figure 2 for the relationship of the zones to the indications on the Weston dial.) For more precise work in measuring very small areas of luminance and working in very weak light, I recommend the SEI Exposure Photometer. My system can also be adapted to other meters such as those manufactured by General Electric. A first-class exposure meter is essential and must be used with care.

Film speeds. The published ASA film ratings are adequate for most work. However, it is sometimes necessary to alter the film speeds due to some effect of the shutter, transmission, or lens flare. I base my effective speeds on the threshold response; that is I expose a smooth sheet of evenly-illuminated paper with its luminance placed on Zone I (U of the Weston scale). With normal development, this exposure should produce a density of between 0.07 and 0.12 above the density of the film base and fog level combined, which is the density of the unexposed edge of the film. If there is less density, I lower the film speed; if more density is obtained, I raise the film-speed rating. If the meter is off standard calibration, some change in the film speed will be required. All equipment should be checked frequently.

Developers. All film speeds are based on a standard development with a relatively high-energy developer. Fine-grain developers almost always reduce film speed, in some cases to a marked degree. Kodak D-25, for instance, reduces effective film speed by 50 percent. A straight paraphenelene developer can reduce film speed to 25 percent. Kodak DK-20 is considered to reduce effective film speed about 30 percent. The addition of potassium bromide to the developer also effectively reduces film speed. Old or highly dilute developers will sometimes lessen the effective film speed to a marked extent. Tests are valid, and subsequent exposure procedures based upon them are valid only if the same meter, film, lens and shutter, and developer are used consistently. Testing with one batch of equipment and photographing with another will not produce precise results. In the tests and recommendations for consistent exposure, I favor the use of Kodak D-23 (Elon-sulfite) at 68 degrees F, or Edwal FG7 developer.

Recalling that the exposure formula is Exposure = Intensity × Time, it is wise to make a simple test to confirm this fact. Take a number of smooth cards—uniform white, black, and several shades of gray— and make luminance readings from all of them. Place each luminance reading upon the "arrow" (Zone V) of the Weston scale. Expose each film to a single card according to the indications of the luminance reading as placed on the exposure scale, and develop all film equally. You will find that all negatives have the same density, although the difference in exposure between the darkest and whitest card may be 1 to 40 or 50. This will clearly indicate the possible control of any one value.

Literally, in relation to the edge of the film which should print maximum black, a white card can be exposed so as to print black, and a black card exposed so as to print white. However, if the luminance value of the card is placed below Zone I, no amount of conventional development will result in sufficient negative density to distinguish tones between the maximum black of the film edge and the subthreshold exposure. With some films having an exceptionally long "toe" the effective threshold may be Zone O, or even below, but this is unusual.

It is important, when placing luminance values on the exposure scale, to remember to expose for the darkest important values and develop for the high values.

EXPOSURE AND DEVELOPMENT

Visualization, in terms of exposure and development of the negative to obtain a negative of proper opacity range, necessitates use of the proper procedure:

1. Those parts of the subject which have been visualized as total black in the print can be placed on Zone O and below on the exposure scale.

2. Those parts of the subject which have been visualized as Zone I, II, or III should be placed on those zones of the exposure scale.

3. If a portrait is being made, and the skin values are of greatest importance, place the illuminated skin (not highlighted or backlighted skin) on Zone VI. It may be necessary to disregard all other placements at this time. We must remember that the zones progress geometrically: 1, 2, 4, 8, 16, or 1, ½, ¼, 1/8, 1/16. If a luminance of 25 is placed on Zone III, Zone VII can carry a luminance of only

400—no more, no less. Refer to the line "Relative exposure for I" in Figure 2.

4. Those parts of the subject which have been visualized as near-white or pure white should be placed on Zones VIII and IX. Perhaps they will "fit" on these zones; perhaps they will not. Let us assume that they do fit. In that case we have a "normal" negative where most of the values fall upon their appropriate zones of the exposure scale.

In order to obtain a negative which will print satisfactorily on a No. 2 paper, a paper with an exposure range of approximately 1 to 50, it will be necessary to develop this negative "normally" for whatever type of printing or enlarging used. A negative of higher contrast is required for ordinary contact printing or enlarging with diffuse light, than for printing with a condenser enlarger.

Just what this "normal" is exactly depends not only on the type of light used for enlarging or printing, but on the personal requirements of the photographer. The zone system provides satisfactory results for a wide range of personal requirements.

NORMAL DEVELOPMENT

At this stage we will say that "normal" development is that degree of development which gives the required opacities for the various luminances of the subject placed on their related zones of the exposure scale.

You should now understand the relationship which exists between awareness of subject values, visualization of print values, and placement of subject luminances on the

exposure scale. But we have discussed only "normal" placement and "normal" development. The next step is to consider the important elements of control through exposure placement and related development.

Figure 6 illustrates the increased contrast produced by processing the negative at different developing times. The central curve (slightly heavier than the others) indicates the normal development contrast. The densities in relation to exposure in this diagram are in no way related to any particular film; yet the effect of different degrees of development applies symbolically to all films. The meaning of Figure 6 is related to the following points:

1. I have mentioned that we should design negatives for a No. 2 paper. The basic exposure relationships are determined by placement of the subject luminances on the exposure scale. I set Zone VI as the "key tone." This is useful in both visualization and execution because it represents the gray-scale value of Caucasian skin and is, therefore, a good point of reference. It represents 32 units of exposure above Zone I (I unit). As the reflectivity of Caucasian skin is about 30-35 percent, this Zone VI placement is both expressively and physically sound. With normal development, all other placements hold their appropriate densities. In recent years I have used the standard gray card, which has an 18 percent reflectance, in relation to Zone V exposure placements.

2. Just what this optimum opacity (density) should be depends upon the photographer's requirements. You should make actual photographs, placing the skin values

---

CHART I

Placement on zone	Total density	Film-base-plus-fog density	Actual density range	Development	Sample developing times (Kodak D-23 developer)
IV	1.22	0.12	1.10	Normal++	20 min.
V	1.21	0.11	1.10	Normal+	16.5 min.
VI	1.20	1.10	1.10	Normal	11 min.
VII	1.19	0.09	1.10	Normal−	9.5 min.
VIII	1.18	0.08	1.10	Normal−−	7.5 min.

on Zone VI of the exposure scale, and developing a group of similar exposures for various times. You then select the one which gives the most satisfactory print, noting the development time, and base your test on the exposure and development of this negative. Merely to follow my suggestions and work for a density of 1.10 above film-base-plus-fog density (opacity range 12.6) might not provide the personally desirable negative quality. I aim for a relatively high Zone VI opacity, such as density 1.30 above film-base-plus-fog. In condenser enlarging, aim for a density of 1.00 or 0.90 above film-base-plus-fog density.

3. In studying Figure 6 the significance of the five curves will become apparent. The object is to obtain optimum opacity for Zone VI subject brightness placed not only on Zone VI, but on Zones IV, V, VII, and VIII. You can accomplish this by varying development time.

See Chart I for information on achieving a density of 1.10 above film-base-plus-fog density, with luminance for a smooth card (neutral color) placed on Zones IV, V, VI, VII, and VIII.

The developing times have no special significance for any particular film. I do not wish to make definite suggestions, as films differ widely in their processing requirements, and the proper times can be determined by adequate tests.

Agitation during development is very important. For developing times of 15 minutes or more, give constant agitation for the first minute and agitate ten seconds for every minute thereafter; for shorter normal developing times (five to ten minutes), give constant agitation for the first minute and 15 seconds every minute thereafter; for very short developing times (five minutes and less) agitate constantly. The actual agitation plan you follow is not as important as keeping to a consistent agitation in both tests and actual work.

4. Remember that when, say, 36 percent luminance values are placed lower than Zone VI on the exposure scale, other important values may fall below the threshold. This must not be overlooked when planning the exposure.

5. Also, when, say, 36 percent luminance values are placed lower on the scale, and development increased, values related to Zones VII and VIII will show as higher densities, sometimes exceeding Density values VIII and IX. This usually can be compensated for in printing. Of course, if a 36 percent luminance value is placed on Zone IV and a very bright object falls on Zone VII, the development required to achieve Density value VI for Zone IV exposure will perhaps result in a Density value IX for the Zone VII placement. As a result, it may be difficult to print this Density value IX other than as a pure white.

It is of great importance to evaluate all luminances of the subject, to know where they fall on the exposure scale, and to determine what their densities may be with different degrees of development. Compromises in placement are often necessary.

7. When a subject of very short luminance scale is to be expanded by normal-plus-two development, the average luminance value should be placed on Zone V, or, in some cases, on Zone IV.

8. Note in Figure 6 that as development is extended, all values increase in density, but the lower values increase proportionally less than the higher values. When development is reduced to about half the normal time, it is usually apparent that the lower values (Zones I to IV) will not have sufficient density separation to be satisfactorily printed. The water-bath process is advised when you have to narrow the density range. Figure 7 shows the recording of some actual exposures and the developing instructions.

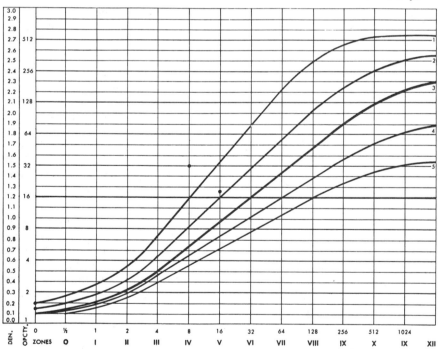

Figure 6. *A group of curves suggesting effects of different times of development in relation to different exposures. The heavy horizontal line represents a density of 1.20—actually a density of 1.10 (opacity 12.5) above film-base-plus-fog density (0.10). The heavy curve symbolizes the exposure-density relationship of the negative when a Zone VI exposure is developed to a density of 1.20 (1.10 above film-base fog). It shows a Zone 1 density of 0.10 above film-base fog and a Zone IX density of 1.80. The density range—from Zones O to IX—is 1.70, or an opacity range of 1 to 50 (approximating the exposure scale of a normal printing paper). Curves 1 and 2, representing long development times, may show a film-base-plus-fog density higher than 0.10, in which case the optimum density for Zone VI should be 1.10 plus whatever this film-base-plus-fog density happens to be.*

OPTIMUM OPACITY CONSIDERATIONS

Preliminary tests for optimum opacity should be made for purely expressive objectives. I suggest the following:

1. Take a portrait head in sun-

EXPOSURE RECORD
Designed and Copyright by
ANSEL ADAMS

	PLACEMENT OF SUBJECT INTENSITIES ON EXPOSURE SCALE									
SHEET NO. X	REL. LENS STOP F/	64	45	32	22	16	11	8	5.6	4	2.8
FILM X	REL. EXP. FOR V	1/32	1/16	1/8	1/4	1/2	1	2	4	8	16
SIZE X	REL. EXP. FOR I	1/2	1	2	4	8	16	32	64	128	256
DATE LOADED X	WESTON SCALE	–	U	–	–	A	↓	C	–	O	–
DATE EXPOSED X										

NO.	SUBJECT	0	I	II	III	IV	V	VI	VII	VIII	IX	FILM TYPE OR SPEED	F.L.	EXT.	X	FILTER NO.	X	STOP	EXP.	DEVELOPMENT
1	Mountain Landscape			25		100	200		800			50	8	–	–	K2	2	f/22	1/10	Normal
2	Portrait in sunlight				50	100		400			1600	100	12	–	–	–	–	f/16	1/100	Normal
3	Architectural detail, soft lt.				6.5		25	50				24	5	7	2	–	–	f/16 22	1 s	Normal +
4	Forest scene – much contrast			3.2		25				400		50	12	–	–	–	–	f/8	1/25	Normal –
5	Distant landscape in flat lt.				50		200		800			50	24	–	–	23A	4+	F/16	1/10	Normal +
6	TEST for optimum Opacity Nor.							X												NORMAL
7	ditto less than Normal Pl.						X													NORMAL +
8	ditto ditto					X														NORMAL ++
9	ditto more than Normal Pl.							X												NORMAL –
10	ditto ditto								X											NORMAL – –
11	ditto Threshold Test		X																	NORMAL
12	ditto Total development						X													TOTAL ($\gamma\infty$)

PHOTOGRAPHER: | PLACE: | JOB: | REMARKS OVERLEAF

Figure 7. *Exposure-record chart, available in blank sets. See text for explanation.*

light. The subject should be posed so the sun strikes the plane of the face at a 45-degree angle. Adjust the shadow values, by diffuse reflectors if necessary, so that the luminance ratio of shadow and flat sunlight is about 1 to 4. Do not include the brilliant highlights on the skin as they will vary with different types of skin and facial structure, and with the direction of the sun.

2. Measure the luminance of the sunlit portion of the head, avoiding the highlights and small shadows, and place this luminance on Zone VI of the exposure scale. Make 12 identical negatives.

3. Develop these negatives as follows: If the manufacturer advises 15 minutes for a given developer, develop the 12 identical exposures for 9, 10, 11, 12, 13, 14, 15, 16, 17, 18, 19, and 20 minutes.

4. Try contact printing on a No. 2 paper (No. 1 chloride papers, such as Azo, Convira, or No. 2 papers such as Velour Black, Kodabromide, Cykora). Determine the negative which gives you the best print in a regular print developer and put this negative aside. Note the developing time you gave it.

5. Try enlarging with a diffuse-light enlarger, and select the negative which gives you the best print. Remember, I am speaking of expressive prints, not just technically perfect prints. Put this negative aside, noting the developing time which you gave this one. This negative may be the same one selected for contact printing.

6. Try enlarging with a condenser enlarger, and select the negative which gives you the best print. Put this negative aside, noting the developing data.

7. Now make tests with a gray card, as described below, to establish accurate density (opacity) values. Evaluation with a smooth, continuous gray card is necessary, since it is almost impossible to read accurate densities from a negative with a textured surface such as skin. These values may be determined with a good densitometer.

TESTS FOR OPTIMUM OPACITY

1. Set up a light card and illuminate it evenly. Extend the lens as much as possible (to at least twice its focal length) for better coverage of the negative area. (Be certain to compute the exposure increase.) Daylight may be used only if an assured, constant quality and intensity exist, such as in high, clear sections of the country. Tungsten light is best as its intensity can be regulated by varying its distance from the card. The intensity of the reflected light from the card should read between 25 and 50 on the Weston Meter scale.

2. Set the metered-light value on Zone VI of the exposure scale, and make two or three exposures as indicated. Develop the negatives for the development times determined by the best portrait negatives. After processing take the density measurements of both the exposed areas and the unexposed edges of the films. The differences indicate the actual density of each of the negatives.

Or, if you wish to work directly for an arbitrary density value—

3. Set the metered-light value on Zone VI of the exposure scale and make four identical exposures as indicated. Process one negative in

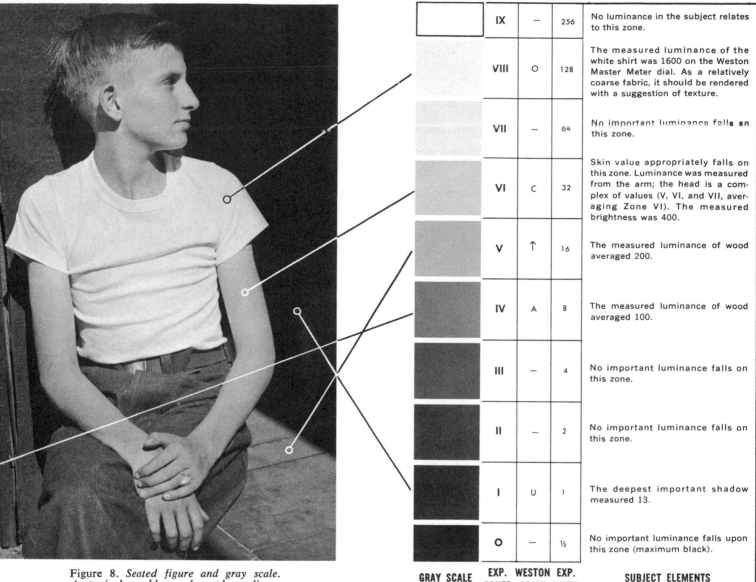

GRAY SCALE	EXP. ZONES	WESTON SCALE	EXP. UNITS	SUBJECT ELEMENTS
	IX	—	256	No luminance in the subject relates to this zone.
	VIII	O	128	The measured luminance of the white shirt was 1600 on the Weston Master Meter dial. As a relatively coarse fabric, it should be rendered with a suggestion of texture.
	VII	—	84	No important luminance falls on this zone.
	VI	C	32	Skin value appropriately falls on this zone. Luminance was measured from the arm; the head is a complex of values (V, VI, and VII, averaging Zone VI). The measured brightness was 400.
	V	↑	16	The measured luminance of wood averaged 200.
	IV	A	8	The measured luminance of wood averaged 100.
	III	—	4	No important luminance falls on this zone.
	II	—	2	No important luminance falls on this zone.
	I	U	1	The deepest important shadow measured 13.
	O	—	½	No important luminance falls upon this zone (maximum black).

Figure 8. *Seated figure and gray scale. A typical problem of outdoor figure photography, selected for demonstration because of its simplicity. The placement of the luminances is obvious. Exposure and development were normal. (From "The Negative: Exposure and Development" / Ansel Adams)*

the selected developer for the time recommended by the manufacturer. If the density is too low, develop the second film for a longer time. If, however, the density of the first negative is too great, develop the second film for a shorter time. Several test developments may be needed to establish the proper density for the printing process and paper used. When the proper density value is obtained, consider the developing time for this negative as normal for that particular film and developer combination. Be certain that the developer and your processing technique are consistent.

4. Next place the metered-light value on Zone V and expose four negatives accordingly. Develop one negative for one and a half times normal time and compare its density with that of the normal, Zone VI, negative. Develop the other three negatives, striving to match the density of the normal, Zone VI, negative. This will establish the developing time for a 36 percent luminance value placed on Zone V of the exposure scale, thereby resulting in more contrast and textural emphasis than possible with the normal procedure.

5. Place the metered-light value on Zone IV and expose four negatives accordingly. Develop one negative for two and a half times normal time and compare it with the normal, Zone VI, negative. Process the other negatives until one matches the density of the normal, Zone VI, negative. This will establish the development factor for a 36 percent luminance value exposed on Zone IV, expanding the values of the negative and providing much greater contrast and textural exaggeration than would be obtained by either the normal procedure or by the procedure described above.

6. Place the metered-light value on Zone VII and expose four negatives accordingly. Develop one negative three fourths of the normal time and compare with the normal, Zone VI, negative. Develop the

other negatives until one matches the density of the normal, Zone VI, negative, thereby establishing the development factor for a 36 percent luminance value placed on Zone VII of the exposure scale. This compresses the values of the image in relation to the value scale of the subject, resulting in less contrast and milder textural effects.

7. Placing 36 percent luminance values on Zone VIII will considerably compress the image values in relation to the value scale of the subject and will require one-half to two-thirds normal development. As the time of development approaches one half of normal, use the alternate water-bath process, or the lower tones of the image will be depressed in contrast and therefore of weak emotional impact.

To sum up, lowering the placement of 36 percent luminance values and giving more development increases the contrast of the image and intensifies the textural effects. Raising the placement and giving less development reduces image contrast and softens the textural effects. But in either case, 36 percent luminance values are maintained at the same value. In relation to threshold value, all values are changed by modification of development time, but the lower values are least affected.

Developing times and factors cannot be determined without testing. The factors suggested above are for test purposes only. The factors obtained for various placements of 36 percent luminance values will apply approximately, with most films, to various placements of 18 percent and 72 percent luminance values. A Zone V exposure can be raised to Density value VII, and a Zone VII exposure can be reduced to Density value V without rendering other Density values unprintable, except with subjects of great luminance range. Some recent films do not permit more than one-zone expansion.

The question may be asked, "Why select Zone VI for the basis of our tests?" Remember that you are concerned not with arbitrary subject luminances and negative opacities, but with the tonal values in the print, and these values are more "emotional" than factual. The importance of visualization, which implies *recognition* of subject values in terms of expressive values in the print, must not be underestimated. I have selected Zone VI as a basis of recognition for average skin values on the assumption that average Caucasian skin is a familiar value, easily compared to other values. Subjects such as gray rock, blue sky, green trees, and white sand are too variable for reference values.

The standard gray card (18 percent reflectance) now has universal recognition, and is directly related to Zone V of the exposure scale. All the tests listed above in relation to Zone VI can be carried out with Zone V. In recent years I have used densities 0.8 or 1.0 (above film-base-fog densities) for Zone V exposure results in relation to condenser-illumination for enlarging, or diffused-light enlarging and contact printing.

We can select any zone on the scale for a test. Anyone anxious to know the full scale of the papers used should make tests for Zone VIII exposure values. The resulting opacity should print as a slight but definite value below the pure white of the paper (when the film-base-fog value prints as full black). Setting an arbitrary density of 1.6 (opacity 40) above film-base-fog density for Zone VIII is a good point of departure for such tests.

I have found that variations in print developers and variations in development time change the effective exposure scale of the paper. Development cannot be prolonged when processing smaller negatives, since the grain will become objectionable. The use of higher contrast papers are indicated in such cases.

THRESHOLD TEST

A further check on meter, shutter, film, and developer performance requires a "threshold" test. Threshold is a term which refers to the lowest negative density, the shortest exposure necessary to produce the first step of printable density on the negative. This value is achieved by placing the subject luminance value on Zone I and exposing accordingly. Develop normally as previously determined. Effective threshold negative density should be about 0.1 above film-base-fog density value. If it is considerably more or less, major adjustments must be made either of film-speed setting or through checking the exposure meter response. This would mean retesting for normal development of Zone VI value. This threshold test should be made before 2, 3, 4, and 5 above are made. In practice a certain amount of lens and camera flare will produce additional threshold density. The minimum density of the average negative (above film-base-fog) usually will be between .10 and .20 and as high as .50 and .60 with multiple air-glass uncoated lenses.

EXTENSION TUBES AND BELLOWS

GEORGE BERKOWITZ
Photographer and author of "Hyperclose-up Photography with the Exakta."
[Because they reveal and magnify details not apparently visible in ordinary photos, extreme close-up photographs have become essential aids in medicine, dentistry and other scientific fields. This article explains the principles of the equipment and how to use it, including formulas for calculation of magnification ratios and lens-to-object distances.]
• *Also see: Bellows; Copying and Close-up Photography; Exposure (Light) Meters; Lighting.*

IF YOU WERE TO EXAMINE YOUR finger with a magnifying glass, you would see lines and whorls resembling deep ruts. Callouses would appear as rough bumps. The unusual size of familiar details may surprise you; even more surprising would be the unfamiliar details which would become visible to you for the first time through the magnifying glass.

Extension tubes and bellows, as well as other optical and mechanical devices that increase the distance normally existing between

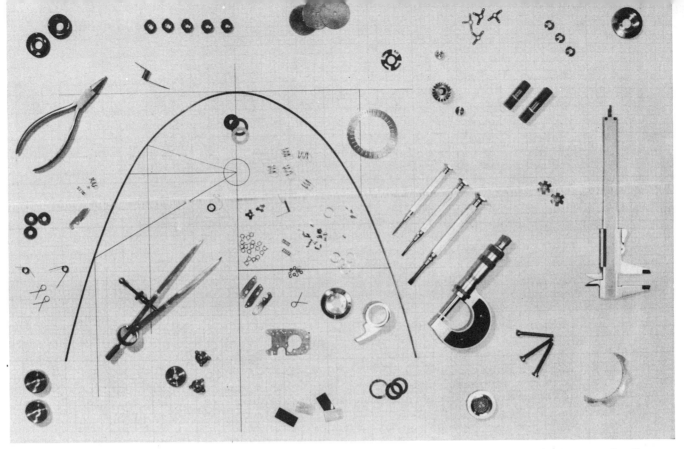

These 8 photographs show a comparison of focal length of lenses on the Contarex camera. This one was taken with the 35mm Zeiss Distagon f/4 at 37-inch distance. (Photos: M. Meuer / Zeiss Ikon)

camera lens and film, have the same effect as a magnifying glass. They make it possible for a camera lens to magnify the image of part of an object far beyond its ordinary capability and to produce a hyperclose-up photograph (macrophotograph, as it frequently is called).

Such photographs are provocative and occasionally astounding. They are more than just visual stimuli and adventures because they reveal details apparently not visible in ordinary photos. By magnifying a detail, macrophotography has become an essential aid in medicine and dentistry, in business and industry, and in education and research.

DESCRIPTION AND FUNCTIONS

Extension tubes and bellows are the devices perhaps most frequently used by photographers to obtain the image magnification required for hyperclose-up photography. They are accessories designed for insertion between the camera body and lens to increase the distance between the lens and film.

Tubes are nothing more than cylinders of varying length, usually threaded at both ends so they can be screwed together and combined

for longer extension if needed. They are usually made of lightweight metal, although they can be cardboard or any other material that is light-tight.

Accessory bellows are a more versatile and convenient variation of tubes. They serve the same purpose but have the advantages of speed and simplicity of operation. The length of the extension can be varied quickly, within the range of the bellows, simply by racking it in or out. Extension bellows are usually made of paper, cloth, or plastic, and closely resemble the bellows used on old-fashioned folding cameras and on modern press and view cameras.

Both extension devices require an adapter at each end, one to form a light-tight connection with the camera and the other to accept the camera lens. These adapters are in separate units for tubes but in most cases are built into extension bellows. It is possible to use a set of tubes on different brands of cameras of the same film size, as long as the appropriate adapters are available.

A bellows ordinarily can be used only with the specific camera or cameras for which it is designed. However, a few bellows are available with interchangeable adapters or front- and rear-panel boards, making it possible to use them on a variety of cameras of the same film size.

IMAGE MAGNIFICATION

You don't have to use an extension tube or bellows in all cases to magnify an image. There are several ways of getting the same result, to a limited degree, without using such accessories.

Basically a camera lens normally transmits to the film an image of the subject which is smaller than life-size. Because the size of the film is generally small, the size of the image in the film frame is also small, and a contact print of it will not be large enough to show any minute detail.

The image can be enlarged or magnified by printing so that more detail is discernible, but projection enlargement and the film itself have their limitations. Beyond a certain magnification, the image is likely to "fall apart"; that is quality and definition will be poor. This can be avoided if the *required* area of the image—and only this part—is magnified as much as possible in the film frame before the picture is taken. When it is enlarged, it will not suffer appreciable loss of quality.

The size of the image in the film frame (the amount the camera lens reduces or magnifies it) depends upon such factors as the lens' focal length, its focusing capabilities, and the distance between it and the subject. Altering any of these factors affects the image size.

FOCAL LENGTH

The longer the focal length of the lens, the larger the image transmitted by it to the film. The focal length of a lens, technically speaking, is the distance from the plane in which the lens forms an image of objects at infinity to the node of emission.

Roughly this is the distance from the film plane (the plane in which the film is located in the camera) to the optical center of the lens (usually considered to be location of the lens diaphragm). The focal length is customarily engraved on the lens

50mm Zeiss Planar f/2 at 35 inches.

mount in millimeters (sometimes in centimeters or inches), with the letter "f" usually preceding the number.

LENSES

All cameras normally are supplied with a "standard" lens, one in which the focal length is equal to, and covers the diagonal of, the film frame or negative. A lens that is twice the focal length of a standard lens, but is designed to cover the same diagonal, will transmit an image magnified twice the size of the image provided by the standard lens. But less of the subject area will be covered, because the film-frame size remains the same. A lens that has three times the focal length of the standard lens will magnify the image three times, but even less subject area will be covered. Whenever the image is magnified, less subject area is included within the frame.

It is apparent that the image of an object can be magnified if the standard lens is replaced with one of longer focal length. This is not always practicable, as the lenses of some cameras are fixed permanently in place.

Conversion accessory l e n s e s, which are attached to the original

lens and combine with it to form a longer focal length, are available for some cameras with fixed lenses.

Supplementary lenses also can be used over the fixed camera lens. If a positive lens is used, the focal length of the original lens is shortened, and the camera must be brought closer to the subject to focus sharply and to provide a large image.

A negative supplementary lens, on the other hand, will increase the focal length of the original lens so the distance between the lens and film plane must be increased to get a magnified image in sharp focus. Such lenses generally are uncorrected elements of the eyeglass-type (both surfaces are curved), and they introduce aberrations as well as alter the correction of the original lens, thus adversely affecting the quality of the image. A meniscus supplementary lens (one side concave, the other side convex) is better, but still degrades the quality of the original lens to some degree.

Fully corrected supplementary lenses are available and provide definition almost equal to that of the original lens. However, supplementary lenses introduce a focusing problem. Unless the camera has some provision for film-plane or

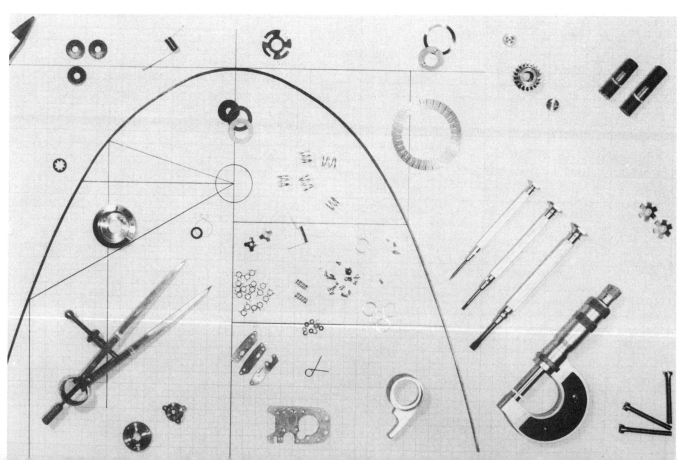

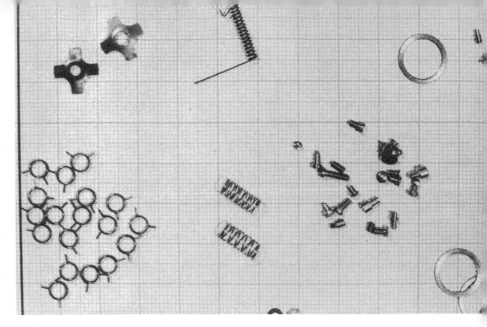

reflex-groundglass viewing, precise measurements must be made to ensure sharp focus, since the rangefinder on the camera body, in these cases, becomes useless. If the camera has a mount that permits the lens to be interchanged, the standard lens can be replaced with a longer one. The longer lens cannot be focused with the camera as close to the object as a standard lens. This may be an advantage if perspective and the heat of lights are important. The long lens is heavier, more cumbersome, and more difficult to use because it must be mounted on a tripod. It usually has a smaller maximum aperture which requires longer exposures. Finally, since many long lenses are costly, owning several may involve a considerable investment.

LENSES FOR 35 mm CAMERAS

In recent years, zoom lenses incorporating variable focus in the lens have become available for 35 mm cameras. Simply by changing the separation of the elements of these lenses, a range of focal lengths is available.

The Voigtländer-Zoomar, the first of these lenses produced for the 35 mm camera, offers a continuous variable focal-length range from 36mm to 82mm. Others have been introduced with a range in the longer focal lengths; one is now available with a range from 60mm to 500mm. Such lenses offer the possibility of magnification without extension accessories, but they are large, heavy, and expensive.

FOCUSING

The image of an object can be magnified to some degree without the use of extension tubes or accessories if the lens can be focused (in effect, if the distance between the film plane and the optical center of the lens can be varied). A camera lens forms an image on the film in the back of the camera. The image of the object is sharp, however, only when the distance between the lens and film is correct for the focal length of the lens and the distance of the object from the lens.

When the lens is focused at infinity, the distance between the film plane and the optical center of the lens is equal to the focal length of the lens. In order to focus with sharpness on objects closer than infinity, the distance must be increased. Changing this distance by extending the lens is known as focusing. All cameras, except the simple, inexpensive "box-type," have some method of focusing.

Focusing of 35 mm cameras is usually done with the lens, which generally has a helical (turning) mount allowing the front portion of the lens to be screwed forward or backward, thus increasing or decreasing the extension. Bellows-type cameras are focused by racking the bellows and lens forward or backward. Twin-lens reflex cameras are focused by moving the entire lens panel out or in. Other types of

50mm Zeiss Planar f/2 at 11.8 inches.

cameras have provision for back focusing, in which the film plane is moved forward or backward, or for changing the separation of the lens elements.

If a lens could be extended without limit, it would have unlimited range and there would be no need for extension tubes, bellows, or other accessories for hyper-close-up photography. Lenses must be limited in extension for practical reasons of weight, convenience, complexity, and economy. Until recently it was customary for the near limit of the focusing range of a short focal-length lens to be between two and three feet, and of a long focal-length lens to be from about five or ten feet to as much as 65 feet in extreme cases.

The more a lens is extended by

50mm Zeiss Planar f/2 close-up lens.

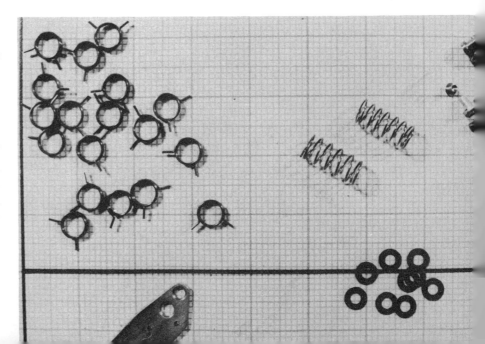

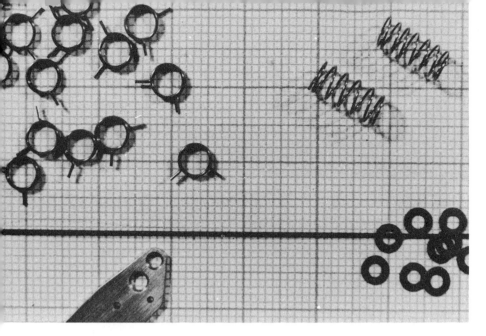

35mm Zeiss Distagon f/4 at 7.6 inches.

focusing (the more the distance between the film plane and optical center is increased), the more the image is magnified and the smaller the object area covered. However, a lens extended to the near limit of its normal focusing range, say three feet, would still transmit a smaller-than-life-size image to the film.

The increasing popularity of 35 mm cameras (particularly of the single-lens reflex type) and of hyper-close-up photography has brought about manufacture of lenses with wider-than-normal focusing ranges.

The target was a 1:1 ratio. When the distance between the optical center of the lens and the film plane is twice the focal length of the lens, the image of the object and the object are equal in size. The problem was to increase suffi-

50mm Zeiss Planar f/2 with bellows attachment, 1:1.6.

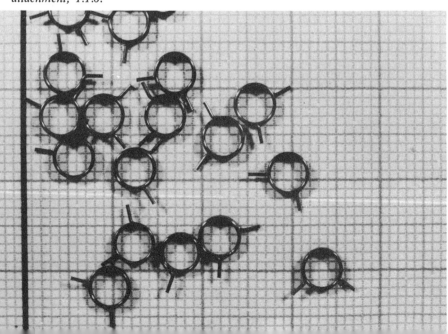

ciently the normal focusing range of a short focal length lens to achieve this ratio; it was solved by the development of double helical focusing mounts.

First to appear, in 1953, was the 40mm Kilfitt Makro-Kilar, designed for 35 mm cameras. Two models were available. One provides continuous focusing from infinity to four inches from the subject (the distance is measured from the end of the lens mount). It has an object-to-image ratio of 1:0.5, that is, the image transmitted at the nearest limit of the normal focusing range is half the life-size of the object. The other model focuses from infinity to two inches from the subject, providing a 1:0.99 ratio or slightly less than life-size.

A third model, the 90mm Kilfitt Makro-Kilar, designed primarily for 2¼ × 2¼ single-lens reflex cam-

eras, appeared later. It provides a 1:0.93 ratio with such cameras, but goes to 1:1 when used on a 35 mm camera.

Many more close-focusing lenses have been introduced in recent years. Among them are the 50mm Macro-Extenar for the Exakta and the 55mm Micro-Nikkor for the Nikon, both of which provide a maximum 1:1 ratio. Another is the 50mm Macro-Rokkor for the Minolta SR cameras which provides a 1:0.5 ratio normally, but is supplied with a small extension tube which extends the ratio to 1:1.

As you extend the lens by focusing, you must decrease the distance between the lens and object. The closer you come to the object, the more its image is magnified and the smaller the area covered. You can demonstrate this with any camera equipped with a focusing lens. Merely start out with the lens focused on an object at infinity and slowly walk closer to the object, keeping it in focus. You will see the image magnify and the area covered decrease as the lens is extended. In addition, the distance between the film plane and optical center of the lens increases as you get closer to the subject.

OTHER METHODS OF MAGNIFICATION

There are other methods of image magnification without using accessory extension devices. Press and view cameras can be used because they generally have a bellows that can be extended considerably. If you prefer the larger film size of such cameras, some are available with a double-extension and triple-extension bellows. Stretching the double-extension bellows to its maximum normal limit will give you a 1:1 ratio with a standard lens and greater image magnification with a shorter focal-length lens.

The lower range of image magnifications above 1:1 is usually covered by such cameras without extra accessory extension equipment. Short focal-length lenses, however, can provide higher magnifications.

Enlargers that can be converted into cameras by the removal of the lamphouse and insertion of a camera back, or by similar arrangements, also can be used for low-range magnification. The length of the bellows extension on such equipment determines how much the image of the object can be magnified. Copy and slide-duplicating outfits, and even view or press cameras used front-to-back, can be used for making hyperclose-ups.

35 mm CAMERAS

With the exception of press and view cameras, if you want image magnifications above life-size and up to about 30 times the object size, you'll have to use either accessory extension tubes or bellows. Many photographers today seem to prefer the 35 mm camera for this type of work because the equipment is relatively light and compact, easy to handle, focus, and operate. Although the film format is small (24×36 mm), it is economical. In addition, there is a staggering array of equipment available at all prices, much more than for any other size camera.

Extension tubes usually come in sets of varying length. Leitz, for instance, supplies tubes of 7 mm, 15 mm, 30 mm, 45 mm, 60 mm, and 90 mm lengths which can be used singly or in combination. Other camera manufacturers offer tubes of the same or slightly different lengths. It is possible to make your own tubes out of cardboard, but you must be certain they are light-tight and that the inside is painted dull black to eliminate light reflection.

ADAPTERS

Photographers using Kilfitt lenses can utilize the Kilfitt Macro-Adapter, a type of extension equipment that combines the features of tubes with the helical focusing of a lens mount. A mount at one end fits the camera; a threaded section at the other end accepts the camera lens. This adapter can be extended over a narrow range by means of helical focusing. With an additional adapter placed between the Macro-Adapter and the lens, the full focusing range of the lens can be used. The 90mm Makro-Kilar with the Macro-Adapter will provide a maximum ratio of 1:1; the 135mm and 150mm Kilars, a ratio of 1:0.38; and the 300mm Tele-Kilar, a ratio of 1:0.25.

EXTENSION BELLOWS

Many different kinds of extension bellows are available. They vary in maximum extension from as little as three and one-quarter inches to as much as eight and three-quarter inches. Some provide scales to make macrophotography easier, or they may have special features—such as interchangeable front and back panels or a pistol grip.

Choosing the focal length of the lens to use with your tubes or bellows is not always an easy decision. A short lens is lighter, faster and easier to work with than a long lens. It also has a wider angle of view. Because it is short, however, you may have to work very close to the subject, and the heat and intensity of the lights may make you uncomfortable.

A long lens cannot be focused as close to the object, so the lights may not affect you as much. A

Above: *50mm Zeiss Planar f/2 with bellows attachment, 4:1.*

Below: *35mm Zeiss Distagon f/4 with bellows attachment, 4:1.*

Great detail is revealed in extreme close-ups made with extension tubes or bellows.

long lens also offers the advantage of proper perspective, if this is important in your picture. However, if the object you are photographing, and thus the lights, must be shifted continually, a long lens can be more inconvenient than a short one. Long lenses are also heavier, more cumbersome, more difficult to handle, and require a tripod. They cannot be conveniently used for higher magnifications. They have smaller maximum apertures than short lenses, thus requiring longer exposures. And, in most cases, they are more expensive.

PREPARATIONS

Before you start photographing, you can save time if you consider the size of the object you want to photograph and decide how much of it you want on the negative.

Macrophotography is usually approached from one of two directions. Some photographers calculate what they want to get before they set up their equipment. Others decide what they want by looking through the viewfinder.

Working by visual means alone is accurate enough; it simplifies matters because it eliminates calculations. After setting up your equipment and the subject, start with the smallest extension and add tubes or extend the bellows until the image you see on the groundglass is the size you want. This method can be time-consuming if you are using extension tubes.

Calculating what you want may seem to take longer than the visual method, but it usually saves time, particularly when the object is tiny

and the magnification is to be great. You simply aim for a specific object-to-image ratio.

RATIOS

If the subject is one inch long, but measures only one tenth of an inch on the groundglass, the image will be reduced ten times. The ratio or relationship between the object size and image size is 1:0.1.

If the object is one tenth of an inch and is magnified to measure one inch on the groundglass, it will be increased ten times. The ratio of object-to-image size is 1:10.

There is some inconsistency in the way ratios are stated by various sources; it is advisable to study ratios carefully to make certain they mean what you think they do. Some

writers always state the object size on the left and the image size on the right of the ratio, using a zero in front of the decimal when either number is below 1. Others avoid the zero by always stating the image size as 1 when it is smaller than life-size (reduced below 1:1); they then switch, always stating the object size as 1 when the image is larger than life-size (magnified greater than 1:1).

You can use either system as long as you are consistent. Some writers confuse the ratio by using a number greater than 1 for the image, even though it is smaller than life-size. For example, a 2 is used for 0.5 (½ life-size); a 3 is used for 0.33 ($^1/_3$ life-size); and a 4 is used for 0.25 (¼ life-size). This should be avoided. Be consistent, whichever system you use, so you can tell in reading a ratio which number refers to the object and which one to the image.

Once you have decided on the ratio you want, it's a simple matter to determine whether you can get in the film frame the magnification of the object area you want. Dividing the largest dimension of the object area (length or width) into the largest dimension of the film

The macrophotograph is an indispensable tool in many scientific fields. Made with 135mm lens by electronic flash. (Photo: Karl Muller)

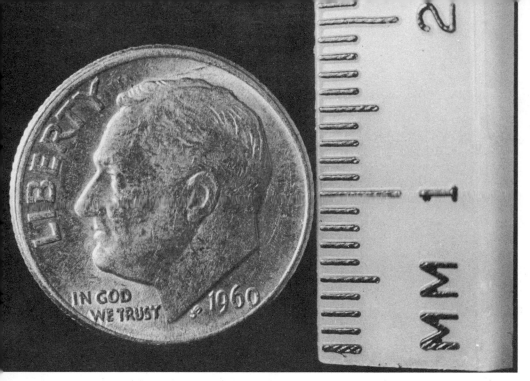

frame will give you the answer.

For instance, suppose you want to photograph a section ½ inch long, and you want to have a horizontal format on a 35 mm film frame (which is 24×36 mm or roughly $1 \times 1\frac{1}{2}$ inches in size). Dividing 1½ by ½ you get 3, the maximum magnification obtainable of an area ½ inch long on a film frame $1 \times 1\frac{1}{2}$ inches in size.

More magnification is possible, of course, if less of the subject is photographed. If only half of the ½-inch section is required in the picture, for example, you can magnify it 6 times on a film frame of the same size (1½ divided by ¼ equals 6). If the given area is only $^1/_8$ inch long, you can magnify it 12 times.

If you need a larger magnification than the film size and desired subject area will permit, the image can be further magnified by projection enlargement.

A ½-inch detail will be magnified about 18 times its original size if the image on the film is 3 times the detail's actual size and the negative is then enlarged to an 8×10 print. An 11×14 enlargement would provide a 27-times magnification, a 16×20 print about a 39-times enlargement.

The idea is to magnify the image as much as possible and fill the film frame with it. However, the dimen-

sions of the frame may not always permit filling it completely; if you have a square area and your film frame is a rectangle, you cannot fill the entire frame with the object. All you can do is take the largest dimension of the area and magnify it to the limits of the frame.

DATA FOR MACROPHOTOGRAPHY

In macrophotography you will have to know the length of the extension required for the magnfication you want, the distance between the film plane and optical center of the lens, the distance between the lens and object, and the required exposure increase. Manufacturers of cameras, lenses, and extension accessories often provide tables containing all this information. Find out if they are available for your equipment, because they will save you considerable time and calculation.

If you are unable to use the data tables (see chart) and cannot obtain suitable ones for your equipment, you'll have to calculate the data you need. If you do any amount of macrophotography, you will find it helpful to make up your own tables for the lens focal lengths you use, if they are not otherwise available.

Certain standard data on film-lens-object distances can be helpful. If you want the image and object to have the same size (1:1 relationship) you know that the film must be twice the focal length of the lens distant from the optical center of the lens. At this extension, the lens also must be twice the focal length distance from the object.

Therefore instead of trying to find the 1:1 relationship by trial and error, simply multiply the focal length by four, and your answer is the distance the film plane should be from the object. The optical center of the lens should be exactly halfway between the two. You can check this with a ruler.

If the distance between film plane and optical center of the lens is three focal lengths, the image will be twice as large as the object. If

Above: *The Minolta Macro-Rokkor lens.*

Below: *Kilfitt 40mm Makro-Kilar lenses.*

CLOSE-UP DATA FOR 50-MM. LENSES

Length of extension in mm.	Distance from subject to lens in mm.*	Distance from lens to film in mm.†	Total distance from film to subject in mm.‡	Scale of subject image to life size§	Required exposure increase*
0	infinity	50	infinity	variable	1.00
5	550	55	605	0.1	1.21
10	300	60	360	0.2	1.44
15	217	65	282	0.3	1.69
20	175	70	245	0.4	1.96
25	150	75	225	0.5	2.25
30	133	80	213	0.6	2.56
35	121	85	206	0.7	2.89
40	113	90	203	0.8	3.24
45	106	95	201	0.9	3.61
50	100	100	200	1.0	4.00
60	92	110	202	1.2	4.84
70	86	120	206	1.4	5.76
80	81	130	211	1.6	6.76
90	78	140	218	1.8	7.84
100	75	150	225	2.0	9.00
110	73	160	233	2.2	10.20
120	71	170	241	2.4	11.60
130	69	180	249	2.6	13.00
140	68	190	258	2.8	14.40
150	67	200	267	3.0	16.00

CLOSE-UP DATA FOR 105-MM. LENSES

Length of extension in mm.	Distance from subject to lens in mm.*	Distance from lens to film in mm.†	Total distance from film to subject in mm.‡	Scale of subject image to life size§	Required exposure increase*
0	infinity	105	infinity	variable	1.00
5	2310	110	2420	0.05	1.10
10	1208	115	1323	0.10	1.21
15	840	120	960	0.14	1.30
20	656	125	781	0.19	1.42
25	546	130	676	0.22	1.49
30	473	135	608	0.29	1.66
35	420	140	560	0.33	1.77
40	381	145	526	0.38	1.90
45	350	150	500	0.43	2.05
50	326	155	481	0.48	2.19
60	289	165	454	0.57	2.47
70	263	175	438	0.67	2.79
80	243	185	428	0.76	3.10
90	228	195	423	0.86	3.46
100	215	205	420	0.95	3.80
110	205	215	420	1.05	4.20
120	197	225	422	1.14	4.58
130	190	235	425	1.24	5.02
140	184	245	429	1.33	5.43
150	178	255	433	1.43	5.91

CLOSE-UP DATA FOR 58-MM. LENSES

Length of extension in mm.	Distance from subject to lens in mm.*	Distance from lens to film in mm.†	Total distance from film to subject in mm.‡	Scale of subject image to life size§	Required exposure increase*
0	infinity	58	infinity	variable	1.00
5	731	63	794	0.09	1.18
10	394	68	462	0.17	1.37
15	282	73	355	0.26	1.59
20	226	78	304	0.35	1.81
25	192	83	275	0.43	2.05
30	170	88	258	0.52	2.30
35	154	93	247	0.60	2.60
40	142	98	240	0.69	2.85
45	133	103	236	0.78	3.17
50	125	108	233	0.86	3.46
60	114	118	232	1.03	4.14
70	106	128	234	1.21	4.87
80	100	138	238	1.38	5.66
90	95	148	243	1.55	6.51
100	92	158	250	1.72	7.42
110	89	168	257	1.90	8.39
120	86	178	264	2.07	9.42
130	84	188	272	2.24	10.50
140	82	198	280	2.41	11.70
150	80	208	288	2.58	12.90

CLOSE-UP DATA FOR 135-MM. LENSES

Length of extension in mm.	Distance from subject to lens in mm.*	Distance from lens to film in mm.†	Total distance from film to subject in mm.‡	Scale of subject image to life size§	Required exposure increase*
0	infinity	135	infinity	variable	1.00
5	3780	140	3920	0.04	1.07
10	1958	145	2103	0.07	1.15
15	1350	150	1500	0.11	1.23
20	1046	155	1201	0.15	1.32
25	864	160	1024	0.19	1.40
30	743	165	908	0.22	1.49
35	656	170	826	0.26	1.59
40	591	175	766	0.30	1.68
45	540	180	720	0.33	1.78
50	500	185	685	0.37	1.88
60	439	195	634	0.44	2.09
70	395	205	600	0.52	2.30
80	363	215	578	0.59	2.54
90	338	225	563	0.67	2.78
100	317	235	552	0.74	3.03
110	301	245	546	0.82	3.29
120	287	255	542	0.89	3.57
130	275	265	540	0.96	3.85
140	265	275	540	1.03	4.12
150	256	285	541	1.12	4.49

These tables have been computed mathematically. You may find that the figures are not precise for your lens. Minor variations exist because all lenses differ slightly, even those of the same focal length. Therefore, use this data as a guide rather than as absolute measurement. If greater accuracy is required, the necessary data can be computed quickly with the formulas given in the text of this booklet. All lengths are given in millimeters. To convert to inches, multiply by 0.03937.

* The customary point of measurement of the lens is the center, usually considered to be iris diaphragm plane.

† This distance is the sum of the extension and the focal length of the lens. It is measured from the center of the lens (diaphragm) to the film plane in the camera.

‡ The sum of columns two and three.

§ The ratio of the size of the subject's image on film to the actual size of the subject.

* This column shows by how much the basic exposure time, computed for the lens without additional extension, must be multiplied to compensate for the extension used.

Leica M3, Visoflex II and 90-degree magnifier, 90mm Elmar lens unit and short focusing mount; standard magnifier to right.

the distance is four focal lengths, the image will be three times as large as the object. This rule also works in reverse. If the film plane is only 1½ focal lengths from the optical center of the lens, the image is half the size of the object. These proportions are true for any focal length of lens.

Whenever you use extension tubes or bellows, you need a ruler or tape measure because the distance scale on the camera or lens is no longer accurate when an extension device is inserted between camera body and lens. If your camera has a built-in rangefinder, it too is no longer usable.

GROUNDGLASS FOCUSING

If the camera has a groundglass back or a through-the-lens viewfinder, you can focus without difficulty. If the camera does not have such a back or finder, you may be able to focus with a piece of groundglass or matte celluloid placed in the back of the camera on the plane normally occupied by the film. This must be done before the film is loaded into the camera.

Reflex housings which can be inserted between the camera body and extension device are available for most 35 mm rangefinder cam-

eras. They change rangefinder cameras into single-lens reflexes.

Reflex housings are extremely versatile and can be used with or without an extension bellows. The Leitz Visoflex II, for instance, can be used with lenses from 35mm to 400mm in length. Intermediate rings provide the hyperclose-up range. The Kilfitt Kilarscope and Kilarflex can be used with the 90mm Makro-Kilar and other Kilars as long as 600mm. Some housings are supplied with long focal-length lenses in special short mounts, to increase their versatility.

Special accessories, which permit the camera to be pushed to one side while the object is focused upon and the picture composed on a focusing screen, are available for some 35 mm rangefinder cameras. Such a unit is the Leitz Focoslide. Another, the Leitz Reprovit II, is actually a copying outfit, but also can be used in macrophotography and other fields because it has a focusing stage. After the focusing has been completed, the camera is returned to taking position and the picture taken. This unit not only permits the focusing to be accomplished when the camera contains film, but keeps the camera rigidly in the same plane during its move-

ment from taking position to the side and back.

ACCURATE FOCUSING

For very precise focusing, you can sometimes replace your regular groundglass with an extra fine one to get delicate detail, or use a magnifier. Extremely fine detail is very hard to see even when a magnifier is used. It may be possible to oil your groundglass, or rub a drop of glycerin on it, to improve detail rendition. The glycerin is preferable, because it is not only bright and odorless, but can be washed off easily.

Many photographers use a photographic glass plate which has been fogged by light and processed to a density of about 0.3. The plate is mounted, emulsion side toward the lens, and a strong magnifier used for critical focus.

If you are unable to use a groundglass with your camera, you will need to know the dimensions of the field size which is the area covered by the lens at various extensions and reproduction ratios. This information is sometimes available from camera manufacturer or makers of supplementary lenses. For some cameras, wire frames are available which attach to the front of the camera and delineate the field covered at specific magnifications and extensions.

Critical focusing is always a problem in macrophotography, because of the limited depth of field. When a camera lens is focused on an object a few feet away, depth of field is measured in feet; when the subject is a few inches away, it is measured in inches or fractions of an inch. Depth of field varies with the focal length of the lens; the range of apparent sharpness decreases as a longer lens is used.

Depth of field also decreases as the camera lens is focused on nearer points, when a larger aperture is used, and as the image magnification increases.

CIRCLE OF CONFUSION

The "circle of confusion" is also a factor in depth of field. When the lens is focused at a predetermined distance, light rays from other distances are not all brought to a focus exactly in the focal (film) plane. Some are focused in the plane, some ahead, and some behind it. If the lens were able to bring objects at varying distances to a sharp focus in one plane, then the objects would be sharply defined as points of light all over the film. Since this is contrary to optical principles, each ray brought to focus in front of or behind the focal plane records not as a point of light, but as a tiny circle called the "circle of confusion."

The circle of confusion is not an inherent quality of a lens, but a measurement, just as Centigrade and Fahrenheit degrees are measurements of temperature. The circle of confusion measures the diameter of the image of an out-of-focus light ray on the film.

The image of the object is composed of many sharp points of light from the plane upon which the lens is focused, plus many overlapping circles of confusion from light reflected from objects near or far from the plane upon which the lens is focused. These may blur the image and degrade definition.

Fortunately, a tiny circle looks like a point to the eye if its diameter is $1/100$ of an inch or less. Therefore this size is the largest permissible circle of confusion when a sharp image is desired. If the circle of confusion is $1/100$ of an inch or smaller in diameter, and the image is 10 inches from the eye when viewed, the image will appear to be sharply focused.

If a negative with an image containing circles of confusion $1/100$ of an inch in diameter is enlarged to twice its size, the relative diameters of the circles of confusion is also doubled, becoming $1/50$ of an inch. The picture loses sharpness proportionately.

For this reason, 35 mm camera negatives, which are always given considerable enlargements, require a tiny circle of confusion. When enlarged ten times, a circle of confusion of $1/1000$ of an inch will become

65mm Elmar f/3.5 lens on Leica M1 with Visoflex II.

$1/100$ of an inch.

When the depth of field is increased and the image magnified the circle of confusion is increased. It is important to keep this fact in mind and maintain a circle of confusion of $1/1000$ of an inch or less whenever possible in macrophotography.

DEPTH OF FIELD

Since depth of field becomes critical at high magnifications, it is important to use depth-of-field tables. A separate depth-of-field table must be calculated for each focal length, for each aperture, and for the specific circle of confusion.

Just as depth of field is critical in macrophotography, so is depth of focus at very close distances. Don't confuse the two. Depth of field refers to the range of acceptable sharpness at the subject. Depth of focus refers to the range at the film plane.

The tolerance of the film plane may be so critical that you may have difficulty getting sharp images if the film plane and focusing screen are not located exactly at the same distances from the lens. For this reason, many macrophotographers prefer glass-plate cameras which hold the film in registration.

Depth of field decreases as you use a wider lens aperture and increases as the lens is stopped down. Definition and resolution depreciate if you stop down too far. Diffraction of light rays occurs at small lens apertures and degrades the image.

The optical design of a specific lens provides it with an optimum aperture at which it will give the best possible definition. This aperture is usually near the widest opening, or sometimes midway, rather than near the smallest.

LIGHTING

The lighting of objects for hyper-close-up photography is a subject of broad scope because the requirements vary from picture to picture and from object to object. Each individual situation must be considered by the photographer on the basis of what must be emphasized, such as shape, texture, or details. There are many different types of light sources, such as daylight, flash, electronic flash, ring lights and other circular flash tubes, reflector floodlamps, spotlights, vertical illuminators (for opaque objects), fluorescent substage illuminators (placed under the object), projection lamps, prefocused flashlight

bulbs, and polarized light, some used with mirrors and other reflectors.

One of the problems in illuminating small subjects is that the light is usually larger than the object. Another is that it is very difficult to position a light near the lens which will fill in the front of the object. Shadows also become a problem, although a "tent" may eliminate these. Try to use only one

light to avoid excess heat. A high-low switch or rheostat arrangement, to control lights and keep them at a low level while you are setting up your equipment, is particularly effective in this type of photography. Use reflectors to keep down the number of lights.

EXPOSURE METER USE

An exposure meter can be used to determine exposure, but accurately reading the light being reflected by, or falling on, a tiny object can be very difficult. You

can use either a reflected- or incident-light meter, but unless it has a very narrow angle of acceptance, its reading will be inaccurate.

One way of handling the situation is to mask off, or otherwise block off, all but a small area of the meter's sensitive cell and take a reading from the camera ground-glass. Another method is to take a reading from a card, such as an 18 percent reflectance gray card placed in the same position with the same illumination. Avoid read-

Leica M3, Visoflex II, OUBIO Adapter, 21.5mm Adapter, and 200mm Telyt f/4 lens.

ing from backgrounds of a different and lighter color than the object or you'll get a wrong reading.

Meters are now being introduced which actually measure the amount of light entering the lens, because they can be positioned inside the camera or are permanently located behind the lens. These innovations will make measurement in hyper-close-up photography more accurate. Another recent innovation, the Beseler Topcon Film Plane Exposure Meter, is unique in that it compensates for bellows extension when it is bayonet-mounted onto the back of the bellows unit in the position of the camera.

Make some advance tests with any meter you plan to use; bracket exposures to get at least one well-exposed photo.

When the lens has been extended beyond its normal length, the image of the object is fainter on the groundglass. You'll have to make an adjustment for this fact in your exposure. The *f*-stop numbers on your lens no longer apply, even at 1:1, because the extension is so much greater and the light reaching the film so much less. The table below gives an idea of the actual aperture of the lens at several magnifications:

Magnification	Indicated aperture	Actual aperture
1×	*f*/4	*f*/8
2×	*f*/4	*f*/12
4×	*f*/4	*f*/20
8×	*f*/4	*f*/36
12×	*f*/4	*f*/52
15×	*f*/4	*f*/64

Many lenses, especially the close-focusing type, and most of the accessory extension bellows, have scales which automatically provide an exposure-increase factor as the lens or bellows is extended. This factor is multiplied by the shutter speed which normally would be used to obtain the exposure required without the extension. The new, short lenses for the Zeiss Contarex camera automatically compensate for extension by a change in the shape of the aperture. For convenience, Table 1 can be used to determine the correction factor for reductions to 20:1 and magnifications to 1:20.

EXPOSURE INCREASE

High magnifications entail long exposures that create other problems. Film emulsions are designed for the normal range of exposure employed by the majority of photographers. If film receives exposures excessively longer than average limits, you may find that the film isn't as fast as it is rated. Color film cannot be used for long exposures without radically changing the color balance of the emulsion (reciprocity law failure). Therefore try to make your exposure as short as possible.

Another hazard of long exposures is camera vibration, the effect of which is increased by the high magnification of the image. Both camera and object should be mounted on solid supports, but this may not help when the simple opening

Kilfitt Macro-Adapter.

Table 1. RATIOS					
REDUCTION			**MAGNIFICATION**		
Ratio of object to image		Correction factor	Ratio of object to image		Correction factor
20	to 1	1.10	1	to 1	4
19	1	1.11	1	1.25	5
18	1	1.12	1	1.50	6
17	1	1.12	1	1.75	7.5
16	1	1.13	1	2	9
15	1	1.14	1	2.25	10.5
14	1	1.15	1	2.5	12
13	1	1.16	1	2.75	14
12	1	1.17	1	3	16
11	1	1.19	1	3.5	20
10	1	1.21	1	4	25
9	1	1.24	1	4.5	30
8	1	1.27	1	5	36
7	1	1.31	1	6	49
6	1	1.36	1	7	64
5	1	1.44	1	8	81
4.5	1	1.50	1	9	100
4	1	1.56	1	10	121
3.5	1	1.65	1	11	144
3	1	1.78	1	12	169
2.75	1	1.86	1	13	196
2.5	1	1.96	1	14	225
2.25	1	2.09	1	15	256
2	1	2.25	1	16	289
1.75	1	2.47	1	17	324
1.5	1	2.78	1	18	361
1.25	1	3.24	1	19	400
1	1	4.00	1	20	441

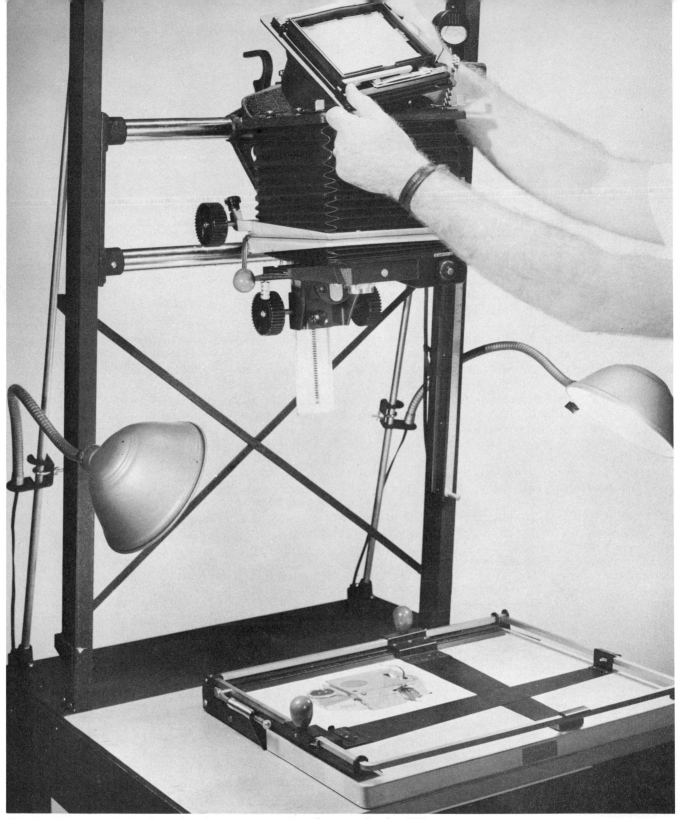

The Beseler camera back takes only a few moments to install on any Beseler 4 X 5 enlarger. It locks in place and provides perfect alignment between the film plane, lens, and easel. The regular enlarging easel holds objects perfectly flat. Lights attach to frame for even lighting.

and closing of the lens causes waves of movement. One way to avoid this problem is to set up your equipment in a room which can be made completely dark. When you are ready to take the picture, turn off the lights, open the camera shutter, wait for a minute or two until the vibration stops, switch on the lights, make the exposure, switch off the lights and close the shutter. Arranging the lights through a control panel with a single switch helps.

FORMULAS FOR MACROPHOTOGRAPHY

Explanation of symbols:

F = Focal length of the lens.
M = Magnification of the image.
When there is a reduction (the image is smaller than the object),

the magnification is less than 1. For an actual magnification (the image is larger than the subject), the magnification is greater than 1.

D = The lens-to-image distance. With small cameras which do not have bellows, add the focal length of the lens and the length of the extension tube or tubes to find the lens-to-image distance.

I = Size of the image on the film.

O = Size of the object.

Lens to object distance: What is the lens-to-object distance when the ratio of magnification is to be 2:1 (the image is to be twice as large as the subject)? The focal length of the lens is 4 inches. Lens-to-object distance =

$$F + \frac{F}{M} = 4 + \frac{4}{2} = 6 \text{ inches.}$$

What is the lens-to-object distance when the ratio of reduction is 1:2 (the image is half the size of the subject, so the ratio of magnification would be 0.5)? The focal length of the lens is 4 inches. Lens-to-object distance =

$$F + \frac{F}{M} = 4 + \frac{4}{0.5} = 4 + 8 = 12.$$

Increase in exposure: What is the increase in exposure (exposure factor) when a 4-inch lens and extension tubes are used so that the distance from the lens to the film is 12 inches? Increase in exposure (exposure factor) =

$$\frac{D^2}{F^2} = \frac{12 \times 12}{4 \times 4} = \frac{3 \times 3}{1 \times 1} = 9.$$

The exposure factor is 9. The exposure necessary is 9 times more than normal.

Ratio of reduction: (When the image is smaller than the object.) What is the ratio of reduction when the lens-to-film distance is 6 inches and a 4-inch lens is being used? Ratio of reduction =

$$\frac{D-F}{F} = \frac{I}{O} = \frac{6-4}{4} = \frac{2}{4} = \frac{1}{2}.$$

The ratio of reduction is 1:2. The image is half the size of the object.

Ratio of magnification: (When the image is larger than the object.) What is the ratio of magnification when the lens-to-film distance is 12 inches and a 4-inch lens is being used? Ratio of magnification =

$$\frac{F}{D-F} = \frac{O}{I} = \frac{4}{12-4} = \frac{4}{8} = \frac{1}{2}.$$

The ratio of magnification is 2:1. The image is twice the size of the object.

The set-up demonstrates how the use of a longer focal length lens provides more area between camera and subject so lights can be more easily arranged. The 100mm lens is attached to extension tubes.

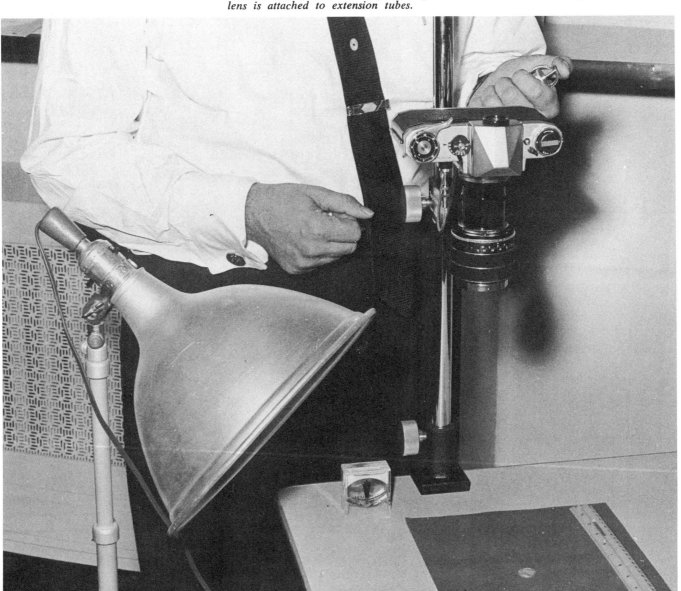

FABRIC PRINTING

There is a continual interest in the printing of photographs on fabrics of various kinds, and over a period of many years a number of processes have been developed for this purpose.

Silver images can be produced on fabrics, provided the fabrics are first well sized to avoid excessive absorption of the silver. An example is to be found in the following method which combines sizing and "salting" in one bath.

Arrowroot
290 grains   20 grams
Sodium chloride
290 grains   20 grams
Acetic acid, glacial (99%)
2½ ounces   80 cc
Tannic acid
290 grains   20 grams
Distilled water to make
32 ounces   1 liter

After sizing, the cloth is immersed in the sensitizer:
Silver nitrate
145 grains   10 grams
Nitric acid (10% sol.)
15 minims   1 cc
Water (distilled)
3¼ ounces   100 cc

The cloth is then dried in total darkness. When dry it is exposed under a negative to sunlight or arc light and subsequently toned and fixed as any ordinary silver printing-out paper.

Since the image is produced by contact printing, an enlarged negative is needed. For enlargements, a faster emulsion of the bromide type is required.

For the advanced amateur who would like to attempt the making of a bromide emulsion, the following will serve as a starting point:

PRESENSITIZER

Potassium bromide
60 grains   4 grams
Cadmium bromide
190 grains   12.5 grams
Potassium iodide
60 grains   4 grams
Distilled water to make
32 ounces   1 liter

SENSITIZER

Silver nitrate
¾ oz., 78 gr   28 grams
Citric acid
½ ounce   7 grams
Distilled water
32 ounces   1 liter

CHART 1

Feertype Sensitizer A

Sodium toluoldiazosulfonate	365 grains	25 grams
Beta-naphthol	365 grains	25 grams
Sodium hydroxide	½ ounce	8 grams
Water to make	32 ounces	1 liter

Feertype Sensitizer B

Sodium ditolyltetrazosulfonate	365 grains	25 grams
Metaphenylenediamine	290 grains	20 grams
Water to make	32 ounces	1 liter

Feertype Sensitizer C

Sodium ditolyltetrazosulfonate	365 grains	25 grams
Resorcinol	320 grains	22 grams
Sodium hydroxide	½ ounce	15 grams
Water to make	32 ounces	1 liter

Feertype Sensitizer D

Sodium ditolyltetrazosulfonate	1 ounce	30 grams
Resorcinol	290 grains	20 grams
Sodium hydroxide	½ ounce	15 grams
Water to make	32 ounces	1 liter

Feertype Sensitizer E

Sodium ditolyltetrazosulfonate	1 ounce	30 grams
Alpha-naphthol	365 grains	25 grams
Sodium hydroxide	¼ ounce	7.5 grams
Water to make	32 ounces	1 liter

Feertype Sensitizer F

Sodium ditolyltetrazosulfonate	1 ounce	30 grams
Paraphenylene diamine	290 grains	20 grams
Water to make	32 ounces	1 liter

Colors obtained from these solutions:

A — Scarlet red
B — Brown   D E — Violet (mix equal parts)
C — Orange   E F — Blue (mix equal parts)

The procedure which follows must be performed exactly as outlined. All operations including the preparation of the fabric must be carried out in darkness or with a deep red safelight (Wratten Series 2). Absorption of light by the fabric, even before coating, may fog the material.

The fabric is first soaked in soapsuds for about 12 hours, washed well in running water, and *dried in the dark*. Still in darkness or dim red light, it is sprinkled with water and ironed with a moderately hot iron. It is next soaked in the *presensitizing* solution for 20 minutes.

The fabric is again dried in the dark. It is then laid in the bottom of a tray, the sensitizing solution poured over it, and any air bubbles broken up with a glass rod. After about five minutes, the sensitizing solution is poured off and the fabric dried in the dark. Test strips should be cut off and used to determine exposure and development.

The final image lies within the pores of the fabric which will probably withstand gentle washing if necessary. Since no gelatin is used, the print can be dried by heat or ironed gently to remove wrinkles.

DYE PROCESSES

A second class of fabric sensitizers produces a dye image within the fabric. The best known of these are the Primuline Process and the Feertype Process.

The Primuline Process is based

on the use of a diazo coupler with primuline (*not* primuline yellow, which is one of the dyestuffs produced by this process). Depending on the coupler used, a variety of different colored images is obtained. The process is as follows:

First soak the fabric in the primuline solution, made as follows:

Primuline
    1 oz., 45 grains 33 grams
Water to make
    32 ounces 1 liter

The solution should be made in hot water and the fabric immersed for about ten minutes. It is then washed thoroughly and immersed for five minutes in the following bath:

Sodium nitrite
    96 grains 6.6 grams
Hydrochloric acid
    ½ ounce 55 cc
Cold water to make
    32 ounces 1 liter

Dry in the dark.

This is a contact printing process and requires strong daylight or arc light. Test strips are necessary to determine the correct exposure. The process produces a positive from a positive; therefore exposure must be done under a positive image. An enlarged positive may be made on film from the original negative if enlargements are desired.

The fabric is exposed under a positive as mentioned. It is then thoroughly washed in cold water, after which it is developed in one of the following developers, depending on the color required:

RED
Beta-naphthol
    145 grains 10 grams
Sodium hydroxide
    190 grains 13 grams
Water to make
    32 ounces 1 liter

ORANGE
Resorcinol
    37 grains 2.5 grams
Sodium hydroxide
    160 grains 11 grams
Water to make
    32 ounces 1 liter

PURPLE
Alpha-naphthylamine
    290 grains 20 grams
Hydrochloric acid
    ¾ fl. drams 3 cc
Water to make
    32 ounces 1 liter

BLACK
Eikonogen (1-amino-2-naphthol-6-sulfonic acid)
    190 grains 13 grams
Water to make
    32 ounces 1 liter

BROWN
Pyrogallol
    175 grains 12 grams
Water to make
    32 ounces 1 liter

After development, the prints must be well washed and ironed before quite dry. The whites, in this process, always have some slight tone; it is impossible to obtain clean whites.

FEERTYPE PROCESS

The Feertype Process is similar to the Primuline Process, but does not require the preparation of an intermediate positive; it produces positive prints from a negative. Printing must be done by contact with sunlight or arc light.

There are a number of different Feertype sensitizers, producing a range of colored dyes. They are shown in Chart 1.

The fabric is soaked in the sensitizer and dried in the dark. It is exposed under a negative to bright sunlight. The approximate exposure under an average negative is about five minutes. After exposure, the prints are washed in a one-percent hydrochloric acid solution and dried.

FADED PHOTOGRAPHS

IRA B. CURRENT
Manager, Photographic Engineering Department, General Analine & Film Corp. Binghamton, N.Y.

[A faded print is almost invariably the result of improper fixing or washing. In this article, the causes and prevention of fading are discussed. Information is also given about fading in color prints and restoration of faded prints.]

• *Also see: Copying and Close-up Photography; Fixing; Hypo Elimination; Printing Technique.*

ANY SERIOUS PHOTOGRAPHER WANTS his work to be permanent. Even pictures taken for a specific commercial or illustrative purpose should have enough permanence to outlast their immediate usefulness. The average person expects his photographic portraits and group pictures to withstand the ravages of time, but too often today the term "faded" must be applied to the photograph taken 20 or more years ago. That this need not be so is

One of the first courtroom photographs, this picture was taken at the famous Scopes trial in 1927. William Jennings Bryan and Clarence Darrow are in the center. Consider the loss if a photograph of such value and interest were damaged because of fading. (Photo: Courier-Journal and Louisville Times)

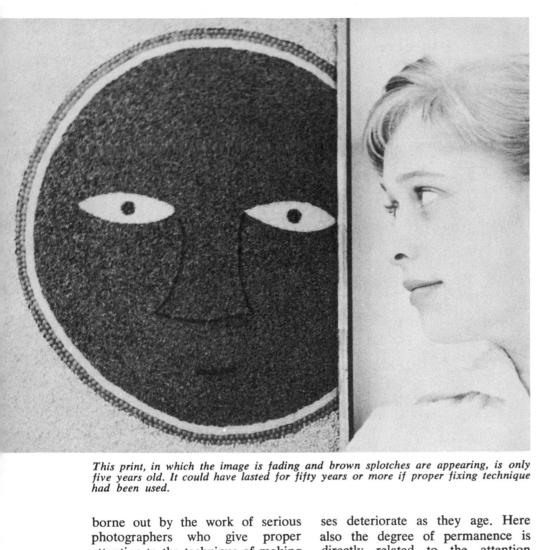

This print, in which the image is fading and brown splotches are appearing, is only five years old. It could have lasted for fifty years or more if proper fixing technique had been used.

borne out by the work of serious photographers who give proper attention to the technique of making the final print.

Early workers made use of albumen and collodion papers and processes that employed such metals as gold and platinum. However, during the last half of the young life of photography there has been an almost exclusive use of gelatino-silver-halide emulsions on paper for the making of monochrome opaque prints. Pigments color-printing processes have given way to those employing dyes, usually in or on gelatin layers.

Extreme care in the fixing and washing of prints can be expected to provide permanence approaching that of the print paper base itself. Anything less than thorough attention to these details will produce prints that will fade or discolor in a few months or a few years. The images made up of the dyes employed in the various color proces-

ses deteriorate as they age. Here also the degree of permanence is directly related to the attention given to processing—including bleaching, fixing, washing, and stabilization.

CAUSES OF FADING

The fading of untoned monochrome prints, the yellowish-brown sulfiding or modification of the silver image, and accompanying general loss of detail are primarily the result of incorrect fixing and washing. Other factors contributing to the instability of print images include the tone of the silver image, the type of paper base employed, the type of protection given to the print, and atmospheric conditions. Fading is sometimes hastened by prolonged exposure to bright daylight or direct sunshine. The presence of moisture (a high relative humidity) tends to hasten the chemical processes involved in fading, and the presence of sulfur com-

pounds, such as those found near oil fields or factories utilizing petroleums or natural gas, will contribute to fading.

Sulfide or selenium-toned prints are more stable than untoned prints because the silver sulfide or selenide images have already been formed by the chemical combination of the silver and sulfur or selenium. Sulfur enters into most of the reactions resulting in fading. Once formed, silver sulfide is one of the most stable of silver compounds. Gold- or platinum-toned prints are also more stable than silver prints. Prints toned by other processes employing common metals, such as iron or copper, are usually less stable than untoned silver prints.

Warm-toned papers usually achieve their color as the result of the finer structure or "grain" of the silver making up their images. A fine structure exposes a much greater surface of silver to chemical oxidants than does the coarse structure of the cold-toned papers.

In some cases, as a result of the chemical reaction involved in fading, the fine-grained silver structure is reconverted into a silver having an even more finely divided character. It is more colored and less dense than the original image. The fine-grained colored silver image may then react with sulfur compounds to produce silver sulfides that are also fine-grained and much warmer and lighter in color than the remaining image; hence it is stained or faded. In view of this, some insurance of permanency can be had by selecting a paper that gives a cold image tone, made up of silver having a coarse filamentary structure and a relatively small surface area to be exposed to the chemical processes that cause fading.

The most common cause of fading is that of insufficient or improper fixing and insufficient washing. Both of these conditions cause complex silver and sulfur compounds to be left in the paper. These are subsequently decomposed in the presence of atmospheric gases and moisture to yield substances like sulfurous acid, sulfuric acid, hydrogen sulfide, and free sulfur.

Typical silver accumulation in two-bath fixer system that has been in operation for several cycles.

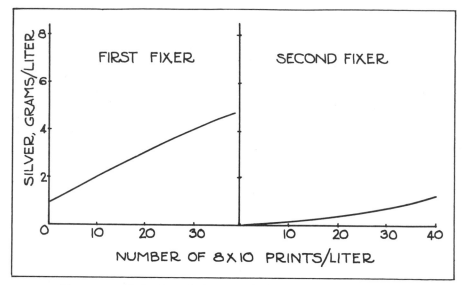

These substances react with the silver image to cause its gradual modification or destruction.

The importance of complete fixation is often overlooked, particularly when expediency is more important than permanency. A determination of adequate washing cannot be made by casual inspection of the prints; it requires carrying out a formal test. The best procedure is faithful attention to fixing and washing details in the first place.

The first requirement is that a maximum of *soluble* silver thiosulfate complex be formed in the fixing process, as far as is practicable. Soluble complexes are more readily removed in the washing process than the less soluble ones formed as the fixing bath, through use, becomes loaded with a greater amount of silver ions. A further complicating factor is the tendency for the complex silver salts to become adsorbed to the gelatin or the paper stock. Because of this, the practical life of a fixing bath is below that based only on reduction of reaction rates as the concentration of silver thiosulfate complexes increases.

The concentration of the fixer is important; the rate of fixing increases as the concentration of sodium thiosulfate in water is increased. Temperature is also important, with the best range between 60 F and 80 F for ordinary photography. Below this range, chemical reactions are slowed considerably. Above this range, increased swelling and softening of the gelatin may affect the diffusion of the fixing solutions, and the emulsion may be more easily damaged.

Agitation is also important in the fixing and washing steps. Agitation during fixing provides constant replacement by fresh chemicals of the products of the chemical reactions, thus encouraging the formation of soluble complexes at a greater,

more uniform rate. Agitation during washing provides a constant replacement of the wash water adjacent to the surface of the print and helps to remove the soluble complexes as they are dissolved.

Prolonged immersion in a strong acid stop bath (two percent acetic acid or stronger) causes adsorption of the acid on the paper fibres; this increases the "mordanting" effect between the fibres and the silver complexes formed. The acidity of acid-fixing baths also tends in this direction, but acid is usually necessary to neutralize developer carryover to prevent sulfurization of the

solution. If an acid stop bath is employed, the acetic-acid strength should be kept below two percent, and the prints should not be allowed to remain in the bath longer than five minutes.

RECOMMENDED FIXING METHOD

When care is taken to replace the fixing bath well before its recommended capacity is reached, or when the bath is rejuvenated and controlled by laboratory methods and all the other precautions followed, a single fixing bath is usually adequate. However, in all other situations, the two-bath fixing

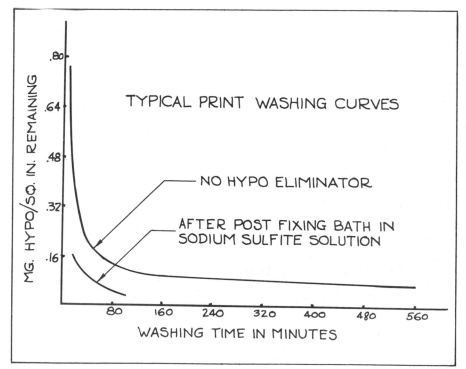

Typical print-washing curves showing washing times in relation to amounts of hypo remaining in the paper. See text for full details.

procedure is recommended.

Here, the prints are first put into a fixing bath that is *partially* used. Under no circumstances should it be an exhausted fixer. Then, after five minutes of freqent agitation in the first bath, the prints are transferred to a fresh fixing solution. As the second solution becomes partially exhausted, it is substituted for the previous first fixer, and a new fresh bath introduced. The original first fixer is then discarded.

Prints should not be allowed to accumulate in either of the baths, and they should be constantly leafed over to insure free access of the fixing solution to the print surfaces. Constant mechanical agitation, such as that provided by some of the print-rocker systems, is the most reliable method of agitation.

A test that can be applied to the first fixer to determine its exhaustion consists of adding one part of a four percent solution of potassium iodide to ten parts of the fixer in question. If a yellow precipitate is formed, the bath is exhausted.

A fixer that has been used for films should not be used also for prints in which permanency is desired. The higher proportion of iodide and the presence of anti-halation and other dyes in some film emulsions may eventually have a staining effect, even though they are decolorized in the fixing bath.

WASHING

When fixing has been completed, and the soluble silver complexes formed, careful washing is required to make sure that these complexes are all removed from the emulsion (or gelatin layer), and from the paper fibres and baryta coating as well. The complexes are removed from the emulsion layer at a rate comparable to that for film; but the rate of removal from the paper fibres and the baryta layer (which tends to adsorb the complexes) is much lower, particularly after gross quantities of silver thiosulfate complexes have been removed in the first few minutes of washing.

Double-weight papers which have approximately twice as much base thickness require approximately twice the time for removal of salts as do single-weight papers. The double-weight paper cell structure and sizing permit very slow diffusion of the wash water and salt solutions; extremely prolonged washing is necessary to insure that all of the silver complexes are removed.

However, for all practical purposes, single-weight papers may be given a washing time of 30 minutes in running water with constant agitation, or six changes of water five minutes apart. Double-weight papers should be washed for a minimum of 60 minutes in running water with agitation, or given 12 changes of water five minutes apart with thorough agitation during each change.

Under no circumstances should the volume of prints in a tray or washer be so great that the prints become matted together with little chance for water circulation. For greater assurance of permanence of the image, washing times twice as long as these, or even longer, are

Mathew Brady photographed Thomas A. Edison in 1877, just after he invented the phonograph. Today, after almost a century, the picture remains without a trace of fading.

This picture of a Vermont winter scene with its large areas of light tones would be utterly ruined if yellow splotches began to appear. Here proper procedure preserves the subtle beauty of the original scene. (Photo: L. F. Hechenberger)

recommended.

Washing is accelerated if the prints, following fixing, are washed for about two minutes in running water with constant agitation, and then transferred to the following bath and agitated in it for three minutes:

Sodium sulfite 20 grams
Sodium bisulfite 5 grams
Water to make 1 liter

After this, the washing time for single-weight prints can be reduced to about 10 to 15 minutes; and that for double-weight prints to about 20 to 30 minutes. There are also available commercially prepared hypo eliminators which cut down washing time considerably.

Washing is also accelerated if the prints are soaked, with agitation, in a one percent solution of sodium carbonate prior to final washing (after the bulk of the fixing salts have been removed in the first five minutes of washing). Following this treatment, washing should continue for another 10 to 15 minutes for single-weight papers, and 20 to 30 minutes for double-weight. However, the use of carbonate solutions may reduce the hardening of the emulsion of some papers. This can lead to excessive tackiness, a tend-

ency toward sticking to dryer belts or dryer cloths, or the accumulation of lint during drying.

Both this treatment and the two percent sodium sulfite treatment, with the washing recommended, give a residual thiosulfate complex content about equal to that achieved by normal washing for 30 minutes and 60 minutes, respectively. While the wash water itself need not be potable, it should be free of oxidiz-

The few extra minutes spent in washing a print thoroughly may mean the difference between a lifetime photo or a faded and damaged print. Notice the splotches in the light area.

ing substances. It is best to filter the wash water, not only to remove solids that might have a chemical effect on the image, but also to remove any particles that would mar the surface of the prints during or after drying. Slightly hard water may have some advantage over soft water; the minerals causing the hardness have a hypo-eliminating effect, and provide added stability to color prints.

TEST FOR RESIDUAL SILVER

The presence of silver thiosulfate complexes (or any form of silver) in paper prints can be detected by means of a simple sulfide or selenide test. This is done by placing a drop of a 0.2 percent solution of sodium sulfide on a clear (unexposed) portion of the print. Any silver present will react with the sulfide to form silver sulfide. The solution is allowed to react for two minutes and is then blotted off. The degree of brown stain remaining is an indication of the relative amount of silver in the paper. A well-fixed and well-washed print should show practically no stain. Ansco Flemish R Toner which contains selenium, or one of the selenium toners on the market, can be similarly used to replace the sodium sulfide solution. The toner should be diluted about 1:20 with water for use in the manner described above.

TEST FOR DEGREE OF WASHING

The amount of sodium thiosulfate remaining in wash-water drippings can be determined by means of the following solution:

Potassium permanganate 0.3 grams
Sodium hydroxide 0.6 grams
Distilled water to make 250 cc

One cc of this solution is added to 250 cc of water. If wash water drained from one of the prints is permitted to drip into this solution and the color of the solution remains unchanged, the print may be considered to be well washed as far as soluble thiosulfates are concerned. On the other hand, if the permanganate solution is decolorized, more washing is required.

Before the wash water comes into contact with the prints, it should be tested with the solution, for oxidizable substances in the water may themselves cause decolorization. It must be remembered that this test determines whether the wash water is free of *soluble* thiosulfates and thiosulfate complexes; if the fixing has not been adequate the less soluble ones may not be removed. Their retention will later cause "fading" of the print.

PRESERVATION OF PRINTS

Prints exhibited under glass in frames may generally be expected to last longer than those in folders, since the glass protects the prints from harmful fumes. There is some evidence that lacquering of the prints, both front and back, will slow down the effects of atmospheric gases on the image; but there have also been cases in which lacquered prints appear to have faded more rapidly than unlacquered ones. The following formula is suggested as a varnish for print protection:

Sandarac 1 ounce
Benzol 4 ounces
Acetone 4 ounces
Absolute alcohol 2 ounces

Spray lacquers in pressurized cans also may be obtained for coating prints.

File prints should be stored in a cool, dry place, preferably with interleaving paper, such as a good grade of bond or black photograph album paper. These sheets separate the surface of one print from the back of the next one; any absorbed silver complexes in the stock of one print will not contribute to the destruction of the image of the adjacent one.

RESTORATION OF FADED PRINTS

There is no certain method for the restoration of faded prints, but sometimes a bleach followed by redevelopment will be effective. The following bleach is employed until the image is converted to a barely visible image of uniform color:

1) Potassium permanganate
   5.0 grams
   Water to make 1 liter
2) Sodium chloride 75.0 grams
   Water 1 liter
   Sulfuric acid, CP 16.0 cc

These two solutions are mixed in the order given. A working solution consists of equal parts of the first and second.

Next, the print is rinsed in water to remove most of the superfluous bleach solution and then bathed for one minute with agitation in a one percent solution of sodium bisulfite. After another wash in running water for five minutes, the print is redeveloped in a standard print developer. This is followed by a final rinse of five minutes in running water.

Perhaps a less hazardous course is to make a photographic copy of the faded print. This is the preferred method because the print may have become cracked or otherwise physically damaged; the copy negative can be retouched to remove the visual effect of such damage. A filter may also be employed on the camera to "drop out" any stains. Adjustment in contrast can be made by selection of the proper grade of paper, or the proper filter if using a variable contrast paper.

COLOR PRINTS

The processing recommendations by manufacturers of color print materials have been worked out to produce optimum results. Since the images making up color prints are usually dyes (pigment-color printing has been largely replaced by dye-printing processes) and the silver has been removed by fixing, different considerations must be made for them than for monochrome silver images.

Residual silver complexes present after bleaching and fixing must be carefully removed to prevent the generation of stain in any of the dye layers. Residual thiosulfate causes deterioration of the dye layers in some color films; variations in pH beyond acceptable limits may also cause fading. The processing procedures are generally designed to provide optimum pH conditions and stabilizer concentrations in the final images. These instructions should be strictly adhered to for best results with any given material.

Color-print dye images are also affected by the acidity caused by certain gases in the atmosphere. The presence of moisture greatly accelerates the rapidity with which the chemical reactions involved in dye destruction occur. Bright daylight or direct sunshine also have a destructive effect on many of the dyes. This is more pronounced on some dye layers than it is on the other layers making up a print. The ultraviolet component of sunlight has the most destructive effect; the use of a UV absorbing foil or lacquer is recommended for protection from it. Storage places for files of color prints should be cool and dry; and, again, interleaving paper between the prints is recommended for best permanence.

FARM PHOTOGRAPHY

BOB TAYLOR

[A well-known agricultural photographer discusses factors for success in creating stock files which will satisfy editorial and advertising needs in farm publishing. The modern approach to mechanized and scientific agricultural photography is explained with special emphasis on people and the land.]

All photographs by Bob Taylor.
• *Also see: Livestock Photography.*

TODAY WE FIND THAT THE FARMER, as we once knew him, is fast disappearing. He is no longer the rugged individualist farming a hundred acres with a few milk cows, a flock of chickens, and a litter of pigs. Today farms and ranches have been almost completely mechanized with farmers becoming specialists in the types of crops they grow and in the way they conduct their business. We find farmers operating individual feedlots with automatic machinery so that one man can do the work of five or six. Many not only feed their own livestock, but are now custom feeding for their neighbors, making a paying specialty out of this procedure. We find farmers who grow wheat, cotton, grain, sorghums, and other crops, using thousands of acres. They own several large tractors, harvesting combines, and other farming implements and employ several helpers in the busy seasons when the work must be done immediately.

The modern farmer is conducting as big a business as his city associates. His children graduate from the best universities. He and his family travel extensively during their vacation periods. In some parts of the country farmers even have town homes and become part of the urban complex. Therefore, as we photograph farm folks, we must keep these things in mind, and remember above all that the country-bumpkin approach is no longer valid.

FARM PEOPLE

The inclusion of people in a farm photograph generally adds interest to the scene. The photographer must decide whether the person is to be just a "prop" to add to the subject interest or whether the person is to be the center of attention. If the subject is busy at something with which he is familiar, he will be at ease in front of the camera, and many interesting poses will develop.

If you are photographing a group of people, be sure to arrange them

The best way to make the over-all field picture is from a ladder or car platform. The high angle often makes it possible to eliminate distracting backgrounds or a bald sky. Made with a 4×5 press camera on medium pan film.

in an interesting formation. Don't let them line up in a fence-post string. If one person in the group is demonstrating something to the others, or if one is talking to a group, a center will be created for the photograph.

Another thing: when photographing people, be selective about where you photograph them. Make sure the setting adds authenticity and interest to the picture. Also, the background should be carefully chosen so it will contrast in tone with the principal subject.

FARM NEWS

Pictures of newsworthy events are in demand. Farm publications are always looking for a cover picture connected with some sort of news interest. One of the most popular news photographs shows the farmer or his wife performing a task in a labor-saving way. Usually this involves a gadget invented by the farmer to conserve time and do the job more efficiently. Another good subject for this type of story is the remodeling of a farmhouse into a modern home—with good before-and-after shots. When submitting such pictures, the photographer must consider the geographic location serviced by the publication. A New England publication has little use for pictures made in the Southwest.

LIVESTOCK

The second most important group of farm subjects is livestock. Today, more and more farms are raising livestock on a commercial basis. The raising of livestock and poultry is a highly specialized, income-producing business. In turn, farm photographers are inclined to specialization as well. Some of them take pictures only of beef cattle; others concentrate on dairy activities, hog raising, horses, or chickens.

Farm publications are eager for photographs showing how farmers have improved their feeding operation or rearranged their feedlots to save time and labor. They also want animal pictures which show breed characteristics, markings, and general conditions. Beef cattle and horses should have a natural, level

A farm photographer's stock files should be crammed with a wide and inclusive variety of farm subjects—from the sweeping vista to the extreme close-up, in both black-and-white and color. This close-up, identifying plant characteristics, is most valuable to scientific and farm editors.

stance so that backline and quarters show to advantage. Udder capacity and other pertinent features should show in dairy cows. The farm editor will be much more receptive to animal pictures with unobtrusive backgrounds, such as sky and pasture, instead of fences or a posing canvas. The city editor, however, wants a more picturesque quality—horses silhouetted against a colorful sunset, or a touching scene between mother and child in the cow pasture.

Poultry photography is another specialty in which the editor of a magazine devoted to the subject will insist that the pictures show clear representations of various breeds. (The more generalized magazine is inclined toward a mass show of baby chicks with a pretty girl or child.) Poultry pictures must be taken with back- or sidelighting to emphasize feather texture. Flashbulb or electronic flash will help when you need high shutter speeds and small lens apertures. Close-up head shots are also popular with the publications using poultry pictures.

It takes patience and perseverance to get animal shots like this one which has been used as a cover for more than 15 publications. Made with a twin-lens reflex, pan film, 1/100 of a second at f/11.

severe perspective is always an eye-catcher. Along with the low angle are the close-up and the extreme close-up photographs which are valuable in illustrating the differences in varieties of crops such as grain, sorghum, or wheat.

When root depth is part of the story, the photographer must combine the skill of a dissectionist with that of a cameraman. He must carefully dig and wash away the soil until an entire root can be shot against a soil-strata background, with the plant projected against the sky. It requires patience and time, but such pictures are scarce and in demand. Cross- or backlighting is best for showing detail in plants, and here the green filter is used to lighten the foliage tones.

There are times when it is necessary to show soil deficiencies in crops. With black-and-white film, it will probably be necessary to use filters to emphasize variations in the color of the plants. It is also a good idea to carry a white cardboard to use as a reflector when needed. Use colored cardboards for background when a better picture can be made by isolating the plant.

Besides field shots of crops, there are the cultivating and harvesting scenes, offering the photographer a multitude of different effects—including action and good composition. Here, either the crop or the harvesting operation can dominate the composition. Again, the use of high and low angle or back- and sidelighting provide the dramatic emphasis for the scene.

CROPS

Photographs of crops constitute a large segment of farm photography. There are a multitude of different opportunities for interesting photographs in this category. Over-all field shots often provide the photographer with beautiful scenics. Usually, for this type of picture, a ladder or an elevated car platform is necessary to cover a large field. For an interesting sky effect, use a yellow, orange, or red filter to make the clouds stand out in dramatic contrast.

Of course, you cannot always expect a cloud-filled sky at the time the crop is ready to be photographed. The experienced photographer anticipates this problem by having a file of good cloud negatives on hand to use for combination printing. In fact, many photographers of agriculture add to the cloud file whenever they can.

Often sidelighting or backlighting will illuminate a crop much better than frontlighting. The same is true of early morning or late afternoon light which add interesting shadows to the pictorial quality.

Low-angle pictures of crops give punch to an ordinary scene. Their

FARM EQUIPMENT

When featuring farm machinery show the equipment in actual operation under the best possible conditions. If you want to interest the manufacturer in the photographs, the equipment must be shown operating according to the manufacturer's directions. The photographer should check to be sure that every lever, chain, and pulley is in its correct position. Correct safety measures must also be apparent in the photo.

The photographer should choose a modern farm for his photographs, because any manufacturer wants to demonstrate that his product is being used by the best farms and ranches in the locality. It is up to the photographer to see that the area is clean and clear of distracting elements.

Another type of picture is that showing the farmer doing a particular job with his machines. Many times such photographs can be made more dramatic by the choice of lighting and camera angle. If it is necessary to show great detail in the machine, use flash to lighten the shadows.

FARM STRUCTURES

Farm buildings can often be used to create dramatic pictures. Unless there is some editorial reason for including an old building, only attractive farm buildings should be shown. Sometimes a series of pictures may be needed to point out the before-and-after effect of an improved or modernized farm building. Show the relationship of the building to the over-all farm layout to illustrate how the farmer is conserving effort and improving efficiency with his arrangement.

FARM MANAGEMENT

The question of methods and management is another subject division which should be mentioned briefly. Here, we use a combination of the techniques already discussed as we attempt to show graphically how the farm family handles its land, crops, stock, and equipment to achieve a satisfactory rural life. All farm publications welcome the farm handiwork pictures. The photographer must clearly show the how-to aspect of the project. He must also include a short description of how the construction or procedures benefit the farmer.

One type of equipment picture is that which shows the farmer doing a particular or unusual job, such as this picture of machines working under artificial illumination. These photographs gain dramatic impact through lighting and camera angle.

SERIES PICTURES

Picture stories usually make a better and more convincing statement than the printed word alone. Photographers who want to create picture stories can take a tip from the movie world by using their formula of distant shot, middle shot and close-up. The setting of the story is established with one or more over-all or general distant-view shots. A closer look with more details is achieved by the medium-range view. Then, to isolate the subject, the close-up shot is used.

The photographer must also realize that the picture story, like a good novel, must have a begin-

The farm photographer must always be on the alert for pictures that tell a story, whether it be of a seasonal activity or something that happens once in a while.

ning, a middle, and an end. The natural action of the story and the "seeing eye" of the cameraman usually provide one impact shot which holds the essence of the story. All others enlarge on the theme and carry the story to a logical end.

One very good reason for making picture stories is that they command a far better price than the single shot. Some publications pay per print while others compute the price according to page rates. Either way, it is more profitable to deal in picture stories.

A picture story gives the photographer a chance to be original and to use some unusual approaches in his work. A picture story can be completely candid, or it can be staged and formal. The photographer has to determine which ap-

proach will be more harmonious with the mood of the story. Seldom can the two approaches be used in the same story.

EQUIPMENT FOR FARM PHOTOGRAPHY

Good equipment that will be rugged enough to stand up under rough conditions and all sorts of weather is a necessity for farm photography. A 35 mm camera or twin-lens reflex is good for action work when equipment must be light and easily handled. These can be hand-held in most situations, except for time exposures when a sturdy tripod is used. A 4×5 press-type camera is often needed, especially when shooting in color. The 4×5 view camera, with several lenses, is probably the most useful of all. It will be needed whenever architectural work is done; correct per-

spective can be maintained with its various swings and tilts.

Among lenses, the 90mm wide-angle, the 135mm, an 8- or 8½-inch lens and, if possible, a 15-inch telephoto are the most needed. Filters for all situations (color and black-and-white), lens shade, and several tripods are also on the essential list. All lenses should be in shutters that are synchronized for both bulb and electronic flash. A reliable exposure meter which covers a wide range of situations is necessary.

For lighting, a flashgun with four or more extensions and a number of serviceable extension cords will do for a start. Later, a 200-watt-second electronic flash and one slave unit that will operate from the power pack will be enormously helpful. Where power is available, a selection of reflectors, various sized photoflood and spot-lamps, and stands or clamp-on sockets will add versatility to the outfit.

Most photographers who do farm and scenic photography have a platform on top of their car. The platform is helpful in photographing fields and crops, especially if the produce is tall, as with corn or wheat. A lightweight aluminum ladder about three feet tall is very helpful in many situations.

APPROACH

Always be courteous and friendly when approaching farmers for permission to photograph them or their property. Always be sure to secure this permission and to get signed releases from each and every person who appears in the photographs.

Remember that you are imposing on a very busy person's time. He may be harvesting a year's worth of effort in a few days, and if bad weather comes along he could lose a year's income. Therefore after you get permission, do try to take as many pictures as possible without stopping the work that is being done. If it is necessary to stop the work, have everything planned so there is no waste motion.

Always give the farmer a set of prints of anything you take. He is proud of his farm, crops, and other possessions, and will appreciate

Getting animals such as chicks, lambs, calves, and pigs to look animated or in a certain direction is always a problem. One way of solving this is to suddenly confront the subject with another animal or person.

such a gift. It takes only a little extra time and expense to make a duplicate set but it is certainly worthwhile in establishing good relations with the farmer.

PHOTOGRAPHY FOR PUBLICATION

The farm photographer must always be on the lookout for the unusual. Sometimes the unusual can be manufactured, other times it just happens naturally. It is the unique which most easily attracts the attention of the editor. And a photographer who submits such pictures consistently will soon have the editors asking for his services.

The photographer should always consider color when photographing a scene or subject. A tremendous amount of color is being used in farm publications today, both inside and on covers. If possible, all color work should be duplicated in black-and-white. Color commands higher prices, but it is still the monochrome print which is the backbone of income.

Print quality is important when photographs are being submitted for publication. They should be sharp and crisp in tone. The 8 × 10 print on double-weight stock is standard. Photographs submitted for publication should carry an identification number and caption. The photographer should also have his name and address stamped on the back of each print. When mailing, the prints should be well packaged, and if being sent on speculation, return postage should be enclosed.

New York's Central Park, larger than the principality of Monaco, is a convenient and versatile location for H. Landshoff. Male models are often used as romantic background interest, as in this photo for Mademoiselle.

FASHION PHOTOGRAPHY

PHILLIP ANDREWS
Photographer, Editor, Publisher
[The author, who has been an editor of both photographic and women's magazines, traces the history and development of fashion photography, outlines the requirement of fashion photography in terms of those who have achieved success in the field, and discusses techniques of lighting and composition with particular reference to qualities needed for reproduction, backgrounds, and staging. Children's fashions and fashion accessories are also covered.]
• *Also see: Advertising Photography; Color Photography for Advertising.*

FASHION PHOTOGRAPHY, IN A SENSE, is as old as photography itself. Four years prior to the public announcement of the Daguerre process in 1839, Fox Talbot, working in England, had produced "photogenic drawings" on sensitized paper; the technique was similar to that now used in making photograms. The results resembled the paper-negative prints of a later day (which, in fact, they were, as nothing approaching the modern film or glass plate had yet been developed). Significantly, one of Talbot's first subjects was a fashion accessory—a piece of lace.

Later, during the 1840's, D. O. Hill made his classic photograph, "The Sisters," in which the subjects' clothes seem to dominate the composition. One sister has her head turned away from the camera, as though to show off the line of the shawl she is wearing; the pattern of the second sister's dress is sharp and clear (remarkably so for a print that is now more than a century old), as though to accentuate the design and texture of the fabric.

Another early photograph emphasizing fashion is a portrait of Lola Montez, made by Southworth and Hawes in 1851. Though certainly not intended as a fashion photograph, it must have induced many of the women who saw it to drape their shawls in a manner emulating that of the famous Spanish dancer, and indeed, it probably stimulated the sale of shawls in general.

Subjects of 19th-century portraits usually wore their choicest finery for sittings; clothes were a prominent feature of many daguerreotypes. Although not conceived as such, many of these were fashion photographs in the sense that they established trends and encouraged emulation, especially if the subject was a celebrity. These pictures are frequently consulted today by dress designers in search of inspiration, ideas, and motifs.

DECLINE OF FASHION PHOTOGRAPHS

By the turn of the century, however, portrait photographers began to concentrate their lights and lenses on the sitters' faces. Clothes were minimized, even obscured, by means of soft focus or by placing them in Rembrandt-like shadow. Fashion and photography had come to a temporary parting of the ways.

Although 19th-century photographs may have influenced styles to some extent, just as paintings had done in previous centuries, their audiences were limited. Prints could not be made from daguerreotypes, and Talbot's process called "calotype" permitted reproduction in only relatively small quantities. (Another limitation of the daguerreotype was that it produced a reversed image, making it appear that many ladies used their left hands instead of their right to hold fans or other accessories—a right to left reversal of the fashion which no modern art director or fashion editor would tolerate.)

This inability to reproduce photos in quantity represented a basic inadequacy in their use for fashion illustrations, for the basic purpose of the fashion photograph is to *sell* the particular style, pattern, fabric, garment, or accessory pictured. The illustration, therefore, must be widely distributed and this, in turn, implies publication.

Because books, journals and newspapers of the day were illustrated with wood engravings, it was logical to utilize the same medium for the purpose of portraying fashion. From it evolved a system of printed salesmanship that reached its provocative perfection in *Godey's Lady's Book.*

Wood engravings were preferable to photographs, not only because they could be reproduced in virtually unlimited quantities, but also because they permitted use of the important additional dimension of color. Moreover, the process made it possible to idealize both the model and her clothes (wash or line drawings are frequently used today for the same reasons).

RENAISSANCE OF FASHION PHOTOGRAPHY

With the development of the photoengraving process, photographs began to appear on the pages of the world's press, penetrating eventually to the fashion sections, where they usually depicted some well known and fashionably attired personality. In addition, there was a widespread belief that the camera could not lie; this implied integrity perhaps contributed more than any other factor to the development of a profession that has become one of the most exacting and profitable in the entire field of photography.

FASHION PHOTOGRAPHY REQUIREMENTS

Because a fashion photograph, whether it appears in the editorial or advertising pages of a publication, is primarily intended to *sell* something, the photographer's relationship with editors, art directors, publishers, and advertising executives is understandably a close one.

The late Condé Nast, publisher of *Vogue* and the memorable *Vanity Fair,* has been referred to as the father of modern fashion photography; he induced Edward Steichen, Baron de Mayer, George Hoyningen-Huene, Cecil Beaton, Man Ray, Anton Bruehl, Toni Frissell, and Gjon Mili, among others, to train their lenses on the fashion scene.

That these personalities possessed widely disparate talents and photographic philosophies is, in itself, evidence of fashion photography's wide scope and diverse opportunities. Gjon Mili, for example, was an early exponent of stroboscopic lighting; Toni Frissell emerged from the editorial department armed only with a 35 mm camera.

In the Condé Nast tradition, editors and art directors today continue to wield the balance of power in fashion photography. They are always looking to discover and employ new talents. Fashion photography, as well as fashion itself, is a world of constant change and innovation. Last year's dress may be no more out of date than last year's picture of it.

The photographer is often limited by the necessity of highlighting a specific point of fashion—the cut of a collar, the flare of a skirt, or the design and texture of a fabric. He may be instructed to conform to a prepared layout while a fashion "coordinator" hovers in the background to be sure that he captures the sheen of a model's hair (the beauty department has a coiffure "credit" involved). Even so, he is expected to astonish and surprise the editor, art director, fashion designer, manufacturer—and readers of the publication.

TASTE—A PRIMARY QUALIFICATION

Taste and imagination, accordingly, take precedence over technique in the criteria applied to fashion photographers. Richard Avedon's work, for example, has been described as "containing all the rudimentary faults of a beginner's snapshots." Blurred and distorted as some of his photographs may seem, they are, however, the result of careful planning. Avedon, who began wearing glasses at the age of six, was aware of two optical worlds—one sharp and clear, the other blurred and distorted. Combining the two in his viewfinder, foreground subjects loomed dramatically in contrast to hazy backgrounds which dissolved abruptly into infinity. When nature would not, or could not, cooperate in achieving Avedon's objectives—in his studio assignments, for example —he resorted, as early as 1945, to electric fans for the purpose of agitating still air and destroying the vacuum of formality.

A SENSE FOR CLOTHES

John Rawlings, himself an accomplished technician, refers to a fashion photographer "who could not read a light meter yet made a success of his profession because he had an unerring instinct for clothes."

"An invaluable exercise," Rawlings suggests, "is to observe elegant, well-dressed women and re-create in the studio their gestures and attitudes."

"Beautiful clothes," writes Geri Trotta (who has served as an editor of two leading fashion magazines, *Mademoiselle* and *Harper's Bazaar*) "are a tremendous source of inspiration. Yet such is the skill of the eye, the sense of style of a competent photographer, that a mediocre and often misshapen rayon sack is transformed before the lens into a dress of taste and line.

"The dress will not only look attractive but a thousand women will want to wear it...a first-rate photographer sells the fashion idea in addition to the specific merchandise pictured. To effect this minor miracle, he must have patience, energy, and technical proficiency.

"He must move in a world of music, the theater, ballet, books, taste, and ideas. He must particularly have a knowledge and appreciation of fine painting, as fashion work probably stems from it more than any other branch of photography. Beyond all else, he must have an intuitive feeling for fashion. He must know how women want to look and that, in turn, implies knowing everything about them... how they walk and think and live— or want to live."

FASHION PHOTOGRAPHY AND PHOTOJOURNALISM

Irving Penn, who admits to influences ranging from the Civil War photographs of Mathew Brady to the metaphysical paintings of Giorgio di Chirico, gives precedence to Brady in that he regards "fashion photographers as journalists rather than artists."

Moreover, according to Penn, "In the editorial pages our first problem is to jolt the readers in order to win back the interest dulled by the luxurious advertisements that precede us." Penn's method of accomplishing this purpose is to inject liberal doses of what he calls "poison"—some "startling or perverse element, such as an ugly black bug on a delicate pink flower."

The photojournalist approach to fashion photography is shared by Avedon, who often relates his subject to some real occurrence. On one occasion, encountering a group of French cyclists returning from a race, he posed his model in their midst—and transformed a conventional fashion shot into a picture with all the implicit urgency of a spot news photo.

IMAGINATION AND TECHNIQUE

All fashion photographers who have attained any notable degree of success seem to have two things in common: cameras and imagination. Imaginative minds appear to have very little difficulty in evolving adequate techniques, but photographic technicians lacking in imagination have rarely enjoyed continuing success as fashion photographers.

Many leading photojournalists, portraitists, and commercial photographers have emerged from their apprenticeships in darkrooms and studios, but a number of other successful fashion photographers have entered the field directly from art studios, designing rooms, and even editorial copy desks—developing their technique *after* receiving their first assignments, or, in some instances, depending upon assistants or specialists for such technical aspects as processing and printing.

FASHION PHOTOGRAPHY—A GROUP EFFORT

Although artistic imagination is a priceless ingredient it cannot, for long, give way to artistic temperament. A pleasing personality, patience, and the ability to get along with people are qualities which most eminent fashion photographers seem to possess to a marked degree.

These characteristics are not merely a means of making life more

Men's fashions are more standardized, much less subject to change than women's fashions, consequently may require more elaborate settings to provide interest. Here, William Ward has employed a library and a pretty girl to build a situation for displaying men's slacks which are tailored along traditional lines.

Photographs of men's fashions are frequently given a humorous or light-hearted touch because men, presumably, may like to be well dressed but may be considered foppish if they take their clothes too seriously. (Photo: William Ward)

pleasant for the photographer and the people around him, but may have a bearing on the quality of his work because a significant fashion photograph is seldom the product of one individual's efforts. Art directors, editors, designers, models—all play an important role. Fortunately their tastes often har-monize with those of the photog-rapher and there are few such prob-lems as may be encountered by the commercial photographer working with more prosaic products. People who have devoted their lifetimes to designing glamorous clothes by writing and talking about them or, as in the case of models, wearing them, are inclined to be more sym-pathetic toward innovation than the client whose mission in life is selling dog biscuits or detergents. They are well aware of the photographer's importance in presenting the subject to the best possible advantage and of his ability to transform a "garment" into a "creation" coveted by every woman who sees it. (Baron Hoyningen-Huene, it has been said, "could make a roll of toilet tissue look like a bolt of satin ribbon.")

It is rare enough to be a nontemperamental g e n i u s—but the fashion photographer who aspires to eminence in the field must also be a businessman and efficiency expert. One of the most important commodities he must consider and conserve is time—not only his own, but that of the accompanying fashion editor, models, and employes of the dress manufacturer waiting for the samples to be returned.

He must be well organized. In a single day, he may conceivably meet with editors to discuss a new assignment, interview models for another, photograph a third, process preliminary prints for a fourth, and prepare the final prints or color transparencies for a fifth.

At other times he may have days, weeks, and even months of relative inactivity, for the fashion business is a seasonal one. Usually he must accept all the work he can get when it is offered; unless he enjoys a truly outstanding reputation, there are others potentially his equal who are eager to take over his space in a particular magazine on a regular basis.

FAME AND FORTUNE

Although the requirements for a top fashion photographer are stringent, the remunerations are commensurate. The space his pictures occupy is expensive, especially when printed in color. He is working with other highly paid people; and even if the clothing is relatively inexpensive, a considerable investment is involved in its manufacture. Accordingly, the fashion photographer whose work appears in a major publication, either in the form of editorial or advertising space, is highly paid.

In addition to being perhaps the most remunerative branch of the profession, fashion photography offers other rewards. There are frequent opportunities for travel, because magazines and advertisers are always seeking new and exotic backgrounds. His subjects are attractive; his associates and clients are usually interesting, intelligent, and understand his craft. He receives recognition not only in the form of a credit line printed adjacent to his work, but in the opportunity to produce pictures which, despite the number of people involved, are essentially his and recognizable as such.

"The inventive fashion photographer," writes Geri Trotta, "is perpetually pressing the limits of his medium. As he stretches his stride, he evolves his personal formula which is individualized to the extent that no one familiar with the field need glance at a credit line to identify the photographer.

"The melting luminosity...of a Dahl-Wolfe, the gold-toned elegance of a John Rawlings, the arrogant humility of a Penn composition, the female perception of a Frances McLaughlin, the high-key informality of a Mark Shaw, the flat-of-the-hand impact of a Landshoff... these are signatures and standards unto themselves."

LUCK AND THE BEGINNER

For the aspiring fashion photographer, or for the cameraman who desires to change his status from that of a general practitioner to specialization in this glamorous and rewarding profession, there is no single highway that leads to success, no one key that opens all doors.

As has been previously noted, a knowledge of the fashion industry itself, coupled with taste and imagination, are more important in the beginning than technical proficiency.

A well-known graphic artist, for example, had developed migraine headaches from long hours at the drawing board and decided that photography, particularly in the fashion field, would provide some relief without interrupting his sources of income. Taking a twin-lens reflex camera, of which he had only the most rudimentary working knowledge, and a suitcase filled with film, he set out on a long cross-country tour, stopping along the way to shoot anything and everything that provided exceptional photographic interest.

Returning with more than a hundred rolls of exposed film, he had 11×14-inch enlargements made of a dozen or so which he considered outstanding and unusual, mounted them in an impressive portfolio and started out on his rounds of magazine art directors. The first one he visited gave him an assignment. He has since returned to his drawing board—but only because his headaches disappeared, and not for lack of opportunity to pursue the photographic phase of his career.

Conversely, another photographer who had demonstrated his abilities with landscapes, still lifes, and portraits of consistently high quality was given a "trial" by one of the major fashion magazines. This consisted of being assigned a studio and a model with several changes of costume. Being the kind of photographer who would wait for hours until the sun reached a desired position for a street scene or landscape, or who would search for days to find a particular item for a still-life composition, he failed the "test."

Subsequently, however, he became a highly successful photographer of fashion accessories—a field in which he was basically able to work alone at his own measured pace, experimenting at will.

EQUIPMENT

Fashion photography requires special skills and special knowledge, and within the field of fashion itself there is a high order of specialization. Consequently, the methods of any one photographer reflect only one aspect of the profession.

Conversely, an outline of the entire field results in confusing contradictions—large cameras as opposed to miniatures, elaborate studio sets as against whatever is offered by the neighboring streets or a country road, batteries of lights versus the sun at high noon or filtered through a translucent skylight.

Cecil Beaton, for example, is said not to use a light meter, trusting experience on exposures, and has reportedly made many of his pictures with a Brownie. Yet few photographers have ever achieved Beaton's atmosphere of elegance.

On the other hand, a cursory examination of another prominent fashion photographer's studio revealed four 5000-watt, two 400-watt, and six 250-watt spotlights, one 10,000-watt and two 5000-watt floodlights, plus elaborate strobe equipment. His cameras run the gamut from 35 mm to large view types.

A photographer whose work has appeared regularly in the pages of *Vogue* used an ancient Kodak fitted with a German lens for a number of years, and presumably still does. For lighting he combines a 5000-watt sunlamp with a flood.

One prominent fashion photographer uses only two cameras—an 8 × 10-inch view and a twin-lens reflex. The former permits accurate composition and observation of tone values on the groundglass; the smaller camera, having similar characteristics, is used when faster speeds and greater portability are required. Since an increasing number of fashion photographs are being made outside the studio, and frequently on location in faraway places, portability and light weight are important considerations.

Landshoff, for example, does nearly all of his assignments on location, using a twin-lens reflex for all black-and-white work. For color he uses a 5 × 7 Linhof, but

Editorial fashion photographs must compete for attention with dramatic advertisements, many of which are in full color. Photographers, consequently, are constantly in search of new devices to lend subject interest. One of the most resourceful of fashion photographers is Louis Faurer who here uses a plaster figure to attract attention to fashion lines that are extremely simple.

chooses a smaller (4 × 5) and lighter camera of the same make when it is necessary to travel any considerable distance. Such trips are usually made by air, and excess baggage charges on long flights can be prohibitive.

The smaller camera not only weighs less but frequently can be carried aboard the plane. The weight of the larger camera is increased by the packing necessary to protect it in the baggage compartment or in transit by air freight. The big difference, however, is in the film, which weighs as much as

Models make the picture. Photographers give unlimited credit to models for successful fashion photographs. Jean Patchet (left) and Suzy Parker are two of America's best, most popular, and most highly paid high-fashion models. Their personalities project so that elaborate backgrounds are seldom required to provide photographic interest as, for example, in these two by William Ward. Fashion features are the blouses shown in career-girl poses.

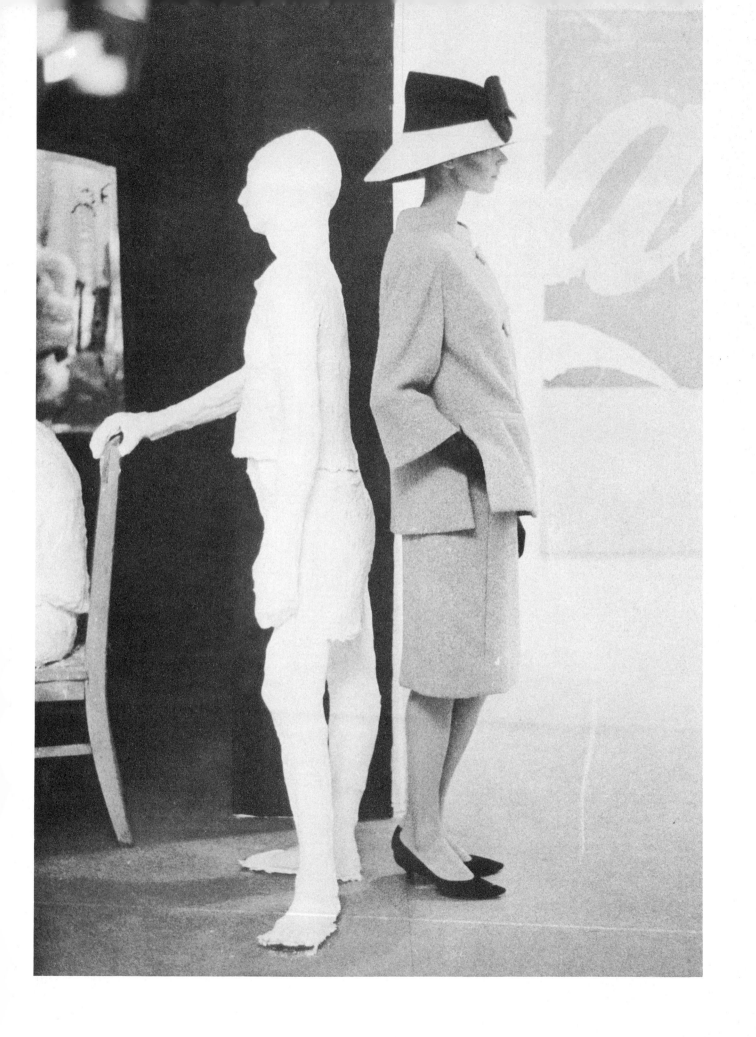

Strobe and conventional lighting were employed by George Barkentin to produce this unusual effect. Strobe lighting alone would have stopped the action of "rain"; it was used here partially to arrest motion.

60 to 70 pounds. The larger camera also requires a heavier tripod, and other accessories are scaled upward in proportion.

Apart from considerations of weight in transit, there is the problem of portability at the scene of action. Even on long trips, however, Landshoff carries such accessories as a 6-step aluminum ladder "to avoid monotony in the horizon line and angle of view" and a large umbrella "useful in shielding the camera in cases where a lens shade is not adequate and to keep models crisp and cool-looking under a sweltering sun."

Small twin-lens reflex cameras are generally favored for outdoor assignments, as the groundglass viewing panel permits careful study of modeling and composition before shooting. Another advantage is that the photographer can submit a number of contact prints for the perusal of the art and fashion editors.

Any film which offers a balanced color sensitivy is adequate, but high-speed films are often used for work outside the studio. (Still another advantage of the smaller camera is that it has a faster lens and higher shutter speeds—both important considerations in available-light photography. The shorter focal lengths of smaller cameras also give a greater depth of field at a given aperture.) Consistent use of one film type will eliminate at least one variable and contribute to quality control, but a few rolls of high-speed film may be useful under limited light conditions.

Obviously, the question of equipment is very much a matter of personal choice, for fashion editors and art directors are concerned only with the end result and not the means by which it was attained.

"If the average photographer," writes Edward Steichen, "could divert his interest in types of cameras, lenses, lights, etc., to *what* he photographs and *why* he photographs it, the world would be filled with good photographers.

"Making better pictures begins with learning to see things as they are, instead of how you would like them to be, then developing speed while photographing so as to be ready to press the button when your subject matter looks right to you. You stand a much better chance of working in an understanding manner in surroundings familiar and close to you, rather than by chasing rainbows all over the place."

FASHION PHOTOGRAPHY TECHNIQUES

Techniques of lighting and composition in fashion photography are essentially the same as for other

When the design in a fabric is very pronounced, as in this fashion photograph by George Barkentin, it is best photographed against a simple background.

categories. There are, however, certain special considerations.

As mentioned previously, fashion photographs are intended primarily, if not exclusively, for purposes of publication. Although each photograph should have all the elements of a good general composition, it is usually intended to highlight some special feature of line, pattern, texture, or color.

As with other types of pictures intended for wide circulation in print, fashion photographs must be considered in terms of the reproduction process used. All fashion magazines, and most other publications in which the photograph appears, are printed on "coated" paper and are reproduced by means of "fine-screen" halftones which retain 85 percent or more of the tonal quality present in the original print. (Some detail, of course, is lost in reproduction, just as a contact print does not reveal all of the qualities present in an enlargement.)

Photos intended for newspaper reproduction will require special care. Tonal quality, shadow, and highlight detail, as well as some of the fashion features, may have a tendency to flatten out. To compensate for these deficiencies, lighting should be arranged to produce definite blacks, a pronounced separation of medium tones, and possibly a slight overexposure of flesh tones.

Coarse-screen halftones, combined with the absorbent characteristics of newsprint, cannot be depended upon to show more than a half-dozen distinct tones, ranging from black or dark gray through one or two middle grays to white or light gray. Subtle definitions of tone will not register as such, but will either show darker than in the original print or be lost completely.

The rotogravure (intaglio) process, extensively used in newspaper magazine supplements, is capable of relatively high-fidelity reproduction, comparable to that of letterpress with fine-screen halftones; but as newsprint paper is generally used, the photograph must have a pronounced definition of tone and detail.

When fashion photographs are intended for extreme enlargement and display use, original tone values should be stronger than usual, and negatives should possess the finest possible grain.

Similar requirements pertain to prints to be shown on television. These, incidentally, should be matte rather than glossy, as the latter will reflect light into the television camera.

Instantaneous light (strobe or flash) is not generally used in fashion photography, although interesting and unusual results can be produced by this means. Strobe or flash can also be used to lighten shadows cast by the sun; reflectors, of course, are also used for this purpose.

In fashion photographs intended for quality reproduction, a full tone range is usually required. Some subjects, however, will require relatively "low-" or "high-key" treatment. A low-key effect can be obtained by placing the main lights to the side or toward the rear of the subject, with secondary illumination being employed to control the shadows. Exposures may be fairly long—as much as a second or two at high-numbered apertures. Film speed and light intensity are important factors; control in development and printing will make longer or shorter exposures feasible.

LIGHT SUBJECTS AND TWEEDS

High-key lighting is often used in rendering white or light-toned subjects as, for example, summer evening dresses, pastel daytime wear, or wedding gowns. Lighting should be broad and sufficiently off-center to provide modeling detail without creating sharp shadows and contrasts.

With fabrics ranging from rough tweeds to shimmering satins, the texture will dictate variations in lighting arrangements. B e c a u s e tweeds usually have larger and stronger patterns than other materials and thus provide some of their own contrast, softer lighting can be employed.

Moreover, as tweeds and other rough materials are associated with an atmosphere of informal comfort, lighting and general treatment should

George Barkentin frequently uses strobe lighting for unusual effects, as in this photo. Strobe not only serves such dramatic purposes as arresting movement of the greyhounds' leashes in mid air, but also prevents blurring of the fashion itself. Note sharp lines of dress.

be in the same mood.

SILKS AND SATINS

Metallic materials may appear harsh in the final print due to "hot" spots and dark shadows. Although it is usually possible to solve such problems by arrangement of lights, some photographers spray the materials with a thin mixture of condensed milk and warm water to cut down extreme highlights. Bright metal buttons and ornaments can be softened by rubbing a small amount of modeling clay on the objectionable highlight sources. As a rule, however, if the designer has conceived a glittering creation, every effort should be made to reflect this characteristic rather than to subdue it.

COLOR IN BLACK-AND-WHITE

Usually a distinct definition is required between background and subject colors on the monochromatic scale. Beige will show to best advantage against dark walls or shaded areas. Red, black, and dark blue contrast best against light walls or an unfiltered sky. Pastel blues, pinks, and grays are most effective against dark walls, the bark of a tree, or foliage. White and yellow garments can be accented by dark backgrounds or a filtered sky.

Deep brown, except in the case of fur or leather, should be treated in the same manner as black. Furs, incidentally, absorb considerable light, and leather causes objectionable reflections under direct light; these materials are photographed best in diffused light.

FASHION—THE CENTER OF INTEREST

Because the fashion photograph often constitutes the major portion of a magazine page and is supplemented only by a brief caption, it must be largely self-explanatory.

Accordingly, the fashion itself must be the center of interest, and any particularly significant detail,

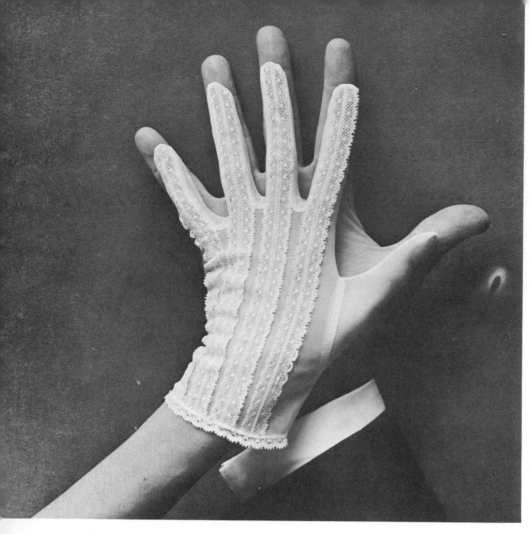

accepts a variety of assignments, his assortment of lighting equipment is relatively extensive. Included are: a trough light for stage effects and backlight; a 5000-watt spotlight, used in combination with other lights for photographing groups or as a sole source of illumination for single subjects; three 2000-watt spots, one of which is fixed on a boom; one flood; and one movie flood, which is used for backlighting.

METER READING

Like other veterans who began their careers prior to the widespread use of exposure meters, Mr. Lynes has developed his "light sense" to the point where he can confidently rely on his long experience for correct exposures.

Experienced photographers temper meter readings with personal judgment in accordance with their desired results. Some fashion photographs may seem under- or overexposed by strictly technical standards, yet serve their purpose well. The generally dramatic effect achieved may more than compensate for loss of some detail in the highlights or shadows.

RETOUCHING OF PRINTS

A fashion photograph which is acceptable in all other respects may be marred by a ruffled sleeve, or blurred flounce, or a lack of detail in some significant aspect of the design. As a result, retouching is frequently required.

If a view camera is used, retouching can be done on the plate, but this is usually not feasible on the 2¼ × 2¼ negatives of twin-reflex cameras favored for black-and-white by the majority of photographers who work on location. Consequently, some retouching on the enlarged print may be required.

As airbrushing is in itself a specialized craft, this work should be handled by a professional. The matter of retouching, however, is usually assigned by the art director and so is not of particular concern to the photographer.

---

such as an unusual neckline or new sleeve length, should be prominently shown. Posing of the model and concentration of light are principal elements of control and, as such, require close and careful attention. Surveys reveal that the model's face is the first element the reader notices; consequently the fashion point of interest must be emphasized in order to compete successfully for its share of attention.

LIGHT ON THE SUBJECT

Although technical proficiency, as previously mentioned, is less important to a successful career in fashion photography than certain other factors, the photographer must have a highly developed "light sense"; he must have full control over his lighting equipment.

As previously noted, lighting arrangements will vary widely with different photographers. Horst, who places "idea" above technique, uses few lights on indoor work, except where a very clear picture is required. "It is not how many or

what kinds of light you use," he suggests, "but how the lights are placed."

A coordinator from a Paris couturier arrived at Horst's studio one day with several creations to be photographed; she produced a small pocket flashlight. When asked what it was for, she replied beseechingly, "I would like just a little light on the gown, please."

George Platt Lynes, who has held a reputation for portraying simple elegance for more than a quarter of a century, suggests a basic geometrical arrangement in which two 200-watt spots form the base of an imaginary triangle, with the model at its apex and a third spot overhead. The function of the two foreground lights is to provide modeling and shadow detail, the overhead light serving as general illumination. The backlight, when used, is likely to be stronger than for other types of photography in order to point up the outline of a fashion design.

Since the versatile Mr. Lynes

Art director, fashion editor, and photographer, incidentally, may not agree on the choice of the best shot in a group of pictures. Some photographers who wish to see what they consider their best work in print mark their preferences on the contact print with a rubber stamp— "Landshoff's choice," for example. Editor and art director will usually give special consideration to prints so marked, but the final decision is theirs.

FASHIONS IN COLOR

Theoretically, the three colors represented in color film are capable of faithfully reproducing any conceivable combination of colors, no matter how varied. In graphic reproduction, a fourth "color" (black) is added synthetically, and the approach to reality (again, theoretically) becomes even closer.

In fact, most color photographs are far from truthful in their color rendition, and, despite the addition of a black "key" plate in printing, there may be little if any improvement in the ultimate result. One reason for this is that a printed page cannot reproduce the luminosity present in a transparency. Another is that color printing is done in "forms," that is, with eight, sixteen, thirty-two, or even sixty-four pages of color subjects being printed at the same time. Under these circumstances it becomes necessary for the printer to compensate for wide color ranges.

One set of plates, for example, may be predominantly red, another may emphasize a particular shade of blue. There are dozens of different "process" ink colors, and the printer must limit his selection to those three (plus black) which best serve the requirements of all plates involved. This means that some of the plates will not be treated as favorably as others. If the photographer tries to encompass a great many shades and hues in his original, the chance of inadequate

The fashion accessories pictured here are Coolray sunglasses. Although apparently taken on location, the nautical background was produced in William Ward's studio by means of a photomural.

reproduction is proportionately increased.

MANY COLORS EQUAL NO COLOR

There is a popular illusion that a photograph, in order to be "colorful," must show as many colors as possible. Scientifically, the reverse is true. The mixing of all known color pigments, or the mixing of even the primary colors (red, yellow, and blue) will produce gray. At a distance, the eye mixes colors. To give a practical example, camouflaged military weapons are made inconspicuous by being painted in rainbow hues.

The application of this optical axiom to fashion photography in color is important. For most subjects, the important considerations are simplicity and contrast. A mixing of many colors will obviously defeat both these photographic aims.

In seeking contrast, however, there is a danger of playing one color against the other too violently. Pink and green, for example, are contrasting colors, but most shades of these two colors do not present a pleasing juxtaposition.

Basically, procedures are the same in color as in black-and-white fashion photography. However, fundamentals of lighting which govern all color photography must be observed, perhaps even more closely on fashion work than with portrai-

Fashion photography is nearly always "out of season" as most fashion magazines and advertising campaigns are planned at least several months in advance of publication. This ski picture was taken on a beach, the negative printed at an angle to give the illusion of a slope. The snow flurry was achieved by sprinkling salt on the paper during enlargement. (Photo: George Barkentin)

ture and illustration. Scarcely perceptible deviations in the final color from that of the styles being pictured may make the photograph unusable.

Fortunately for the photographer, however, considerable control over color can be exercised in making

the engraving. The engraver, in fact, is often given a "swatch" of the material to be used as a guide in etching and finishing.

Inaccuracies in staging and backgrounds, which may not be noticeable in black-and-white pictures, become conspicuous in color.

In general, color requires four or five times as much light as black-and-white. Transparencies usually must be at least 4×5 inches in size. Accordingly, cameras used in color photography generally do not have the shutter or lens speed of the smaller cameras which can be used in black-and-white photography.

At present the majority of fashion photographs are black-and-white, but the ratio of color to monochrome is increasing each year, and in one national women's magazine color is being used almost exclusively.

BACKGROUNDS AND STAGING

Although some photographers specialize in either studio or location work, France McLaughlin-Gill points out that "our ten or twenty *best* fashion photographers excel at both techniques and the student, therefore, should be thoroughly briefed on the requirements of both types of assignment."

There have been, and still are, some portrait photographers whose work can be identified by the background or props employed. And although there are some fashion photographers who have made a trademark of certain kinds of settings, and others for whom background devices are virtually nonexistent, the setting which is appropriate for one picture or for a series of pictures is generally not suitable for the next assignment.

Successful artist-craftsmen in all branches of the profession are usually known for a recognizable style, and the fashion photographer is no exception. But he is also expected to keep pace with, or ahead of, the fashion designer, who is primarily interested in innovation. Settings, which are primarily the photographer's responsibility, are no less important in terms of the over-all composition than the fashion itself.

STUDIO SETTINGS

Indoor backgrounds may range from bare studio walls to the most extravagant rococo decor. In the hands of a Horst, a Hoyningen-Huene, or a Beaton, elaborate

settings have contributed to many striking and memorable pictures. The opportunity for mistakes and bad taste, however, increases in direct proportion to the number of elements involved, and the beginner is well advised to use only such background items as he can effectively control.

A knowledge of the graphic potentialities in furniture, fabrics, and floor coverings, however, can be valuable, as these elements not only attract the eye of the style-conscious reader (and editor), but may relate to the fashion motif. Specifically, period furnishings may complement a design, or, in the eye of a perceptive viewer, may result in an undesirable anachronism. If the gown is an adaptation of a historical design, furnishings of the same period can be effective in calling attention to its source.

FASHION PHOTOGRAPHY AND SOCIOLOGY

From time to time there have been trends toward sociological settings—a smart suit modeled in a tenement doorway, an evening gown photographed in a garment-district cutting room. Fashion photography can, in fact, comment eloquently, though sometimes inadvertently, on times and conditions. "Pictures taken by Paris fashion photographers in 1939," observed Condé Nast, "showed France getting ready for war...the Third Republic on the eve of disaster."

Although the photographer in search of an assignment may get one by suggesting an unusual background or theme, these are usually selected by editorial boards. Even magazines that are primarily devoted to fashions recognize the other interests of their readers.

If an assignment suggests a backstage location, for example, the photographer will probably be told which theater to use; the play or musical must be one that the editors consider of interest to their audiences—and one they assume will still be running when the magazine appears.

The time lapse between photographic assignment and publication date may be a matter of several months, which presents certain

seasonal considerations—swim suits may be photographed outdoors on a windy March day, furs during a July heat wave.

COMMERCIAL CONSIDERATIONS

Because the publishing business is precisely that—a business—there may also be certain advertising considerations. As a result, the photographer will often find that he is expected to show not only the salient features of a new fashion, but must also focus on such "background" items as furniture, drapes, wall coverings—even motor scooters and automobiles.

TRAVEL CREDITS

On fashion locations in which transportation or accommodations are provided, graphic credit must frequently be given to an airline, a steamship company, or a hotel. A test of a photographer's ingenuity is the manner in which he manages to satisfy the commitment without making a picture that looks more like a travel advertisement than a fashion photograph.

SUITABLE SETTINGS

When the choice of backgrounds is left entirely to the photographer, and where no location theme is indicated, the decision can be made purely on a basis of the fashion and its characteristics. In this instance, a complicated subject such as a flowered or veiled hat will usually require a relatively plain background to register detail in the subject. A simple setting can be established by the positioning of lights, or by using screens to form neutral areas of various tones.

More elaborate and ingenious settings are indicated when the garments are not sufficiently interesting in themselves to attract attention.

FASHION MODELS

"Fashion photography with living models," according to one leading cameraman, "is one of the most interesting and exacting of all photographic pursuits. Models, no matter how competent and cooperative, must be humored, coaxed and cajoled—much as a motion-picture director must deal with actors and actresses. In fact, the more elaborate fashion photographs are comparable to a motion-picture sequence."

Dr. Agha, Art Director of *Vogue* for many years, once said of Horst: "He has absolute control of his medium and sitter. By commanding a bend of the spine, by suggesting a tilt of the head, he can squeeze the last ounce of glamour from an exhausted model posing in a fur coat in July under 20,000 watts of light."

A good model is not in herself any assurance of a good photograph, or even a good "likeness." An illustration of this is found in the anecdote about a Paris model who was not recognizable as the same person in twelve pictures taken by a dozen different photographers. Conversely, one cameraman photographed twenty-four show girls, and it was difficult to distinguish one from the other.

MODELS MAKE THE PICTURE

A good model can, however, mean the difference between an ordinary and an outstanding fashion photograph. At her best, she is an actress and the photographer is her director. She will develop beyond her first poses until eventually she is able to express before a photographer's lens the exact nuance of emotion he wishes to record.

"On the highest level, her contribution to the final success of her picture is as real as that of the fashion stylist who stands by to correct details like sagging hems or a straggling hair...freeing the photographer to focus on the major creative problem."

Says Horst of the famous Parisian model known as Lud, "She came to deliver a bathing suit and revolutionized the model type...she was sensual, catlike, and terribly alive as opposed to the cold, remote somnambulist that meant glamour to the early thirties. Lud would never pose in a dress she disliked and she had an aversion to jewels."

MODEL TYPES

The desirable physical characteristics of models will vary according to the age and size for which the fashion is designed and the publication in which the pictures are scheduled to appear. Models of "indeterminate" age are seen in the pages of *Vogue* and *Harper's Bazaar* year after year, and are more sophisticated in appearance than those used for the women's "service" magazines such as *McCall's* and *Ladies' Home Journal.* From *Glamor* and *Mademoiselle* to *Seventeen,* models are progressively younger in appearance.

Frequently, models are selected by the magazine with or without the photographer's approval. When the latter is given the responsibility of selection, it is customary for him to consult with the editors or art director; otherwise the same model may possibly appear in the work of another photographer in the same issue.

Also, magazines have definite conceptions about the "image" of their readers. *Mademoiselle,* for example, is edited primarily for college women, but seldom uses actual students for fashion models. The principal reason for this policy is that magazines prefer to show their readers not as they are, but as they would like to be.

There is also a record of legal complications when nonprofessional models have been used. When amateur models are employed, the photographer should be sure to obtain a "release"; this is a legal document which permits use of the photograph for specific or all purposes. If the model is under age (twenty-one in some states), the release should be signed by a parent or guardian.

PHYSICAL CHARACTERISTICS

Since the camera tends to make people look slightly heavier than they appear in real life, fashion models are usually quite thin. Moreover, the lines of a dress can be defined much more clearly on an angular model, and it is easier to add apparent curves with tufts of tissue paper than to remove excess undesirable poundage. A beautiful woman whose proportions are the classical "perfect thirty six" may win beauty contests and movie contracts, but she is not likely to be seen in the pages of high-fashion magazines.

"To me," says Eileen Ford, of the Ford Model Agency, on the subject of why conventional beauties are not used in fashion photographs, "this affair is just a merchandising problem. And if you understand that the face and figure are props to glamorize the garment, you've hit the secret. The perfect model convinces the reader that anyone can look glamourous in the dress advertised. Can you imagine a clean-cut American girl doing that?

"To use a scrubbed-American-type girl on a high-fashion modeling job would be as sensible as trying to sell a Dior gown through a mail-order house.

"The high-fashion model must satisfy the super-woman instinct in the heart of every female. She must master a mask of elegant disdain and at the same time smile a pleasant come-hither look which has an attached price tag engraved with big dollar marks. The first thing I look for in a model is wide eyes that will photograph in any kind of light. Then I like a nice straight nose that is narrow at the bridge. And if a girl is anemic, I'm really sold!"

MALE MODELS

The modern male is much less fashion-conscious than the female, more conservative in his dress, and more resistant to change. Nevertheless, it is interesting to note that photography of men's clothes parallels that of women's fashions in many ways.

Men's clothes, like women's, were first rendered in paintings and drawings rather than photography, a practice which continued longer than in the case of women's fashions and is still more prevalent. *Esquire Magazine,* for example, has rarely used photographs in its fashion pages, but employs them extensively in another of its publications which is distributed to the men's-wear industry.

The preferred characteristics of male fashion models are similar to those for female models. They are generally thinner than the average man, and their faces tend to be interesting or distinguished rather

"The White and the Black." William Ward has devised his own available light set-up consisting of banks of floods set in a huge box with a diffusing screen of controlled intensity. Note here that black lingerie is given a light background, light lingerie a dark background. Hearts painted on the cheeks of the models are effective accents.

than handsome in the conventional sense. "Real" people are frequently used as male fashion models. Well-known athletes, for example, pose in sportswear; many business and professional men with photographic connections make extra money or find diversion in posing.

Paradoxically, the first fashion photograph to appear in *Vogue* depicted not the sort of lithe, unworldly beauty for which that magazine later became distinguished, but a *man* framed by the convolutions of a buggy whip!

CHILDREN'S FASHIONS

Although this article is primarily concerned with "high fashion" be-

A children's fashion picture is basically a good "kid" picture. William Ward made this photo of his young son for the family album but it could serve as an advertisement for corduroy jumpers.

cause it represents the ultimate in fashion photography, there are other important aspects of the craft. One of the most highly specialized is children's fashions.

Ordinarily, the fashion item to be pictured takes precedence over all other considerations. Children's fashions are a notable exception to the rule. Mothers, to whom most

children's fashion advertising is addressed, are infinitely more interested in children than they are in children's clothes. So a good children's fashion photo is primarily a good "kid" picture.

The spontaneity and restlessness of youngsters is not conducive to good studio photography. Strange surroundings, bright lights, and

artificial backgrounds contribute to a child's self-consciousness. So the most satisfactory children's fashion photos are made outdoors, where the model can be engaged in some typically youthful activity. Then it is up to the photographer to catch the right moment.

Naturally, the children's-wear photograph presents one problem not offered by an ordinary "kid" picture. Any special style feature must be shown clearly, whether that detail lies in the texture or pattern of the material, in tailoring, or in snap-button closure. When the photographer makes a dozen or more negatives, the essential feature must stand out in at least some of the prints.

The picture will, necessarily, assume an air of authenticity and an atmosphere of naturalness if an outdoor setting is employed. This must be novel enough to interest the child, but sufficiently familiar to prevent fright. Beach, zoo, toy department, or circus are ideal for the child past kindergarten age.

Smaller children will, on the other hand, be more at ease in their own backyard or sandbox. If, for reasons of time or weather, the picture must be made in a studio, every effort should still be directed toward an unposed picture. To accomplish this, the child's interest must first be diverted from the camera and focused on some other subject. Toys will distract the young child; games will serve for his older brother or sister; birthday or tea parties can set the stage for any age.

"Poses" should be avoided. In women's fashions, the stilted and obviously staged posture is often used to denote glamour; in children's fashions a feeling of naturalness must be preserved. (See *Child Photography* and *Baby Pictures*.)

The need for spontaneity also dictates to some extent the choice of equipment. The 2¼ × 2¼ twin-lens reflex with its short focal length and extreme depth of field permits freedom of movement for the child and, at the same time, enables the photographer to shoot in sharp focus and at sustained tempo. The ground-glass finder helps to frame the subject accurately enough to bring out the desired fashion feature.

Illumination of children's fashions is also somewhat different from lighting adult fashions. Natural sunlight provides the typical setting for most childhood activities, thus contributing to the naturalness of the final print. When artificial light must be used, strobe or flash provides a satisfactory solution to the problem generally, even though the flatness of such illumination may not be suitable for adult fashion photographs.

FASHION ACCESSORIES

In the photography of fashion accessories the photographer has an opportunity to utilize his full potential of imagination and resourceful-ness. In live fashion photography, the model can make a substantial contribution to the picture, but if accessories are photographed by themselves, the cameraman is solely responsible for the results achieved.

The following suggestions are based on the experience of David Fletcher, former staff photographer with Underwood & Underwood, and more recently associated with Sarra, Inc.

Lighting. Lighting equipment is of particular importance, as the nature of accessories or "small fashions," as they are sometimes called, makes natural illumination generally impractical. Because lighting demands will be virtually un-limited, it is advisable to concentrate on lights of professional quality from the beginning.

The primary light should be a good (though not necessarily expensive) spotlight which can, with a change in bulbs, be used for color work. This spotlight should be at least of 500-watt capacity. Secondary illumination may consist of several flood bulbs for use in clamp-on reflectors.

A "kicker" rear accent light can be made with a regular screw-in socket, snap-switch, and threaded inlet for the cable. A rod or pipe,

This lingerie photograph was made by using one of the studio props as unusual background. (Photo: William Ward)

threaded to fit the socket, can then be fitted with a film clip to make an adjustable clamp-on fixture. By interchanging dim and bright bulbs, almost every basic problem of lighting accent can be solved.

Background and equipment. Unlike the candid technique frequently employed in photographing live models, pictures of fashion accessories depend on carefully prepared backgrounds in order to complement objects which are in themselves usually prosaic.

The following are directions for construction of a versatile homemade background. The first step is to purchase a large sheet of quarter-inch plate glass and have *one* side sandblasted. For most purposes a glass measuring 20×24 inches will be adequate, although it will need to be at least twice that size for furs and other large accessories. This single glass should then be mounted in a wooden frame and fitted with a hinged base which will permit tilting. The variety of backgrounds attainable with this device is virtually endless. With the "kicker" providing backlight, objects such as leaves and lace, for example, can be interposed between the small light and the glass, creating hundreds of shadow backgrounds for merchandise placed before or on top of the glass. Without backlighting, the neutral tone of the glass will serve as a near-white or jet-black background to complement any accessory, depending on how much light you give it.

Because sharp detail is essential for success in photographing fashion accessories, a fairly large view camera is generally preferred. However, any camera fitted with groundglass focusing can be used. Naturally, the extension-bellows type will serve better than the single or twin-lens reflex because it accepts a wide selection of lenses and film types. An exposure meter is considered standard equipment.

With regard to black-and-white film, a portrait panchromatic emulsion will be suitable for most purposes. There will be occasions, however, when an orthochromatic film emulsion may be preferred. Color transparencies should be 4×5 inches or larger.

Props. The word "prop" is derived from the word "property." The meaning has special significance in this instance, for although such items may be rented or borrowed, those which are the property of the photographer are more conveniently available.

These can be assembled over a period of time and stored for eventual use. A piece of driftwood or a large chunk of tree bark, for example, may be just the thing to enhance the interest and relate the function of a shoe. A leafy branch placed behind the groundglass table can suggest the out-of-doors. Cocktail glasses or a sheet of music help tell the story of a dancing shoe.

Sheets of white, medium gray, and black heavy-ply cardboard (in appropriate hues for color photography) have many uses. In glossy and dull finishes, these cardboard sheets will furnish basic backgrounds for accessories; the white ones will double as reflectors for the indirect lighting of jewelry and similar merchandise which cannot be lighted directly.

Eventually more elaborate settings such as pillars and platforms will be required. Simple household items can serve a variety of purposes. Bathroom-cabinet shelves, available in various lengths, can be used as staggered shelves against the upright groundglass table when several items are photographed together.

Other background and display material can be purchased quite economically from commercial display sources. Window decorators for department stores and shops can sometimes be induced to pass along used artificial grass, paper maché tree trunks, and corrugated paper pillars at little or no cost. Yard-goods departments of local stores will provide interesting textiles for backgrounds, and remnant sales can produce bargains in usable props.

Antique stores will usually rent at a nominal fee items ranging from a cigar-store Indian to a Louis XV chair. (One European photographer acquired so many antiques as props that he eventually went into the business and now makes photography his hobby!)

Technique. In the arrangement of subject matter there are no set rules other than those governing all still-life compositions. Lighting should not be too intense, but carefully planned to provide modeling and form to the subject. The spotlight is used for this purpose; the "kicker" controls background effects; floodlights lighten shadows caused by the spotlight.

Apart from technical considerations and more important than technique are taste, imagination, and a knowledge of good design. In this respect it is interesting to note that most specialists in the field have had some training or experience in drawing and painting. Even the photographer who possesses no talent for manual graphics may do well to study composition and the work of still-life painters.

Models. Some fashion accessory subjects cannot be pictured effectively and consistently without the use of a live model. Hats are made to complement the face of the wearer and are best shown on the head of a living model. Hands, rather than artificial forms, show gloves to their best advantage. Lingerie, because it is cut on the bias, is infinitely better suited to display on the human figure than on a table or platform.

When live models are used, techniques applicable to fashion photography should be observed. More light may be required, as it is usually necessary to use small apertures for maximum depth of field.

A final word on the subject of photographing fashion accessories—and this applies to fashion photography in general: the composition should be kept well within the size limits of the negative or transparency. Some cropping may be required for purposes of layout; if the standard dimensions are to prevail, the photographer may indicate his own suggestions for cropping on the final print or transparency.

The most satisfactory children's fashion photos are made outdoors, where the model can be engaged in some typically youthful activity. (Photo: George Barkentin)

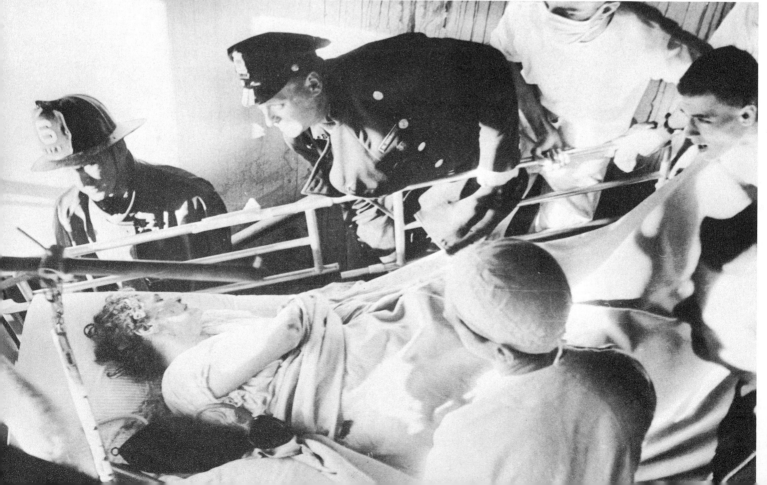

Top Left: MAD RIVER: Living up to its name, Mad River left its mark on Main Street in Winsted, Conn., following a flash flood and two hurricanes. Taken with 4X5 Speed Graphic, Royal Pan film, 1/200 of a second at f/8.

Bottom Left: DESPERATE HOURS: Policeman, fireman, and hospital personnel hurriedly carry patient, bed and all, down stairs during Hartford Hospital fire which claimed 16 lives. Contax with 35mm Biogon f/2.8 lens. Plus-X, 1/125 of a second at f/4. (Photo: Charles J. Vendetti)

Top Right: ON GUARD: Intense backlighting dramatizes lonely vigil of soldier guarding NIKE display in the rain. Rolleiflex with flash behind soldier.

Bottom Right: GLOWING CAGE: Lights attached to helicopter's blades create eerie effect. Taken with 4X5 Speed Graphic with open flash. (Photo: Einar G. Chindmark)

Below: FOR REAL? Finding an icicle stuck in the snow, photographer Bob Pugliese has added watering can to show what might happen during a sudden cold snap. Leica with 90mm Summicron f/2. Panatomic-X, for 1/500 of a second at f/8.

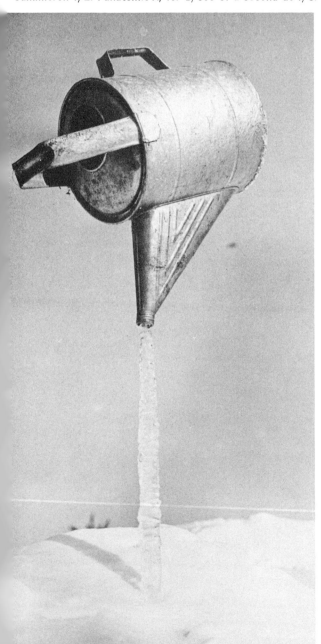

COVERED STILL   **RUSSELL LEE**

The experienced photographer will sometimes bypass the theoretical rules of composition in order to achieve an artistic end. One of the first rules of photographing buildings is to use an off-center angle in order to indicate some idea of the depth and form of the structure. In this photo, however, the photographer has placed his camera almost dead center, rendering the building's facade as if it were a piece of stage scenery with nothing behind it. The only factors which interrupt the sameness are the open windows and the door standing ajar.

The sky is monotoned, except for the faint wisp of smoke rising toward upper right. The convoluted piping at lower left, and especially at lower right, becomes a foil for the basic pattern of the main building, while in the distance, the triangular form of the derrick imparts a feeling of depth to the composition.

FAULTS IN AMATEUR MOVIES

WILLIAM STULL, A.S.C.

[In this article, a former judge in many national and international amateur movie contests discusses what he considers the faults of the average movie maker. The author gives valuable information about panning, exposures, composition, parallax, and titling—what to do and what not to do if you want to hold your movie audiences.]

• *Also see: ABC's of Home Movies; Continuity in Movies; Editing Movie Films; Motion-Picture Composition.*

TO HOME-MOVIE AUDIENCES, THE terrors of the amateur film are the jitterbug school of camera work and its Siamese twin, the garden-hose type of panning. Both of them give the audience the impression that the scene was shot during an earth-quake, for nothing on the screen is steady. In the first case, the earth-quake seems to have been mild: people, buildings, and landscape all weave slowly about the screen, usually with a sort of billowing regularity. In the second, the earth-quake was evidently devastating, for everything on the screen reels drunkenly, and in extreme cases the only thing visible is a confused blur.

Both of these faults stem from excessive belief in the advertising that classifies 16 mm and 8 mm cameras as hand cameras. They really are not, even though some of them are smaller and lighter than the ones we recognize as hand cameras in still work.

USING A TRIPOD

If you want to present a steady scene to a movie audience, you can do so only by using a tripod. Few of us have a genuinely steady hand. If you doubt it, try holding a book

Many of today's movie cameras are equipped with built-in light meters that automatically set the lens diaphragm. However, under certain lighting conditions, it is necessary for the cameraman to make compensations since the meter cannot think for itself.

in your hand at arm's length for even the short time necessary to read a single sentence. The book will waver around—perhaps only a fraction of an inch—as your muscles try to support the weight. In addition, it will probably have a more or less up-and-down motion as you breathe.

The same thing occurs when a movie camera is held in the hand. It wavers slightly, to say nothing of weaving slowly up and down as you breathe. The motion may be small, perhaps infinitesimal, but it will be there. And it is magnified many times, first by the relatively narrow angle of view of the camera's lens, and second by the magnification of projection. A weave which at the camera may actually measure only 1/64 of an inch or less may be magnified to one or more inches when the picture is projected onto a six-foot screen. Use a good, solid tripod to eliminate weave.

A tripod, properly used, will also cure garden-hose panning. Panning should be done slowly or not at all. And it should be done only for a definite reason. Spraying the lens all over a scene or group to give motion to the movie is not sufficient reason. If you use a tripod and make it a rule to pan only when you absolutely cannot avoid doing so—and then pan even slower than what you think is too slow—you'll go far in eliminating this problem and will make your scenes more pleasing to the audience.

Now all of the above is, we know, like Sunday's sermon—little is remembered of it on Monday morning. We have been insisting on tripods for amateur cameras for 20 years and more, and have seen no noticeable increase in their use. We have been inveighing against rapid panning, or for that matter, any kind of panning, and we see almost as many pans as ever in the average home movie.

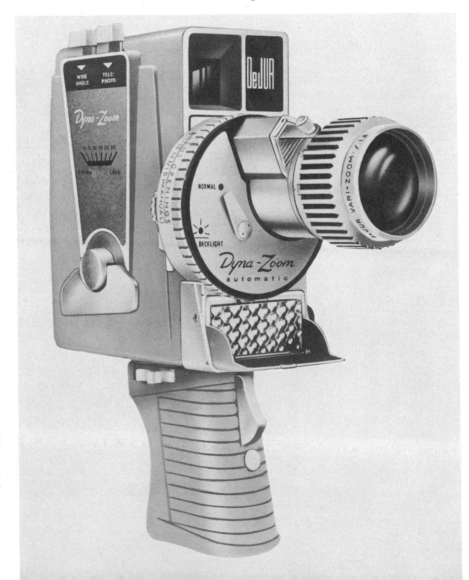

Three effective ways of improving home movies by steadying the picture are to use a tripod, unipod, or pistol grip. Even the slightest movement while shooting the scene is greatly exaggerated when the scene is projected onto the screen. These accessories are particularly useful when panning and zooming where a steady image is of the utmost importance.

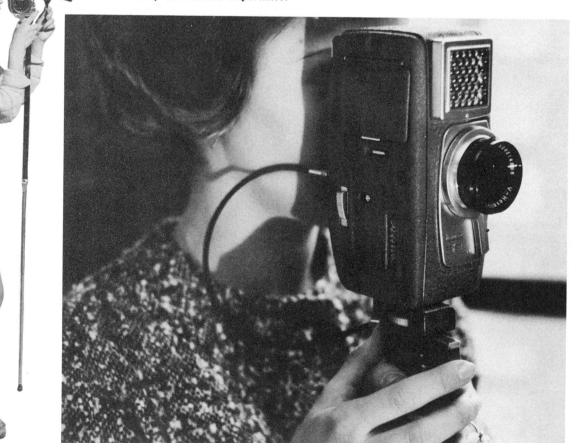

There may be some excuse for the traveler, especially if he is on a tour with a group. Often there is no time to set up a tripod, and in many public places their use is forbidden. Still, there are Belt-Pods, Shoulder-Pods, Unipods, and a host of other ingenious gadgets, any one of which will make a remarkable improvement in the amateur's films.

A tripod will make your films look sharper. If you don't believe this, take a strip of film shot hand-held and examine it, frame by frame, with a magnifier. Every so often, you'll come to a frame which is hopelessly blurred, which means the camera made a small sharp movement at that point. It is something like the old riddle about mixing a barrel of clean water and a barrel of dirty water. What do you get? Two barrels of dirty water. Likewise, when you project a film which has six sharp frames, a blurred one, five sharp frames, a blurred one, and so on, the net result is a movie which appears generally blurred.

BAD EXPOSURE

Today, there seems to be no excuse at all for bad exposure. Excellent exposure meters can be bought for the same price as two rolls of film. Many 8 mm cameras have built-in exposure meters. Some even have exposure meters connected to the lens diaphragm, so the user has nothing to do but point and shoot.

Nevertheless, poor exposure is a major fault in many home movies. There are several easily understood reasons for this. The most common is incorrect use of the meter. In shots where part of the scene is in bright sunlight and part in heavy shadow, the meter can average up the light values of only these two extremes of illumination. If you follow such a reading, important action taking place in one area or the other—especially in the shadows—will be incorrectly exposed. The best remedy is to calculate before shooting just where the important action of the scene will lie, and then to take your meter reading with the meter so positioned that it "sees" only that area.

On other occasions we may get an incorrect exposure by letting the meter's eye "see" too much of the sky or too much of the wall of a white, strongly lit building. The remedy is again to select what the meter's eye is to see. In the case of scenes in which more than the usual amount of sky figures, it is safe to take the reading with the meter pointed slightly downward, with the palms and fingers folded above the meter's cell to produce a sort of sunshade.

Careless use of a meter is another cause of trouble. As many workers grow more experienced in the use of camera and meter, they take a meter reading only at the first camera set-up on a new location, instead of at every shot, trusting experience to keep their exposure right thereafter. They forget that normal daylight changes in intensity from minute to minute and, further, that often only a slight change in the camera's position will give it not only a changed field of view but

Sometimes it is more convenient to steady the camera by clamping it to a support, such as in this arrangement with an open glove compartment.

very greatly changed reflective values. For example, shooting along the shore line at the beach on a sunny day we might have a meter reading of f/16. But swing the camera 45 degrees or 90 degrees shoreward and the reflective values change as sea and sand are replaced by dark green foliage and gray-black rocks. In this set-up, the correct exposure might be one, two, or even three stops larger.

Here is one place where the intelligent use of a built-in meter, with automatic coupling to the diaphragm, can produce results unobtainable any other way. It is quite fascinating to watch the diaphragm control working while the camera is being panned (slowly!) from a dark area to a light one, or conversely. To make the same shot in Hollywood, an assistant would have to ride the camera boom, changing the diaphragm by hand as the camera is moved.

CARELESS COMPOSITION

Another prominent fault, especially among the more advanced filmers who have mastered the rather basic matters of holding the camera, panning, and exposure, is careless composition.

A typical example of poor composition is to be found where some disturbing line or mass in the picture distracts attention from the really important parts of the scene. In innumerable interior scenes, my eye has been forcibly and persistently dragged from the really important action by the intrusion of some pronounced horizontal line in the background—such as a strip of molding, or a mantel on a back wall—making me wonder if by chance the scene has come out of frame in the projector. The remedy is to pay more careful attention to the background of the scene, as well as to its action, and to study the shot through the finder carefully before shooting.

PARALLAX

In close shots, parallax is a perennial trouble maker. It is responsible for trimming off innumerable foreheads, ears, and chins in close shots. The cause, of course, is that the finder and the taking lens are not in the same position. While in more distant shots the fields of view of the two coincide excellently, at closer range—usually six feet or under—the finder's field is noticeably removed from that actually

Titling, or lack of it, is another source of trouble. Here a scene is shot through a transparent screen upon which the title is written.

covered by the lens.

The amateur can thank the manufacturers for their introduction of the "reflex" camera in which the image is viewed through the taking lens. This results in the elimination of parallax; what we see, we get.

ZOOM TROUBLE

The zoom lens is a wonderful invention. Years of optical design have gone into perfecting a lens which provides a continual change in image size without loss of sharp focus at any point. This is wonderful, as we said unless it is misused.

And it is misused most of the time. The real value of the zoom lens is its ability to be set at any focal length to produce the best image size and composition. It takes the place of a whole turret full of separate lenses in providing the exact framing desired. Now and then—yes—now and then, it is permissible to zoom in, slowly, for a closer look at something. This is valuable, for example, in a crowded street scene where a sudden cut to a close-up might confuse the audience.

But an audience watching the average amateur's use of a zoom lens for the first time is apt to get seasick. Often the filmer will zoom in for a close-up, and back out again, sometimes two or three times in a single shot. The net result is that the audience sees less than if the same footage were devoted to a close-up, a medium shot, and a long shot, taken separately.

If the zoom is manually operated, a tripod must be used. It is impossible to hold a camera in the hand and operate a manual zoom lens without jerking the camera. On a tripod, it can be done.

UNEDITED FILMS

Still another thing that irritates an audience is a carelessly edited film that jumps in content over a number of unrelated subjects. Remember that a picture should confine itself to a single basic idea. For example, if you took a vacation trip to the national parks of the northwest, confine your picture to what you saw in those parks. Very

Many pistol grips are available for movie cameras. These steady the picture when other types of support, such as tripod or unipod, are not available.

likely on the same trip you stopped off to visit relatives at various points and shot a few feet of film during each of these visits. Just cut the relatives out of the national park picture; they are nice people, but they don't have anything to do with the park scenery.

Another distinct fault in editing is including too many shots of a favorite scene. One shot of a favorite scene is best; two shots may be effective; three will invariably pall.

TITLING FAULTS

Titling—or lack of it— is another source of painful faults. Everyone knows what a difference good titles make in a picture. If a film is

inherently good—well planned, well photographed, and well edited— titles will add the final touch. If the picture is weak in any of these departments, it needs titles to help pull it together. That much is obvious, but there are several points about titling which are not.

For one thing, home movies often have a good main title, a good end title, and none in between. Many amateurs feel that their pictures should tell their own story, unsupported by titles; but I've noticed that when they show such pictures, they usually keep up a running verbal commentary. Titles would make a much better impression on the audience.

This author has a strong pref-

erence for titles over narration. One reason for this preference is simply that titles are easier on the audience. It is often hard to watch a picture and listen to a commentary at the same time and to make sense of both. Professionals know this, and when they make a film "voice over" they always allow extra footage on each scene so that the viewer can listen, and then watch.

For another thing, amateur narrations are often too complete—something like the book about which the little fifth grader said, "It told me more about penguins than I really wanted to know." The average title is limited, by considerations of legibility, to about 20 words; there are very few scenes which cannot be identified, described, or commented upon within this limit. After that, just let the picture talk for itself.

COLOR TITLES

Naturally titles in a color film should be in color too. Use titles that are simple, almost neutral in tone—white letters on a bluish gray background are excellent. If a touch of color is desired, a single red initial letter starting the title will provide all the contrast needed.

If the titles are superimposed over colored postal cards or other colored pictures, be sure the colored background is not too bright. Often, the background is so full of detail it is hard to distinguish the lettering, harder still to read it. One way to tone this down is to letter the title in white on a celluloid sheet. Then, between the celluloid and the background picture, you can slip a sheet of grayish celluloid which will dull the colors and detail in the back-

ground to any desired extent. These grayish celluloids are sold in art-goods stores under the name of "Bourges Shading Sheets"; they are available in a wide range of solid gray tones.

Finally, there is the question of wording. Try not to tell too much in the title, but rather, simply hint at the following scene. Imagine you are writing telegrams at ten cents per word. For that matter, if you are having your titles made commercially, you will find yourself being economical with words. It is all to the good.

CONCLUSION

This list of typical amateur movie faults could be greatly extended, for as soon as any amateur or professional filmer conquers one set of faults in his work, he finds new ones springing up. But they can all be remedied easily, by the simple process of applying more thought to filming. Movies are unique among the graphic arts, for while the others concern themselves similarly with pictorial effect, and may or may not serve as vehicles for ideas, movies of any sort exist mainly for the purpose of conveying an idea to an audience. And anything which prevents the audience from grasping that idea, or distracts attention from the idea to the mechanics of film making, is a fault. Make it easy for the audience to understand your films, and in the process you will eliminate most of the faults.

☐

FEERTYPE

The Feertype process was invented by Dr. Adolf Feer in 1889. By using the process, paper or fabric may be sensitized with diazo compounds which will form a colored image when exposed to light. The material is exposed under a negative and washed to remove unused chemicals, leaving a positive image in the desired color. For further information, see *Fabric Printing*.

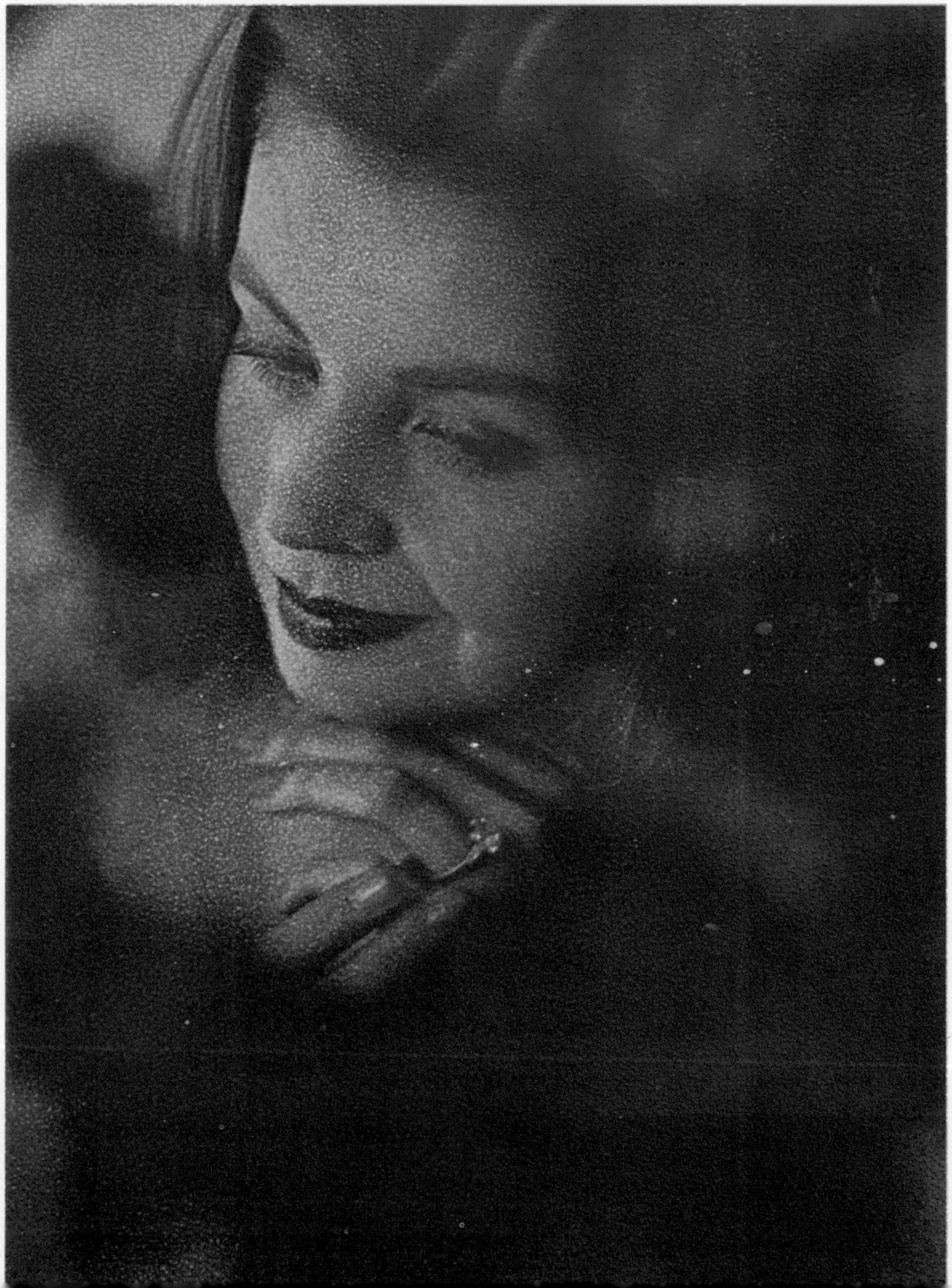

Preceding page: CARL FISCHER / *Wine Cellar*

NORMAN ROTHSCHILD / *The Three Aces*

FILIPPO ACCINI / *Still Life: Tulips*

Barry Hicks / *The Mountains of Mourne*

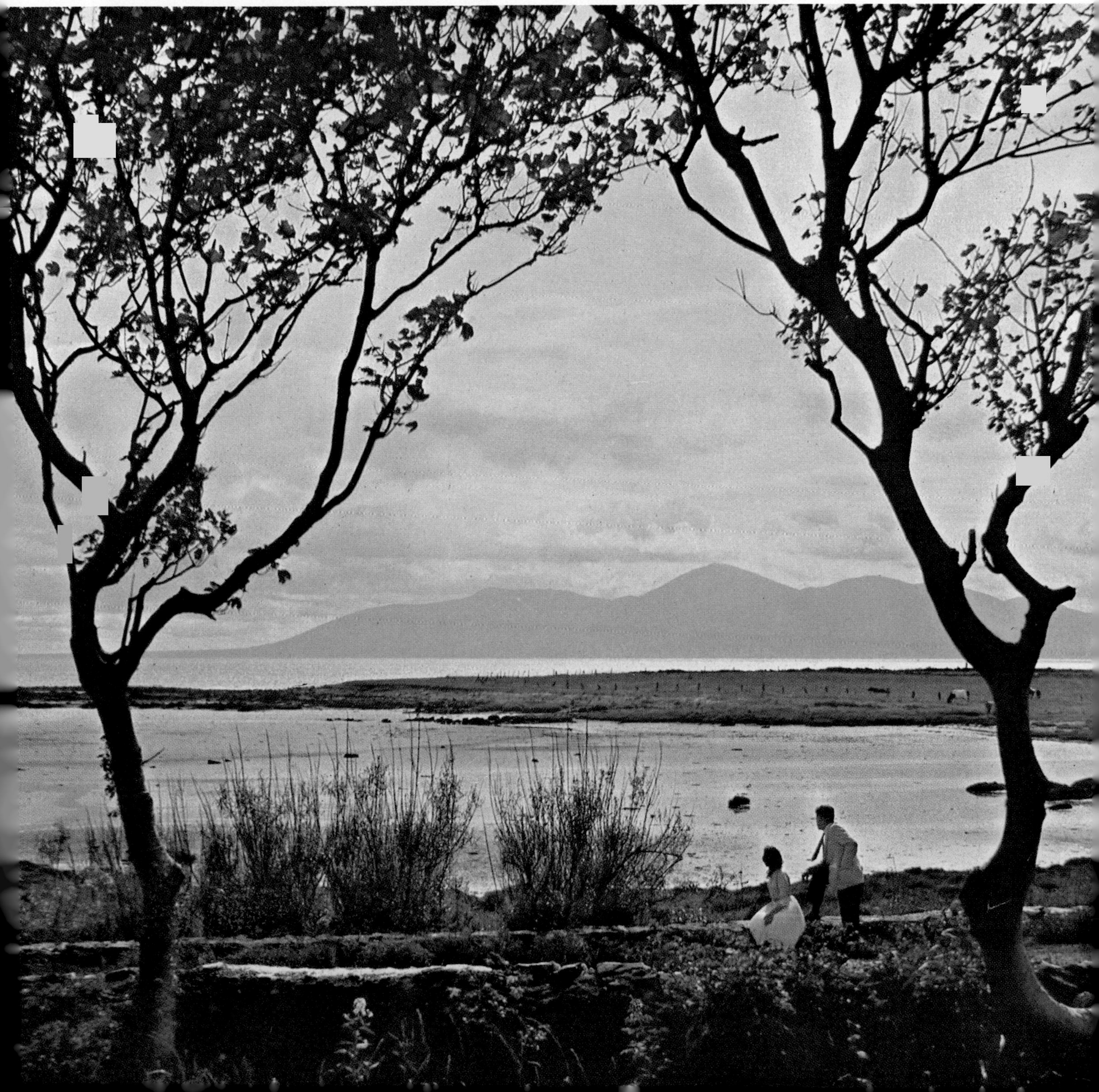

MORT HECHT / *Pastorale at Dusk*

Next page: HORN/GRINER / *Lazy Afternoon*

EDWARD BROWNRIGG / *Castles*

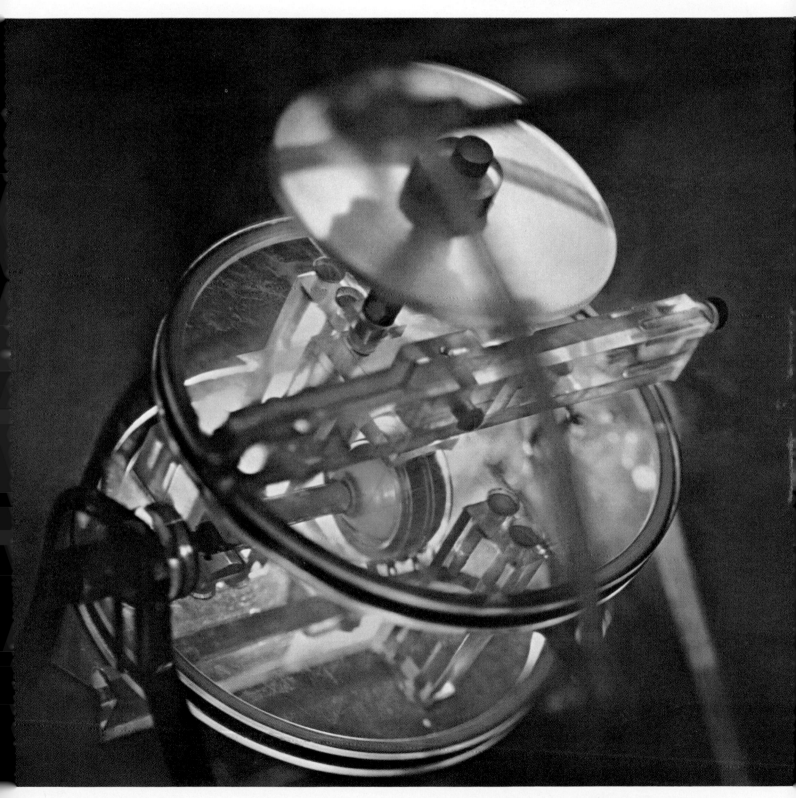

IRVING BAHRT / *Gyroscope*

Next page: A. Kruparz / *Landscape: Rice Paddies*

Sharon Marchant / *Red Harvest*

Final color page: Hy Peskin / *Rodeo*

ANDREAS FEININGER
Biography

Andreas Feininger has succeeded in extending the visual horizons of man. As a photographer, his work has spanned the confining boundaries of human vision; as a teacher, his writings have found wide acceptance throughout the world. Among his books are a series of three textbooks, published in 1954-55 by Prentice-Hall, entitled *Successful Photography, Successful Color Photography,* and *The Creative Photographer.* In the preface to the last of these volumes he states, "This is a summing up. It is the last book on photographic topics the author intends to write. From now on, whatever he has to say, he will say with his photographs."

And since then he has said it, in hundreds of pages of large picture books, the way he wanted to say it —with pictures. *The Face of New York,* published in 1954 and now in its seventh printing, expresses his endless fascination for structure and form as revealed in the buildings, bridges, and streets of the city. Here also Feininger uses the telephoto lens, frequently from a vantage point in the New Jersey meadows or from the cliffs of the Palisades, to provide a powerfully unique group of skyline and river-harbor shots.

His other picture books include: *The Anatomy of Nature,* a study of the function of form and design in the universe (also printed in German, Dutch, and Spanish editions); *Man and Stone,* a photographic journey into the past; and *Maids, Madonnas, and Witches,* a picture book on the sculpture of the female form from prehistoric times to Picasso.

Feininger has had one-man shows at the Corner Gallery of the Museum of Natural History in New York City, the Carl Siembab Gallery in Boston, Mass., the Pratt Institute in Brooklyn, N. Y., and the Smithsonian Institution in Washington, D. C. His photographs have been included in the "Family of Man" and "70 Photographers Look at New York" exhibitions at the Museum of Modern Art in New York City, and in many more museums throughout the United States and Europe.

Andreas B. L. Feininger was born of American parents in Paris in 1906; his father, Lyonel Feininger, was a distinguished artist and sculptor. Andreas attended school in Germany until the age of fifteen when he left to learn the trade of a cabinetmaker at the Bauhaus in Weimar. Three years later he finished his apprenticeship, became a journeyman cabinetmaker, and immediately afterward began to study architecture at Bauschule in Zerbst. He graduated *summa cum laude* and went to work as an architect, first in Germany, then in France.

Finally, in 1933, he moved to Stockholm where he discovered that his real talents lay elsewhere—in architectural photography. For the next six years, he made his living photographing for most of the leading architects and architectural publications of Sweden.

Andreas Feininger / Sectionalized Nautilus Shell.

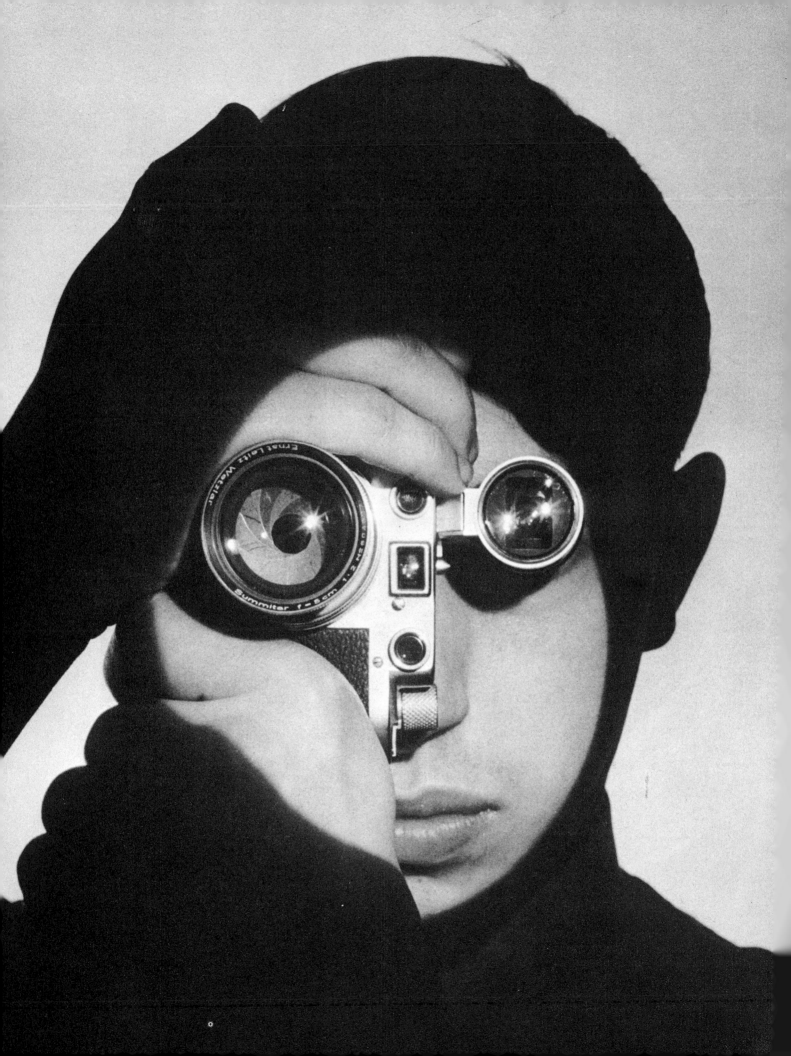

Andreas Feininger / The Photojournalist.

Feininger began his career as an author at the invitation of Walther Heering, owner of the Heering-Verlag in Germany, who asked him to write articles for his magazine, *Der Foto-Spiegel.* Subsequently, Dr. Heering commissioned him to begin writing photographic textbooks. The first of these, *Menschen vor der Kamera,* was published in July, 1934. Five more followed in the next three years. At the same time his love for the city, its buildings, its people drew him more and more to the streets of Stockholm, where, with his camera, he found the material for his first large-size photobook, *Stockholm,* published in 1936 by Albert Bonniers Förlag.

In 1939 Feininger left Sweden to come to New York. After a year of working for the Black Star Photo Agency (at $20 per week), he was discovered by *Life* magazine, and became a full-time *Life* staff photographer in 1943. He held this position for 19 years, resigning recently to devote his time and talents to his books.

Feininger's pictures are distinguished by a meticulous attention to detail and composition, by the sudden, unexpected, confounding shifts of perspective, **the accurate play of light.** His subjects are most often taken from nature—now a tree, now a stone, now a detail of an insect's body—suggesting always the basic functional design of the universe.

Always fascinated by the problems and possibilities of unusual perspective, Feininger was quick to recognize the basic superiority of the camera lens to the human eye. He explains this superiority and its application to his own photographic style and philosophy in the following quotation from *U. S. Camera* (1958):

"Sharp, detailed human vision begins approximately eight inches from the eye and extends for a few hundred feet. Objects that are closer cannot be seen clearly; those that are farther away appear less and less detailed as subject distance increases and image size diminishes. But the camera, in conjunction with lenses of shorter or longer than standard focal length, makes it possible to obtain large-scale, sharply detailed pictures of objects as near as fractions of an inch or as far away as the horizon....Macro- and telephotographs, pictures taken from unusual and revealing angles and points of view, close-ups showing the very essence of a subject, speedlight shots arresting rapid motion, patterns disclosed through abstract black-and-white are examples of the kind of creative photography...that widens one's intellectual and emotional horizons."

Three articles by Andreas Feininger appear elsewhere in this Encyclopedia. They are: *Perspective, Photographic Control Processes,* and *Telephotography.*

□

FERROTYPING

Ferrotyping derives its name from the smooth ferrotype tin surface used in the print-glazing process, but the term also is applied to the use of chromium-plated steel tins and other similar surfaces. (The ferrotype process of glazing prints should not be confused with the ferrotype or tintype which was a wet collodion photo process.)

In ferrotyping, photographic papers which have a special glossy emulsion are pressed into firm contact with a smooth surface and, while drying, the fibres of the gelatin become compressed. This forms a smooth glossy print surface. Glossy prints are especially good for newspaper or magazine reproduction, as the surface reflects a maximum of light and loses a minimum of contrast.

FERROTYPING SURFACES

The surface of the print takes the form of the surface onto which it is pressed; therefore it is extremely important that the ferrotype be smooth and free from defects. There are a number of possible surfaces. The original ferrotype "tins," which still are used for small-scale work, consisted of steel sheets coated with a smooth, brilliant enamel. Chromium-plated sheets are very popular, while sheets of polished copper, stainless steel, plate glass, and Kodapak Sheet also have been used. Ferrotyping large numbers of prints is usually done on heated chromium-plated drums.

While the black and the chromium-plated ferrotype tins are the easiest to maintain and use, glass may be an effective substitute. Mirror plate glass is preferable, as the glass must be uniform and free from surface defects. It must be well cleaned by several washings with hot water and soap.

Transparent Kodapak Sheet is also capable of giving good gloss and is relatively inexpensive, though it has the disadvantage of easily scratched surfaces. The .0075-inch (and thinner) Kodapak sheets are not stiff enough for use without

Use the hand to wipe the surfaces of washed prints while they are still in the water. Wiping them will remove air bells attached to the emulsion.

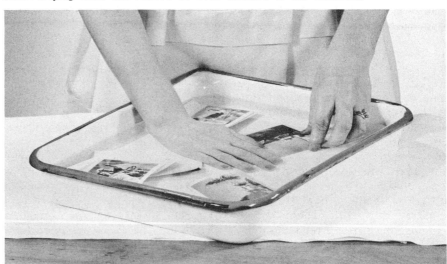

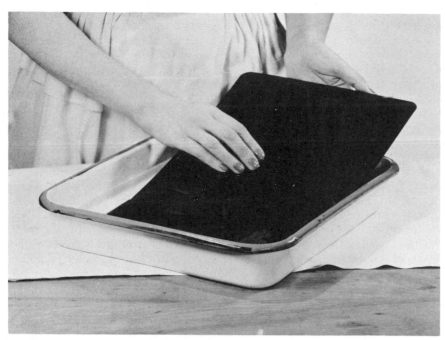

New ferrotype tins are washed with a mild soap, rinsed, dried, coated with wax, and then polished. This is repeated occasionally as tins are used. Before ferrotyping prints, the tin may be flooded with water and washed with finger tips to remove dust and scum and to eliminate air pockets.

backing but will prove satisfactory if backed with metal or glass. This is done by trimming the Kodapak Sheet to the same size as the sheet of metal and then fastening them together with cellulose tape or adhesive tape.

CLEANING FERROTYPES

New ferrotyping surfaces must be thoroughly cleaned or prints will glaze imperfectly and stick. Glass and japanned (black-enamel) surfaces may be cleaned by rubbing gently with a soft material dipped in hot water and soap or in a dilute ammonia solution. Chrome tins can be cleaned with mild soap and water. Great care must be exercised not to scratch the surface.

It is usually better to wax enamel or glass surfaces. Kodak Ferrotype Plate Polish is convenient and simple to use. The plate should first be washed with warm water to remove any particles of gelatin, or other residue adhering to the surface. Then a few drops of the polish are applied to the surface and rubbed in lightly; a final high gloss is given with soft cheesecloth, a chamois, or a silk rag. Chromium and Kodapak surfaces may be used without waxing; a thin layer of

vaseline is often applied to the Kodapak Sheet instead.

Only occasional further treatment is needed once the surface has been prepared properly. The important thing is to avoid scratching, and this requires that handling of the ferrotype be kept to a minimum. The plates should be stored in a rack or carefully interleaved with heavy paper and placed in a drawer.

Enameled or glass surfaces should be washed periodically with soap or ammonia and rewaxed occasionally. Some photographers dust the surface with talcum powder, rubbing gently. Wax or talcum fills in the minute furrows caused by scratching. In the absence of wax, the print gelatin is pressed into the furrows, increasing the adhesion and preventing the prints from stripping off easily. Chromium tins should be cleaned occasionally with a mild soap, especially if the prints show a tendency to stick.

Heated chromium-plated drums can become extremely dirty due to the adherence of gelatin particles, fibre, dust and metallic particles. If prints stick, even after cleaning the drum, the following procedure should be used:

Obtain a carborundum product

known as Aloxite Grade A, No. 1 Fine Buffing Powder. Any other type of aloxite powder will *not* do. Make a thin, watery paste of the powder. Apply it with a soft cloth over a small portion of the drum at a time, and continue to rub until there is no break in the water film. This must be done while the drum is cold. Allow it to dry, then wipe off with a clean, soft cloth. Polish the drum with a mild soap until the water beads, indicating a high degree of water repellency over the entire surface. Allow the soap to dry, then wipe the powder off the drum. This procedure should be used when prints persistently stick and not as a daily routine.

FERROTYPING PROCEDURE

Applying the print. It is very important to have an even layer of water remain under the print and to avoid trapping air bells between the print and the ferrotyping surface. The most dependable method of applying prints is to rinse and swab the tin thoroughly with the finger tips. Wipe the print with the hands while the print is still in the water to remove any air bells clinging to the emulsion. Pick up the print by two adjacent corners and lower it, face down, so that one edge is in contact with the tin. Then lower it further in order to "roll" the print onto the ferrotyping surface. After a short draining period, the print should be squeegeed into contact.

Squeegeeing. This operation presses the print into contact with the ferrotyping surface. All air bells must be eliminated, uniform contact obtained, and tearing of the print avoided. One very good system is to lay the tins bearing the prints on a level surface, place a sheet of rubber or canvas over the back of the prints to avoid injury, and then apply the squeegee, wiping alternately in both directions. Excess water is then blotted off and the prints set to dry. The sheet may be attached to the edge of a table so that it hangs down when not in use and has a chance to dry.

Several types of squeegees are available, including single-roller, double-roller, straight-edge or "win-

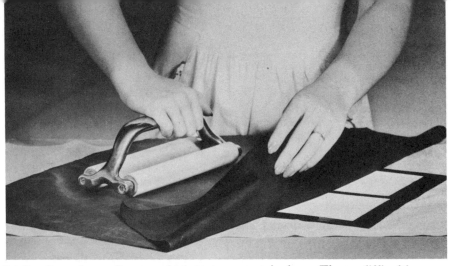

The tin is laid on a flat surface and covered with a sheet of rubber, a blotter, or a cloth and squeegeed.

dow-wiper" type, and wringer-roller. An ordinary washing-machine wringer functions very well and will normally accommodate the 10 × 14-inch ferrotype tin. But the squeegeeing action should not be interrupted while there is a print between the rollers or the finished print may have a clearly defined line of pits or flecks.

Drying. If great speed is not required, the prints can be dried by simply placing the ferrotype tin on edge or by laying it flat, print side up. The prints ordinarily pop off. They may be readily pulled off, but this should not be done until the prints are almost dry or an imperfect gloss will result.

After the prints have been allowed to dry naturally for 15 or more minutes, a mild stream of air may be directed on the tin from a fan and, if desired, a moderate degree of heat may be applied, such as from a radiant electric heater placed several feet away from the tin. Irregular and poor gloss will result if the drying is too rapid, especially during the initial period. Temperatures of over 150 F injure japanned tins, and appreciably higher temperatures melt the print gelatin, causing the prints to stick to the plate. More rapid drying can be accomplished by putting the print in an alcohol bath (one part denatured alcohol to one part of water) before squeegeeing.

Final rinse. A number of different chemicals can be employed in the final print rinse after washing to aid uniform adhesion, prevent sticking, prevent excessive or uneven drying, and further harden (or sometimes soften) the print. Kodak Photo-Flo Solution uniformly wets the ferrotyping tin and the paper surface, ensuring uniform glazing. Kodak Print Flattening Solution, or glycerin in a five-to-ten-percent solution, prevents the print from drying unevenly and prevents curl. It may be combined with a wetting agent.

Hardening agents are usually not necessary if a hardening fixing bath, such as Kodak Acid Fixer or Kodak Fixing Bath F-5 or F-6, has been used. When rapid drying is essential, prints can be bathed in a 50-percent solution of denatured alcohol before squeegeeing and then dried before a fan. Heat should not be applied for the first few minutes. Warm air may be used later.

DEFECTS IN FERROTYPING

The perfect ferrotyping of prints requires care and some experience. A number of difficulties may occur, especially during cold weather when the humidity of the average work-room is low. These difficulties are due to lack of cleanliness, irregular or too rapid drying, too much heat, or too little, or too much hardening of the gelatin coating.

Sticking. If the dried print sticks to the ferrotype plate and is difficult to remove or tears on removal, this is a sign that either 1) the gelatin coating was too soft, which can be caused by insufficient fixing or by use of an exhausted fixer or a fixer without hardener; 2) too much heat was applied; 3) insufficient time was allowed for drying; or 4) the plate was dirty. Softening may be prevented by fixing the print for at least ten minutes in a fresh acid fixing bath, being careful to agitate well; by keeping the temperature of the wash water at 65 to 75 F; and by not applying too much heat while drying.

Adhering prints usually tear if pulled from the ferrotyping surface. To avoid tearing, the tin and prints should be soaked in warm water until they are easily separated. The prints should then be hardened in a fresh fixing bath and washed thoroughly. The ferrotype plate should be cleaned and waxed before referrotyping.

Unglazed spots. Circular or oval unglazed areas or blisters are caused by entrapped air bells which have kept the print from coming into contact with the plate. They may be prevented by ensuring that the entire print surface is covered with a layer of water when applied and by careful and thorough squeegeeing. A final bath containing a wetting agent, such as Kodak

Place prints face down by touching one edge to the plate and then lowering the remainder onto the ferrotyping surface.

Photo-Flo Solution, is helpful. These spots can be removed by soaking and referrotyping.

"Oyster-shell" markings. The print may strip from the plate in steps, creating a series of ridges much like those of an oyster shell. In extreme cases these will occur as actual cracks in the gelatin coating of the print. This is due to irregular and too rapid drying and is most likely to occur during the winter when the humidity is low. They may be prevented by drying slowly in a moist atmosphere, by bathing the print in Kodak Print Flattening Solution or in a five-to-ten-percent solution of glycerin before drying, or by covering the back of the print with a blotter during the first part of the drying period.

Edge lift. The edges of the print may dry rapidly, lifting from the plate before gloss has been achieved. This also is a low-humidity problem and may be acute with double-weight prints. It is prevented in the same manner as are oyster-shell markings, and by dampening the edges with water or Kodak Print Flattening Solution during the drying period.

Insufficient gloss. This is caused by a dull ferrotyping surface, by stripping before the gelatin surface is dry, and by excessive hardening. It may be prevented by waxing the surface and drying the print more slowly, especially during the initial period. If insufficient gloss was due to excessive hardening, small unglazed flecks, especially likely to occur when the wash water is very cold, may be noted. Warmer wash water or a final bath in hot water should be used.

Tone changes. When the drying temperature is too high, especially when the print has not been thoroughly fixed and washed, residual hypo may sulfide the image, causing the tone to become brownish and possibly depositing yellow-highlight stain. This can be avoided by thorough fixing and washing, aided by the use of Kodak Hypo Clearing Agent, and by drying at a lower temperature.

(Reproduced with permission from copyrighted Kodak pamphlet Number G-10.)

FIBRE OPTICS

We are all familiar with the fact that a rod of Lucite, or similar substance, can transmit light from one place to another, even around corners. A ray of light entering one end of the rod is trapped within it, with the light being reflected from one side of the rod to the other until it finally emerges from the opposite end.

The efficiency of the system depends on how completely reflection takes place each time the light ray touches the inner surface of the fibre. Minute defects and contamination at the surface can cause leakage of light. This leakage is not serious in the case of a prism, since only one reflection takes place. But in fibres where a great many reflections occur as the light rays travel through the fibre, these losses must be eliminated.

This elimination is accomplished by "cladding" the fibres with another type of glass of different refractive index. Cladding eliminates leakage of light and "cross-talk," or leakage of light from one fibre to another, which would degrade the contrast of the image being transmitted.

LIGHT PATTERN

If a great many fibres of extreme thinness are arranged in a bundle so that they are in the same order at each end of the bundle, a pattern of light (such as the image produced by a lens) at one end of the bundle would appear at the opposite end of the bundle in the same form. This would be the case even if the bundle were bent around corners, or if the fibres were loosely arranged or mixed up between the ends.

There are two other possibilities: a fibre bundle can be made in which the arrangement at each end is completely random; or, the arrangement of fibres can be altered in a definite way between the input and output ends.

The random arrangement of fibres can be used to conduct light from one place to another when no image forming is required. Scrambling the fibres can be an advantage. For example, it is used in motion-picture printing machines between light source and printing aperture, both to conduct light efficiently and to secure as uniform a printing light as possible at the printing plane.

The second arrangement, in which

Fibres gathered and cemented together in a sleeve at one end and fanned out at the other show their light-transmitting powers.

Figure 1. *A laboratory timer dial photographed through a flexible fibrescope.*

mm square, which would just accommodate the usual 16 mm film image area (8×10.5 mm). The image quality possible through such a device is seen in Figure 1 which shows the dial of a laboratory clock photographed through a fibrescope.

It is possible to fuse bundles of fibres, when flexibility is not required and where an image needs to be transmitted only a short distance and in a straight line. Fused fibres can be used for the face plates of oscillograph tubes, so the image can be photographed by placing a film in contact with the face plate, eliminating lenses and the loss of light resulting from them. They can also be used as elements of lens systems; a recent high-speed camera lens having an aperture of $f/0.58$ has a fibre bundle as one of its elements.

OTHER FIBRE-OPTICS USES

Fibre optics and the fibrescope can be used to transmit radiation from possible fires in aircraft around protective barriers to sensing devices placed in safer areas. Bundles as long as 100 feet have been used for this purpose.

Another use of fibre optics is in borescopes for examining and photographing the insides of hollow objects into which a camera cannot be placed. Thus the inside of a boiler can be photographed through a small hole. The gasoline-level indicator in a fuel tank can be photographed through the filler hole of the tank. Medical uses of fibre optics are numerous.

the fibres are arranged in a definite but different manner at each end, is useful to produce images which are distorted in a desired manner. A rectangular image can be spread out into a single line to reduce the film running speed in a high-speed movie camera. Or, an image may be scrambled until it is unrecognizable and unscrambled by transmitting it backward through the same fibre bundle or through another made in the same manner. The latter method is used in cryptography and for coding signatures for bank identification.

PHOTOGRAPHIC USES

The most familiar form of fibre optical system is the "flexible fibrescope" which can be made as long as 13 feet and has fibre elements as small as ten microns in diameter ($1/_{100}$ mm). This device has an image resolution of at least 50 lines per mm, which puts it in the class of practical photographic devices. The actual resolution is somewhat less because there is some misalignment of fibres in the bundle,

and because there usually are some defective or broken fibres which produce gaps or dark spots in the image.

Nonetheless, the device provides a handy means for viewing or photographing objects which are otherwise inaccessible. Currently the largest cross section of fibrescope which can be supplied is about 10

A flexible fibrescope with objective lens at one end and eyepiece at the other end.

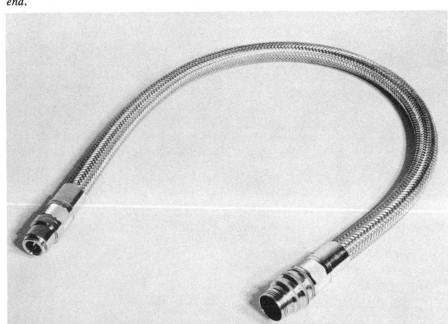

FILING SYSTEMS FOR NEGATIVES, SLIDES, AND PRINTS

BARTON BACHMANN

[A collection of photographs—historic, artistic, or commercial—is valuable only in proportion to its use, and a carefully planned filing system can save the photographer many hours of searching for the exact shot he needs. This article should be read by everyone who handles large numbers of photographs and negatives.]

A COLLECTION OF NEGATIVES, slides, or prints, should be filed for safekeeping and indexed, if utter chaos in handling them is to be avoided. This recommendation applies to the amateur photographer's collection of hundreds of negatives as well as to the tens of thousands accumulated by a commercial establishment.

If a print is misplaced or destroyed, another can be made from the negative. But if a negative or a transparency is lost or irremediably damaged, that picture is gone forever.

There are many types of filing systems. Some are best for general use, when a variety of subjects and pictures are to be dealt with. Others are most useful when the items to

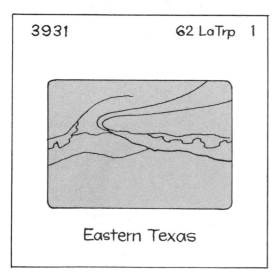

The preferable way of titling and numbering a slide.

MASTER LIST

Ident. Number	Date	Title	Category No.	
3927	5/29/62	Army helicopter at Air Show	NwsSpEv	291
3928	6/3/62	Wide leather belting in operation	Indus	372
3929	6/3/62	Gates Co. V-type belting in operation	Indus	373
3930	7/10/62	Opening new section of freeway	NwsSpEv	292
3931	8/5/62	Eastern Texas	62LaTrp	1
3932	8/7/62	Nachitoches, Louisiana	62LaTrp	4
3933	8/7/62	Magnolia Plantation house	62LaTrp	5
3934	8/10/62	Lake Bistineau	62LaTrp	3
3935	8/12/62	The Red River at Shreveport	62LaTrp	2

NEWS AND SPECIAL EVENTS (NwsSpEv)

Category Number	Title	Ident. Number	Date
291	Army helicopter at Air Show	3927	5/29/62
292	Opening new section of freeway	3930	7/10/62

INDUSTRIAL SHOTS (Indus)

Category Number	Title	Ident. Number	Date
372	Wide leather belting in operation	3928	6/3/62
373	Gates Co. V-type belting in operation	3929	6/3/62

1962 MOTOR TRIP TO LOUISIANA (62LaTrp)

Category Number	Title	Ident. Number	Date
1	Eastern Texas	3931	8/5/62
2	The Red River at Shreveport	3935	8/12/62
3	Lake Bistineau	3934	8/10/62
4	Nachitoches, Louisiana	3932	8/7/62
5	Magnolia Plantation house	3933	8/7/62

be filed are confined to a specialized field, as in astronomical or medical photography, or for the studio engaging almost exclusively in portraiture. Sometimes the speed with which a negative or a print can be located is the primary consideration, as in the photo file of a newspaper. Sometimes safekeeping is the most important factor, as with documentary or historical photographs or negatives.

Any effective negative, print, or slide file must be carefully and systematically arranged and indexed while avoiding overelaboration and complexity. Some sort of classification will, in most instances, be useful if not necessary. But if such classifications are too involved, the file is apt to depend too much upon the memory of one person.

A good filing system should

Entries on the master list and corresponding entries on category lists for a negative and slide filing system.

1) provide safe and convenient storage for each negative, print, or slide, to protect it from dust, scratches, or other damage and 2) make it possible to locate any item easily and quickly. Some types of commercial establishments that accumulate huge numbers of negatives and/or prints find that many of them are seldom used. In such cases it is best to establish both a storage file and an active file.

NEGATIVE FILING EQUIPMENT

Standard metal filing drawers and cabinets, if judiciously selected, are suitable for storage of negatives. One advantage is that, having been constructed to a standard pattern, additional matching equipment is readily available. This is particularly important to a commercial firm whose files are continually growing.

Files should be chosen which are, as far as possible, dustproof and fire resistant. The photographer should investigate the type of insulation used in heat resistant cabinets. At high temperatures some types of insulation release water vapor which could seriously damage negatives. The dimensions of stock equipment should depend on the size of the negative enclosures to be used. In addition to standard office equipment, filing cabinets, drawers, and boxes especially designed for photographic items are available.

NEGATIVE ENCLOSURES

Before being placed in a file, each negative should be enclosed in a suitable jacket or envelope to protect the delicate surfaces of the film. Negative envelopes are available in different sizes and of various materials such as paper (opaque), glassine (translucent), or cellulose acetate (transparent). Stock manila or white bond envelopes also may be used.

However, it should be remembered that photographic negatives are very susceptible to chemical contamination. Some papers, even some seam cements, contain residual chemicals which may have a harmful effect upon negatives kept in close contact with them for a long time. For information on storage of especially valuable or important negatives, consult *The*

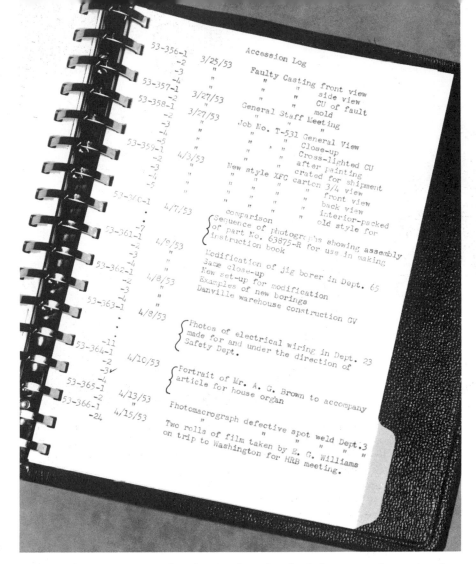

Sample page from log book for entry of negative data.

American Standard Requirements for Photographic Filing Envelopes which may be obtained from the American Standards Association, Inc., 70 East 45th Street, New York 17, N. Y.

Seamless envelopes are preferable for negative storage; side-seam envelopes may be used; center-seam envelopes are least suitable. Even if no chemical contamination results from center-seam containers, the pressure of the seam ridge can cause physical damage, especially if the negatives are too tightly packed in the file.

Negative envelopes are available to fit all standard-size negatives. If different-size films are commonly used, it is better to use one size of envelope (the largest needed) for all. A large firm may, however, find it convenient to maintain separate cabinets for different negative and envelope sizes.

An other exception to this principle of uniform negative enclosures may be made when dealing with small negatives such as 35 mm

A light table may be used for numbering negatives.

used for exhibiting only. The selected slides for any given showing are loaded into them and, afterward, each slide is returned to its place in the permanent file.

PRINTS

Sometimes prints are filed as an adjunct to the negative file with their primary purpose being to assist in identifying and locating a given negative. In other instances the print is the pertinent item, as with photos being held for future publication, for records, for industrial use, for historical reasons, or as art works. The amateur may want prints kept simply for his own and his friends' examination and enjoyment.

To file prints for supplemental use, a contact print should be made of each negative before it enters the file. These prints, each carefully marked with the identifying number or letter of the corresponding negative, are then filed either with the negative or separately. Mount the contact prints on an $8 \times 11\frac{1}{2}$ sheet, one, two, or more on each sheet, according to the print size. These sheets then may be filed in a standard letter file or may be put in a loose-leaf notebook, making it very easy to thumb through them.

Prints assembled for use as such, and not necessarily associated with negatives, may be filed in standard filing equipment in the same manner as negatives. Unmounted prints should be enclosed in heavy manila envelopes, possibly with a piece of cardboard corresponding to the print size to keep prints from curling. Mounted prints also may be stored in envelopes.

Prints too large for a standard file are best stored in solander cases—flat, dustproof boxes made for this purpose. These are often used by museums maintaining a collection of photographic art.

Another way of storing prints which are to be frequently shown is to use special albums with acetate envelopes as pages. Each of these envelopes will hold two prints, back to back. These albums are

size. These are best cut into short strips which are then enclosed in narrow envelopes or sleeves manufactured specifically for this purpose. They then can be filed in shallow drawers or boxes obtainable from firms specializing in photographic filing materials.

TRANSPARENCIES

Unmounted transparencies should be placed in envelopes and filed. Color transparencies are even more delicate and susceptible to chemical and physical damage than black-and-white negatives. Extreme care should be exercised in handling and filing color transparencies. Their life will be increased by protecting them from lengthy exposure to bright light.

Mounted transparencies should be filed in drawers or boxes provided with grooves, each of which will hold one glass-mounted slide or two cardboard mounts.

Various models of slide files are available to accommodate all standard sizes: the $3\frac{1}{4} \times 4$ lantern slide, $2\frac{1}{4} \times 2\frac{1}{4}$ slide, and the still more common 2×2 size. They vary in style from flat metal boxes to more elaborate drawer cabinets which may be designed to allow addition of sections as the file grows. A few slide files have, instead of grooves, small compart-

ments holding about twenty slides each. For ease in locating a particular slide, the groove type is preferred.

For large institutions, such as universities, technical schools, industrial laboratories, hospitals, and clinics, where a great number of slides must be kept for quick reference and comparison, the Multiplex file has been designed to hold 6240 slides. It consists of a large cabinet fitted with sliding steel frames, each frame capable of holding 120 2×2-inch slides ready for viewing against a diffusing screen.

Many slide projectors employ some type of magazine or tray for exhibiting slides. This may be employed as a file, since it usually holds from 30 to 40 slides.

However, as the slide collection builds up into the hundreds or thousands, there will be a considerable number of trays. If the magazines used for exhibiting slides also are employed as files, much shifting of slides will be necessary to exhibit different sequences. It will become almost impossible to establish a permanent location for each slide, where it can always be found—something which is indispensable to effective filing.

The preferable procedure is to have several magazines—three, four, or even half a dozen—to be available for prints of several sizes and provide an attractive way of showing prints, either for the amateur or the professional.

FILING AND INDEXING SYSTEMS

Once safe, convenient, and adequate storage has been provided, a system of filing must be established which will make it possible to locate a desired negative, slide, or print speedily and easily.

It is impossible to devise a single filing system that will be the perfect answer to every conceivable filing problem: choose the system that will best meet your particular requirements and circumstances.

A classification based on subject matter, arranged alphabetically under general headings, and thoroughly cross-indexed, is most suitable for the very large photographic firm which handles thousands of negatives and slides. Organizations using photography in a more specialized field, such as clinical or industrial laboratories, will find a file based on technical classifications more useful. The individual photographer, professional or amateur, who does his own filing, will do better with a general file making use of categories into which the pictures naturally fall.

Once adopted, the chosen filing system should be adhered to. At the same time it should be sufficiently flexible to permit occasional changes in, or additions to, its categories without upsetting the whole plan.

The following sections apply to the general filing system mentioned above as being suitable for the individual photographer. The same system is used for slides and for negatives.

CHRONOLOGICAL FILING

Filing slides or negatives chronologically, in the order in which they are made, does not work out very well as the collection grows.

For example, the average amateur will very likely take photographs of his family at various times. These should be filed together, so that

Use of a Kardex filing system provides for the entry of data and contact prints for easy identification of negatives.

they can be easily found. It would be ridiculous to have two or three such negatives filed just ahead of the Memorial Day parade shots, and two or three more following last summer's Niagara Falls pictures, and others scattered here and there throughout the file.

To avoid such confusion, a category system of filing and indexing should be instituted. Its use will make it possible to see at a glance just what pictures are available of a particular place, person, or thing.

For this system of filing, a number of classifications, or "categories," should be established. They should not be too narrow in their classification, nor so broad as to be meaningless. They should certainly apply to the photographic activities of the individual.

A "landscapes" category, to include all scenic pictures, without reference to type or locality, would be too broad to have any significance. But a separate category for each and every place visited on an extended trip would be cutting it far too fine. An amateur, or a free lance professional who occasionally turns his attention to some formal portraiture, might find a "portraits" category suitable and useful. But it would hardly be significant for the portrait studio photographer.

GEOGRAPHICAL FILING

Nearly everyone who uses a camera, professional as well as amateur, will make pictures of his home town's public buildings, parks, street, scenes, historic landmarks,

On more extensive travels—to Europe, Mexico, or the more distant parts of this country—enough pictures probably will be made to constitute a well-rounded and complete set, a picture story of the trip. Such a set is best filed in a closed category to which no further negatives or slides will be added, for even if another journey is made to the same general region, it too probably will result in another complete set.

SUBJECT FILING

Other filing categories may be based upon the type of subject, rather than upon the location. A category which is likely to prove useful to amateur photographers is one or several, under the general heading FAMILY ALBUM. Here will be filed pictures of the home and home events, members of the family, parties, and friends being entertained in the home.

For a while a single category may take ample care of such pictures. But, particularly if photos are taken at the home of other family members, it may be desirable to divide the category into several subcategories: FAMILY AT HOME, FAMILY AT GRANDMOTHER'S, FAMILY ON OUTINGS. Convenient abbreviations for these can be devised. Such subclassifications will help greatly in locating a desired negative or slide rapidly.

Many amateurs—and occasionally a professional on assignment or "on spec"—will make shots of local events, a parade, the opening of a

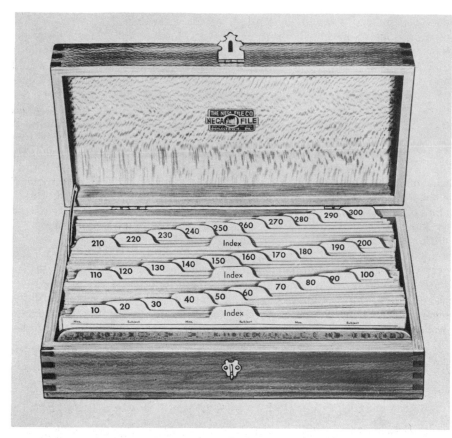

Nega-File for holding 1800 exposures on 35 mm film cut in strips of six and inserted in transparent envelopes.

private residences, and gardens. If done professionally, the photographer may prefer to file such shots according to job assignment. Otherwise he, as well as the amateur, might well file them under a category labelled HOME TOWN, or simply bearing the name of the city itself, as PORTSMOUTH.

A category which many amateurs will find useful is one for filing pictures made on picnics or day trips to near-by localities. It would be clumsy and totally unnecessary to establish a separate category for every point pictured; it is much better to lump them all under a PICNICS AND DAY TRIPS classification which can be abbreviated as PICTRIP.

Pictures made in other cities or particularly interesting regions—not in the immediate vicinity but close enough so that they may be revisited from time to time—are best filed under a category applying to

that city or region. Residents of California, for example, might have in their files such categories as YOSEMITE, DESERT REGIONS, SAN FRANCISCO. Those living on the eastern seaboard might establish categories covering ADIRONDACKS, CAPE COD, WASHINGTON, D. C. Each of these categories would contain pictures made during visits at different times.

This Nega-File accommodates 250 2×2 mounted slides or 750 cardboard mounts. All slots are individually numbered.

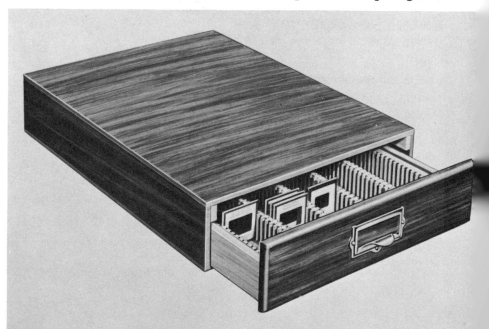

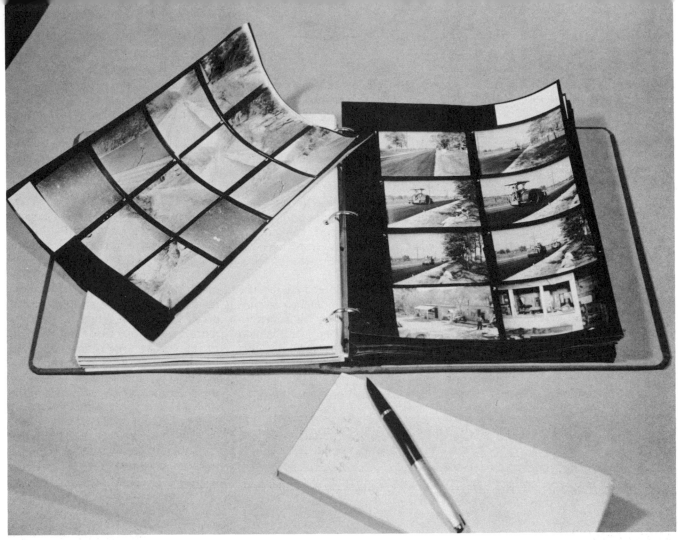

Contact prints may be used to make a master index file. Prints are mounted or contact printed on photographic paper.

new highway, a fire. Such shots should be filed in a NEWS AND SPECIAL EVENTS (NwsSpEv) category.

Those having special interests may establish a filing category for FISHING, GOLF, or SPORTS CAR RACES categories. Sometimes photos of business or professional activities justify the establishment of a category.

When the categories have been decided on, negatives and slides should be classified accordingly. Once in a while a picture may be made which is hard to place in one category. For example, a shot may be made of the family on a day trip to some picturesque spot. Should it be filed under PICNICS AND DAY TRIPS, or under FAMILY OUTINGS? If the primary interest in the picture is the location, or something the people are doing which is definitely related to that location, it should be filed under the former category. If portrayal of the people is of chief importance, the photo belongs in the latter grouping.

This may seem a matter of little importance. But if a negative is to be found without undue searching, a definite policy of classification must be adopted and adhered to rigidly.

MARKING NEGATIVES AND SLIDES

Whatever filing system is employed, it is imperative that every negative and every slide be plainly marked with a permanent identifying number or symbol.

This applies to the large photographic establishment and to the smaller and less elaborate files of the individual photographer, professional or amateur.

A number should appear on the negative envelope and on the negative itself, preferably in the transparent margin, so that the negative can be identified even if left out of the envelope or placed in the wrong one.

It is most convenient to inscribe this number at the upper left hand corner on a negative envelope, or on an inverted, mounted slide, and close enough to that corner so that it can easily be read without the problem of removing negative or slide from the file.

The simplest way of assigning these identifying numbers is to begin with number "1" for the first negative or slide entered in the file and number consecutively from there. Whatever other letters or numbers the negative or slide may bear, according to the system employed, and however and wherever it may be filed, it can always be identified by this permanent number.

When the category system is employed, the category and a number showing exactly where a negative or a slide is to be filed should be inscribed in the extreme upper right hand corner on the negative envelope, or on the slide. Since most projectors require slides to be inserted upside down to be shown on a screen, it is best to do all numbering and titling with the slide in the inverted position.

In addition to these numbers, it is desirable that the negative envelope or slide carry a brief caption indicating the subject of the picture. On a negative envelope there is room for adding, if desired, the date and exposure data, or such information may appear on an index card or in a notebook.

FILE INDEXING

Some files are self-indexing: by the use of tabbed dividers, negatives or slides are separated alphabetically, by classifications, by categories, or by number groups based on dates of acquisition. A desired item then may be located by thumbing through the appropriate section. Such filing requires only that the title or subject name, classification, or approximate date of acquisition be known.

A large file containing many thousands of items should be operated with a card-indexing and cross-indexing system which also has room for technical data and subject information. In working with a smaller file, a loose-leaf notebook will probably prove more effective and convenient.

Card index or notebook, the use of a master list is highly recommended. In this list is entered, chronologically, the identification number and title of each negative or slide, the date it was photographed, and its category number or other indication of where it can be found in the file. This master list will constitute a continuing chronological record of every item in the file, in the order in which it was made.

CATEGORY INDEXING

When a classification or category system is used, another division of the index should contain cards or pages for a separate listing of each such classification or category. It often happens that a set of pictures made on an extended trip, series of occasions, or assignment, can be more reasonably filed and indexed in an order other than that in which the exposures were originally made. The master list will show the chronological sequence; the

This Nega-File will hold up to 900 single 2¼ × 2¼ negatives in glassine envelopes.

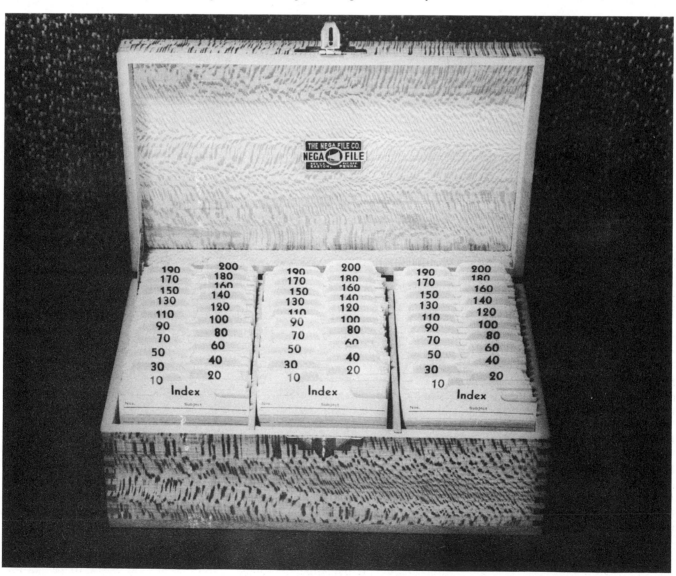

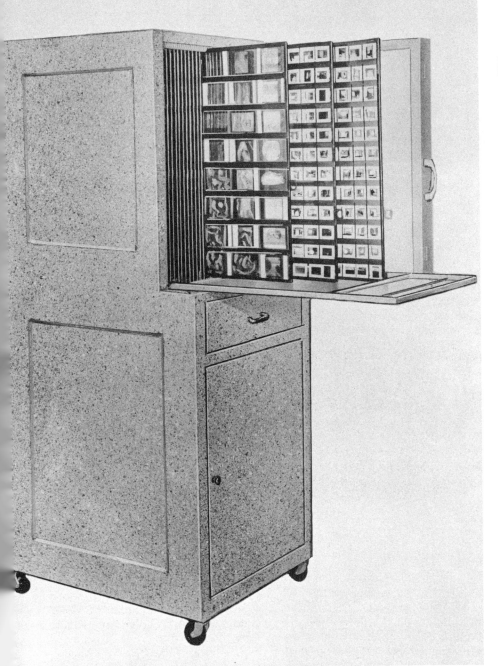

The Multiplex slide cabinet is designed for rapid selection of slides. A fluorescent view box at the rear of the slide panels gives even illumination for viewing. It holds 6240 2×2 slides or 2080 4×3¼ mounted slides.

FILM FESTIVALS

Thomas W. Hope
Assistant Adviser on Non-theatrical Films, Eastman Kodak Company

[All branches of movie making are represented in the many film festivals where the amateur and the professional film makers compete for honors. Here is information about the festivals, prizes, film selection, and a list of important events.]

• *Also see: Experimental and Abstract Film.*

MORE THAN A HUNDRED FILM events, generally called international film festivals, take place each year around the world in cities as widely separated as Acapulco and Zurich. Some are independently sponsored, others are adjuncts to exhibitions and trade fairs.

Most of the major festivals include both theatrical and nontheatrical motion pictures. A number of festivals specialize in a particular subject, such as advertising, medicine, industry, sports, tourism, exploration, religion, labor, or art. Others are limited to films originating in specific regions, such as Asia, Europe, or Latin America. In recent years several festivals concerned entirely with television films have emerged, and categories for television have been established in other festivals.

Major international festivals are held annually in Europe at Cannes, Berlin, Edinburgh, and San Sebastian. The oldest continuous festival is the International Exhibition of Cinematographic Art, established in Venice in 1932 and, with the exception of the war years, held annually ever since. Recently biennial festivals have been held in Moscow and Karlovy-Vary, Czechoslovakia.

Each year the International Federation of Film Producers' Associations examines the regulations of the international film-festival sponsors applying to it for recognition, and recommends events which meet the association's standards.

During the tourist season, film festivals are an additional attraction to those seeking amusement or cul-

categories need not do so.

The first thing to enter on the category listing is the number designating the place of the negative or slide in that category. This should be followed by its title. Then for convenient cross reference with the master list, its permanent identification number should follow. It is often an added convenience to include the date it was photographed on the category list.

It is helpful to employ tabbed dividers to separate category listings from each other, or to group several together under one general heading.

A divider bearing the heading, LOCAL, might include such category listings as HOME TOWN and PICNICS AND DAY TRIPS.

In this indexing system, the master list is a complete and continuing record of all items in the file and, being chronological, provides a means of locating any negative or slide if the approximate date of its making can be ascertained. The great advantage of the category listing is that it will show what pictures are in the files on any subject without your having to pore through the entire master list.

Above: *"Friendly Persuasion," directed by William Wyler for Allied Artists, and starring Gary Cooper and Dorothy McGuire, was a film festival winner.*

tural experience. Often film festivals of a specialized nature are held in conjunction with an annual international congress or conference dealing with special subjects and thus have a ready-made audience of hundreds, or thousands, of keenly interested spectators.

Government sponsorship of major festivals, in which the host government invites the formal participation of governments with which it has diplomatic relations, often means that 40 to 50 countries are represented at a major event. Prizes, trophies, and citations, usually awarded by a jury of international composition, are widely publicized and are eagerly sought after by producers as evidence of their international recognition.

FILM SELECTION

Each participating country has its own method of selecting motion pictures for entry. In the United States there are three mechanisms through which films are entered. The theatrical film entries are selected by the motion-picture industry. Nontheatrical films have, since 1958, been selected by the Committee on International Nontheatrical Events (CINE), which took over this responsibility from the Film Council of America. (CINE is composed of volunteers representing different types of films, such as industrial, experimental, agricultural, and others.) U. S. Government motion pictures are selected by an interdepartmental committee which also nominates official United States delegations to the major international film festivals.

Because the list of film festivals is so extensive, only a selected list of American and European film events can be given.

United States

Academy of Motion Picture Arts and Sciences, March, Hollywood, Calif. Theatrical feature films and short subjects; 35 mm.

American Film Festival (Educational Film Library Association), April, New York City. Nontheatrical educational, business, government, cultural subjects; 16 mm.

Columbus Film Festival (Columbus Film Council), September, Columbus, Ohio. Nontheatrical, business, health, modern medicine, travel, cultural arts, religion and ethics, informational, educational; 16 mm.

Business Film Festival (National Visual Presentation Association), May, New York City. Promotion, industrial relations, public relations, advertising; 16 mm. Sound-slide films on some subjects.

Photographic Society of America, September, different cities. Amateur films in either 16 mm or 8 mm.

San Francisco Film Festival, November, San Francisco, Calif. Theatrical features and short subjects; nontheatrical; 35 mm and 16 mm.

American Society of Travel Agents, October, different cities. All aspects of travel; includes an amateur section; 16 mm and 8 mm.

American TV Commercials Festivals, May, New York City. Film and videotape television commercials; 16 mm.

Europe

International Exhibition of Cinematographic Art, September, Venice, Italy. Feature films only; 35 mm.

Edinburgh Film Festival, August, Edinburgh, Scotland. Feature documentaries, the arts, experimental, scientific; 35 mm and 16 mm.

International Exhibition of the Documentary Film and Short Subject, July and August, Venice, Italy. Newsreel and documentary; 16 mm and 35 mm.

International Festival of Films for Children, July, Venice, Italy. Children's educational and entertainment films by age groups; 35 mm.

Right: *"Long Day's Journey Into Night," a movie from the play by Eugene O'Neill. Embassy Pictures Corp. showed this film at the Cannes Film Festival in 1962; it was the first film in which all four stars received Best Acting awards. From left, they are Jason Robards, Jr., Dean Stockwell, Katherine Hepburn, and Sir Ralph Richardson.*

International Film Festival, June, Berlin, Federal Republic of Germany. Theatrical features, feature-length documentary and cultural films, short documentary and cultural films; 35 mm.

International Film Festival, October, Mannheim, Federal Republic of Germany. Cultural, documentary, industrial, cartoon and puppet, short fictional, first features by directors of documentaries; 35 mm and 16 mm.

International Film Festival, June, San Sebastian, Spain. Features and shorts (under 20 minutes). Non-competitive; informative, cultural and commercial; 35 mm.

In the United States inquiries concerning film festivals should be sent to the Committee on International Nontheatrical (Film) Events, 1201 16th Street N. W., Washington 6, D. C., or to the U. S. Information Agency, Washington 25, D. C.

FILMSTRIPS

AUGUSTUS WOLFMAN
Publisher, "Modern Photography," "Photo Methods for Industry," "Photo Dealer"
[The filmstrip is a series of positive transparencies on one roll of film projected in sequence. It is widely used by commercial firms and schools for visual education and by some amateurs who want to create unusual effects with projected transparencies. An expert here describes in detail how film strips are made and used. Illustrations reprinted from *Handbook for Production of Filmstrips and Records,* by permission of copyright holder, DuKane Corporation.]
• *Also see: Color Slide Shows; Lantern Slides.*

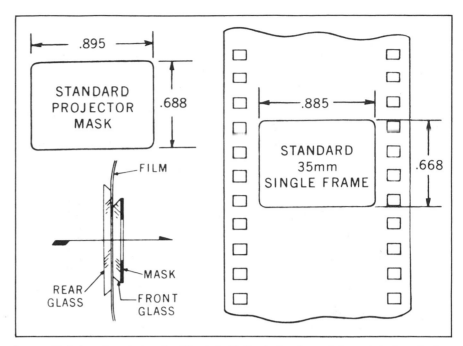

In a well-designed projector the film is held firmly in place at the point of projection by two pieces of glass; one in front of the film and one in back. The projector mask is thus separated from the film by the thickness of the glass. This means that the picture and the edges of the projector mask cannot both be in focus at the same time. To avoid this problem, use the standard frame size of .668 × .885 in making the filmstrip.

A FILMSTRIP IS A SERIES OF pictures printed on 35 mm film and viewed by projection on a screen. This method of viewing photographs has advantages over the usual paper print.

In a paper print, light must first pass through the silver image to reach the paper base. It is then reflected back through the image to the eye, resulting in a loss of some tonal gradation. With filmstrips light is projected through a transparent film so that many of the delicate tones in the positive image can be seen on the screen. Another advantage of the filmstrip is its compact size. As many as 16 pictures can be printed on one foot of 35 mm film; a roll of film about one inch in diameter will contain about 450 pictures. A final advantage of the filmstrip is that it can be seen by a number of people simultaneously.

FILMSTRIP USES

The filmstrip is primarily used in schools where visual methods of teaching are employed. Its relatively low cost and small bulk—which simplifies shipping problems—make the filmstrip a valuable aid in visual education.

In the business world, the filmstrip is used not only for teaching but for sales and promotion as well.

It is not unusual for a salesman to present his "talk" by setting up a small projector and showing a filmstrip with a recorded presentation on a portable tape recorder or phonograph.

SINGLE-FRAME FILMSTRIPS

For educational and commercial uses, the single-frame filmstrip is standard. These strips are almost always printed by mass methods from a one-strip negative, and the result is that the cost of a whole strip, in color, is hardly more than the cost of two or three individual color slides. Where strips must be circulated in quantity, the saving is considerable.

Single-frame filmstrip can be made with any kind of still camera using 35 mm film in the 18 × 24 (single-frame) format with the camera held in horizontal position.

For professional work, however, a more complicated, two-stage process is used. First, all the photography is completed; if color is used, 4 × 5 transparencies or 8 × 10 paper prints are then prepared. In the case of paper prints, airbrush retouching can be done at this stage, and titles can be superimposed by printing in white on celluloid sheets. Diagrams, charts, etc., are drawn on separate cards, and colored if necessary. Captions for drawings are prepared, again, by printing on celluloid for overlaying on the drawing.

Finally, when all the material is prepared for the strip, it is arranged in order and photographed a frame at a time. Usually Eastman Color Negative film, from which the required number of positive strips can be printed on ordinary motion-picture printing equipment, is used.

In commercial studios, the photography is usually done on a standard animation camera and stand; this is equipped with an automatic device which keeps the camera in focus as it slides up and down the column. A projected light beam shows the outlines of the area which will be covered by the camera at any height setting, making it possible to copy many different pieces of art work, all of different sizes, in the standard single-frame format of the slidefilm.

For copying transparencies, the copy table is fitted with a light box; the transparency is placed over the box and then photographed as a piece of flat copy. Filter holders just below the camera lens allow color correction from one frame to the next as needed. Preliminary tests are shot and developed for any difficult copy.

THE 35 mm PICTURE APERTURE

The picture area of a single-frame strip (18 × 24) is only a nominal dimension; the actual dimension of the camera aperture is slightly different, for a special reason. When ordinary 35 mm slides are mounted, they are put into a mask of some kind, usually a cardboard frame or a thin, aluminum-foil cutout. The cutout in the cardboard or foil provides a clean, sharp edge for the projected picture.

Since the aperture plate of the projector is always somewhat smaller than the image on the film in motion-picture projection, it serves the same purpose of providing an edge, though not always a sharply focused one, to the picture. In theaters, the screen itself is usually masked with black velvet, which makes the necessary edge.

The problem of defining the edge of the picture is resolved differently for slidefilms. Most filmstrip projectors have glass plates which hold the film flat in the focal plane. Any masking for the edges of the picture is behind one of the glasses, and is so far out of focus that it cannot at all define the edges of the picture. Its sole purpose is to avoid projecting any part of the adjacent picture. Therefore, to project a picture with a clean sharp edge on the screen, an edge must be provided in the film itself.

For this purpose, filmstrip practice is just the reverse of that followed in motion pictures. The camera aperture, for filmstrips, is always made *smaller* than the projector aperture. In this way the image on the film is surrounded by a black area which acts as a mask for the edges of the picture.

The size of the camera aperture varies with different workers, but all agree on the need for making it smaller than the projector aperture. Some workers who use standard motion-picture animation cameras for slidefilms as well have improvised a quite satisfactory aperture. They simply use the standard "academy" sound aperture, but shift it so that it is centered on the film, instead of being placed to one side (as it is for shooting movies where the side space is needed for the sound track). The projected results are good, but there is a certain amount of wasted space, and the image is smaller than need be.

Actually, only about $1/100$ of an inch is needed top and bottom, and half of that sideways, to accomplish the desired result. Based on this, there is a recommended standard for slidefilms which calls for a projector aperture of .688 × .895 inches, and a camera aperture of .668 × .885 inches. This provides the necessary framing for the image with a minimum waste of film area.

WIDE-SCREEN FORMATS

Since the shape of the image is defined on the film itself, and not by the projector, wide-screen formats can be produced simply by changing the camera mask. To obtain the necessary wider image, a shorter focus lens is used in the projector, or the projector is placed further from the screen.

Two possible formats for use in standard 35 mm slidefilm projectors are shown in Figure 1. The one at the left requires no change at all in the projector; it still pulls down four perforations at each stroke, and the resulting screen image is proportioned 2.2:1. Some film area is wasted, of course, but it is negligible.

For an even wider aspect ratio, coupled with film economy, the arrangement at the right can be used, resulting in a screen aspect ratio of 3:1. In this case, the projector must be modified to pull down two perforations per stroke instead of four. It is possible to get twice as many pictures on a foot of film with this system. The resulting film economy may be of importance in a production having 100 or more frames per strip, and when hundreds of copies are required.

Corresponding to the motion-picture Vista-Vision system, which uses a double-frame image with the film running sidewise through the projector, we can make a so-called "Vista-Strip," with images lying sidewise, and design a special projector for it. One such format is shown in Figure 2; it is exactly two frames long, but has been masked off top and bottom (sides of the film) so as to present an aspect ratio of 2.35:1.

Of course, the whole double-frame image could be used—a return to the still 35 mm 24 × 36 mm frame. The difference, here, is that the camera is *never* turned; all

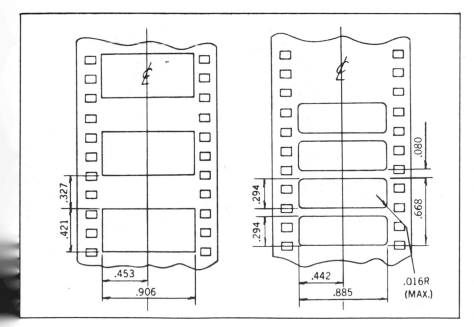

Figure 1. Left: *Film frame size for wide-screen films = .906 × .421 = 2.2:1 aspect ratio four sprocket hole advance. A wide-screen format can be realized for a slidefilm presentation by using the frame size and position indicated above.* Right: *Film frame size for one-half single frame films = .885 × .294 = 3:1 aspect ratio two sprocket hole advance. These dimensions for one half single frame or two sprocket hole advance have been established to meet certain specialized requirements.*

pictures are taken with the long side horizontal. Using the full double-frame format, the aspect ratio is only 1.5:1, which is not much wider than the ordinary filmstrip image (about 1.33:1).

ART WORK AND PHOTOGRAPHY

Commercially, the actual photography of the strip is usually done with animation cameras such as the Acme or Oxberry. But for simple amateur productions a Leica with Focoslide will do; however, it must be adapted to photograph *two* successive frames at a time. The art work is placed under a cardboard cutout, painted black to give the necessary masking around the images.

Before the strip can be shot, all original material must be prepared. Because the pictures are to be rephotographed, resulting in some inevitable loss of detail, a larger camera is generally used for the original photography; most of this work, in fact, is done with a 4 × 5 camera. In using this or any other format, it is important to remember that some work will be done on the final image before it is photographed. Also, the cameraman likes to have a bit of leeway in framing his image, to avoid accidental cropping or showing of unwanted edges.

For this reason, a safe area is always allowed, and the full 4 × 5 film (or other size) is never used.

When the art work is ready, it is photographed on the final 35 mm film. If only a single strip (or at most two or three) is required, the photography can be done on any reversal-type color film such as Kodachrome, Ektachrome, Anscochrome, or Agfachrome. For four or five strips of no more than 30 frames each, it is cheaper to shoot the material five times than it is to make duplicate prints. Each copy being an original, the best possible color reproduction is obtained for reversal films.

In the case of longer shows, of 100 frames or more, where art work varies in size, and where titles may have to be double-exposed over some frames, the amount of photography involved is considerable. It is generally preferable to shoot the film on negative color stock, either Kodacolor or Eastman Color Negative (which is the movie version of the same film). Copies are made by a movie laboratory on a regular movie printer. Usually, the strip is spliced into a loop which runs over and over again through the printer without special attention until the required number of prints are made.

MAKING TITLES

Most amateurs seem to find it difficult to make satisfactory titles for filmstrips. The main problem is usually in preparing the title card.

Professional titles are made by a simple stamping method; the wording is set in type, and the type is then heated to about 225 F. It is then put in a press and the impression is taken through a sheet of pigmented foil or cellophane onto the card or celluloid sheet. The heat causes the pigment to release from the foil and to adhere to the card or celluloid, producing sharp, opaque lettering. Pigment foil is available in a wide range of colors, as well as in black, white, and metallics.

The amateur who owns a small hand printing press may already have tried to print title cards with white ink unsuccessfully. White printing ink is not opaque enough to cover a black or dark-colored card, even with multiple impressions. However, many amateurs have adapted their presses to the use of hot-stamping foil with little additional equipment besides a small electric sandwich grill.

For this work, the ink rollers are removed from the press, the

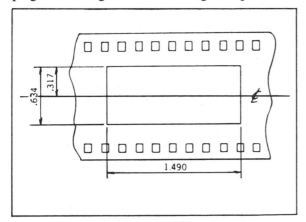

Above: Figure 2. *Film frame size for Vista-Strip (2.35:1). Frame size = 1.490×.634 = 2.35:1 aspect ratio. This "Vista-Strip" aperture has been created to serve the needs of a panoramic type projector in which the picture medium proceeds at a constant rate from right to left across a screen with an aspect ratio the same as one frame. When the animation of the strip is arranged so that no frame line appears between frames, the appearance of a fully continuous strip is given.*

Right: *"Previewer Jr." is a hand-held or desktop viewer for 35 mm single-frame filmstrips; works on a-c, d-c, or batteries; positive framing, threads instantly, always in focus; convex optical viewing screen; carrying handle acts as stand. Viewlex, Inc.*

The "Examiner" is a tabletop, rearview filmstrip projector; 6×8-inch viewing area; coated color-corrected f/3.5 lens; one-knob film advance and framing device with click stops; helical focusing adjustment; instant threading; operates a-c, d-c; on-off switch; 75-watt projection lamp; self-contained unit in carrying case; Camera Optics Mfg. Corp.

slide projectors, but it is equally useful with filmstrip machines. This unit is connected to the projector and to a tape recorder, and the strip is threaded on the first frame. Each time the film advance button is pressed, a tone signal is recorded on the tape; this tone signal is at a frequency high enough to be practically inaudible.

Furthermore, the same unit is attached to the tape recorder and projector when playing back; the sound from the tape goes through a filter on the way to the loudspeaker. The filter separates the tone signals from the spoken sound or music; the tone signal operates a switch which trips the projector to the next picture automatically, but the filter prevents the signal from being heard by the audience.

Similar devices are made by other manufacturers. Some of them use a quarter-inch tape with two tracks, similar to the usual half-track monaural recording. However, in this case, one track is used exclusively for the narration and music, with the other used for the control signals. Here no particular filtering is required, as the tape recorder is fitted with two pickup heads, one for the sound and the other for the control pulses, and each is completely independent.

For commercial use, disk records are preferred over tape; they are more economical, easier to handle, and there is no danger of accidental erasure. With records, the tone signal for automatic operation is mixed with the sound. The tone signal is not superaudible, but rather subaudible, at either 30 or 40 cycles per second.

These deep tones are easy to record on disk, but are not easy to reproduce through the average speaker system; thus the filtering problem is rather simplified. In general, the small speakers used with slidefilm projectors have few useful responses below 150 cycles, so a

type is set in the usual way and locked up in the chase as for printing. The chase is then set on the grill to heat; meanwhile, a sheet of cardboard or celluloid is placed in the press on the gauges, as for printing. A piece of pigment foil is cut and placed over the card, coated side down. When the type is heated to the right temperature (it should be just hot enough to sizzle when touched with a wet finger), the chase is lifted from the grill and inserted in the press. Without delay, the impression is taken. Do not hold the press closed; the best type of impression for this work is a quick "slam." Professional stamping presses have a special cam action to give this kind of quick impression.

For those who do not have printing presses, there are a variety of lettering devices sold at art-goods stores. One of the best is a set of cellophane sheets carrying printed alphabets. Unlike the earlier version, the letters are not cut out of the sheet and stuck down. Instead, the entire sheet is moved around, positioning each letter in turn. The selected letter is rubbed down with a smooth tool, and transfers from the backing

to the card without leaving any edges or adhesive.

Hand lettering is excellent, if it is done well; those who cannot letter freehand may find the Leroy or the Wrico mechanical lettering outfits very useful.

SOUND SLIDEFILMS

Most modern slidefilm shows have sound in the form of a narration, with or without music. Various systems are used to synchronize the sound and film so that the show runs smoothly and professionally.

Where the narration is "live" rather than recorded, the lecturer usually gives some kind of signal, and the picture is changed manually by an operator. With recorded narrations, the same system is sometimes used; the signal is a small bell or "ping" tone recorded on the disk or tape. At each "ping" the operator advances the film to the next frame.

A number of methods have been devised to operate the projector automatically, based on a cue tone or signal on the record or tape. One such device is produced by Kodak as an accessory for their

standard specifications for 35 mm single frame filmstrips

A filmstrip made according to these specifications will conform to a standard now widely accepted in the slidefilm industry. Producers who follow this procedure will find their films can be used on all major lines of equipment and by both skilled and unskilled projectionists with little or no difficulty. The problems which result from lack of uniformity in frame size, length of leader and method of identification, will be virtually eliminated.

The trimming of the leading edge of the film will be a straight cut located between the sprocket holes at 90° (± 3°) with the edge of the film.

Information identifying the filmstrip should appear parallel to the film edge in the four frames following the three "START" frames.

The distance from the cut leading edge of the film to the focus frame is to be no less than frames or approximate 6¾ inches.

START START START FILMSTRIP IDENTIFICATION FOCUS TITLE

The first 3 frames of the film will have the word "START" in large white block letters appearing in each frame.

The focus frame should contain a single design so the projected picture can be accurately located and sharply focused. Instructions about starting the record should also appear in this frame (i.e., ADVANCE TO BLACK FRAME AND START RECORD).

A white dot no less than ⅛″ in diameter will appear in the upper left hand corner.

A filmstrip produced in color will show green as the background of the 3 "START" frames.
A black and white production will use black as the background color.

It is recommended that a black frame appear between the focus frame and the title frame so that the focus frame is not kept in view and the title frame is not revealed until the presentation begins.

The title frame (or information fra will be no less than eleventh frame fr the leading edge of film.

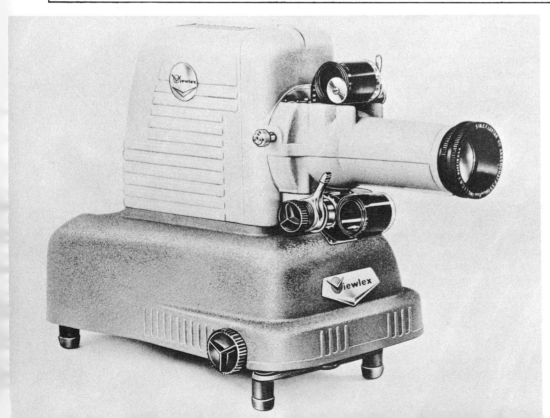

Above and right: Figure 3. *Standard specifications for 35 mm single-frame filmstrips.*

Left: *"Viewlex" slide and filmstrip projector; accepts single- or double-frame 35 mm filmstrip, vertical or horizontal projection; 2×2 and bantam slides in any mount; 5-inch, f/3.5 Luxtar lens; 500-watt projection lamp; motor fan-cooled; automatic slide changer; stereo slide carrier; antihesive aperture plate; pep-up lamp ejector. Also in 300- and 150-watt models; accessories include cases; optional lenses; Viewlex, Inc.*

filter is placed in the amplifier which eliminates all frequencies below this point from the sound channel. If pulses of 30 cycles are recorded on the disk, they will be blocked by the filter from reaching the speaker and will not be heard. Another circuit just ahead of the filter takes these pulses and diverts them to the slide-changing mechanism.

Several different standards have

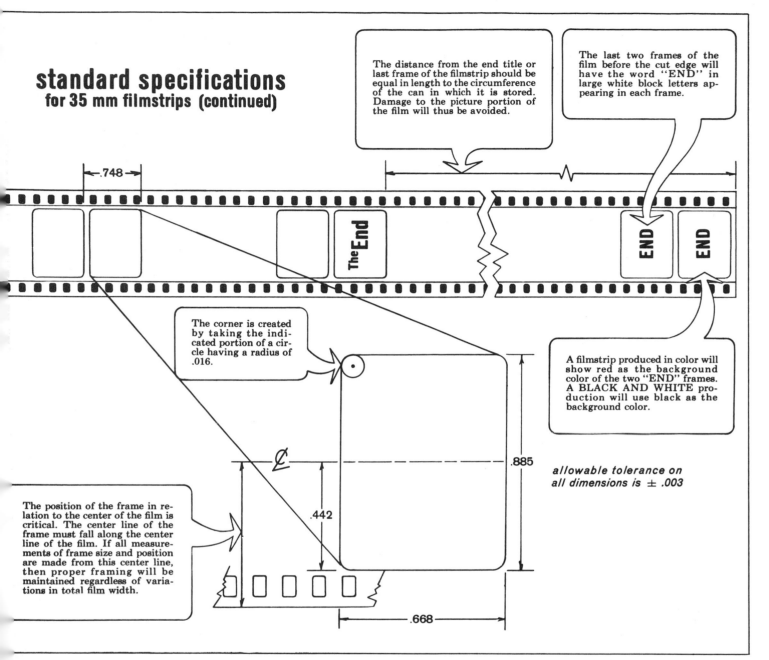

standard specifications
for 35 mm filmstrips (continued)

The distance from the end title or last frame of the filmstrip should be equal in length to the circumference of the can in which it is stored. Damage to the picture portion of the film will thus be avoided.

The last two frames of the film before the cut edge will have the word "END" in large white block letters appearing in each frame.

.748

The End

END

END

The corner is created by taking the indicated portion of a circle having a radius of .016.

A filmstrip produced in color will show red as the background color of the two "END" frames. A BLACK AND WHITE production will use black as the background color.

.885

allowable tolerance on all dimensions is ± .003

℄

.442

The position of the frame in relation to the center of the film is critical. The center line of the frame must fall along the center line of the film. If all measurements of frame size and position are made from this center line, then proper framing will be maintained regardless of variations in total film width.

.668

been used for this purpose; in making slidefilms, check the projector in use to be sure which system is utilized. The earliest of these used a simple pulse at 40 cycles to make the slide change. However, with this system the change was occasionally triggered by a thump or drum beat in the music, and a more reliable system has since been adopted.

In this new system, a steady 50-cycle tone runs along underneath the music and narration; it is a "guard" tone whose purpose is to lock out the change mechanism so it cannot be operated accidentally by any other sound on the disk. At the point where a change is desired, the 50-cycle tone stops, and is replaced by a 30-cycle tone which lasts not less than one second nor more than one and one half seconds. The changing mechanism of the projector is tuned to this 30-cycle tone which causes a slide change. At the end of the 30-cycle pulse, the 50-cycle tone resumes and prevents a change of slide until the next 30-cycle pulse comes along.

The mechanism is timed to the one-and-one-half second pulse; most projectors, if the button is held down longer than one and one half seconds, will change slides a second time. The locking circuit requires a certain amount of time, also, and slide changes should not be timed to occur closer than one and one half seconds apart. This gives the locking and changing devices time to recover.

LEADERS

All slidefilm projectors require a certain amount of film to thread up, and some leader should be provided at each end of the strip for this purpose. The leader also protects the first and last frames of picture from being scratched by the end of the film as it coils up in the receiving chamber of the projector.

The leader can also carry certain

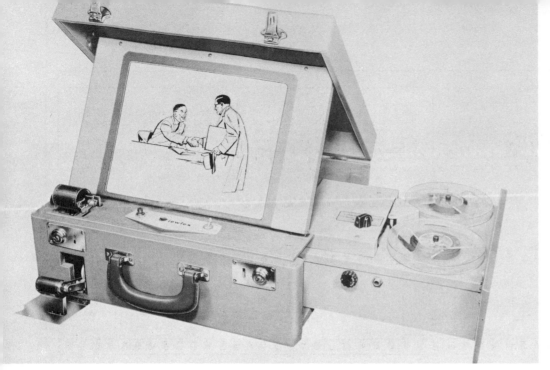

The "Viewtape" is a fully automatic sight-sound, portable presentation unit; rearview screen; 35 mm filmstrip projector synchronized with tape recorder; 8×10-inch screen; light multiplier optical system; instant threading; filmstrip advances automatically by pulse from tape reel to reel (standard 5-inch); Model R2, continuous cartridge (up to 1200 feet) tape speed 3¾ inches per second; self-contained case; Viewlex, Inc.

information which is useful in identifying and projecting the strip. Figure 3 shows a suggested arrangement which has proved practical and is recommended by the DuKane Company, manufacturers of automatic slide projectors. They recommend:

1. Three consecutive frames with the word *Start* at the very beginning of the film. This merely indicates the head end of the film, and is not intended for projection. In color films, the word *Start* will be on a green background; in black-and-white, it will be in white letters on black.

2. The next three frames are combined into one frame on which the title of the strip is printed running lengthwise on the film; also any other information needed by the operator, such as the sound disk, or synchronization method.

3. The next three frames are solid black.

4. The following frame is a focus target of some kind. It is used to set up and focus the projector and to establish a starting point.

5. The following frame is opaque black; it avoids the necessity for holding the "focus" frame on the screen and gives the show a clean

beginning.

6. The next frame is the title of the show, and it is followed in sequence by the pictures of the show itself, finally ending with a *The End* frame.

7. After a *The End* frame, there are a minimum of nine frames of opaque black. This serves to protect the tail of the film from scratches when stored in a can.

8. The film ends with two frames of *End*, indicating that the film is tail up. In color films, the word *End* appears on a red blackground; in black-and-white, it is in white letters on black.

CIRCULATION OF FILMSTRIPS

Where only a few strips are in use, they can be stored in small cans, and the records in regular sleeves, all placed in any ordinary file cabinet.

Libraries will find special equipment for storage of slidefilms and the accompanying records available from Nega-File Corporation, and others. Special shipping containers for disks and filmstrips are available, and are necessary, both for convenience in handling, and for safety in shipping, if strips are circulated to any extent.

FILMS—WHEN AND HOW TO USE THEM

C. W. GIBBS
Photographer and Research Consultant

[For the still-camera photographer, faced with an almost infinite number of brand-name films, the author has some advice. Here latitude, grain, contrast, and color sensitivity are explained. Several charts show at a glance what film to buy and under what conditions to use it.]
• *Also see: Contrast; Development, Background; Emulsion Manufacture; Gamma; Hurter and Driffield.*

PHOTOGRAPHY IS AN INTEGRATION of a number of related and unrelated factors. This multiplicity of factors can be organized under broad headings, making possible such abbreviated, but true, statements as "good pictures consist simply of good composition and good print quality." In the present discussion only factors of technique are to be considered—specifically technique for making good negatives which is the first step in obtaining good quality prints.

PRINT QUALITY

It is a photographic axiom that the best quality prints come from negatives which give the least trouble in printing. While it is true that some fine salon examples in pictorial photography have been made from inferior negatives, these are exceptions and certainly do not represent the ideal. When a negative does not possess the characteristics to produce a good print, we can be sure that if a satisfactory print is obtained, the photographer achieved the result only after sacrifice of time, materials, and patience.

By understanding the characteristics of films and how to adapt film properties to subject requirements, one major quality factor is solved. There are several variables to be considered—emulsion speed, inherent emulsion contrast, color sensitivity, latitude, graininess, sharpness, and resolving power. Through intelligent application of these variables to different subject conditions, it is possible to arrive at consistently satisfactory negative quality.

For example, if we are about to photograph a distant mountain scene with a 35 mm camera, and in the final print we wish to show only a portion of a certain snow-capped peak in bold contrast with the background, we can decide immediately which film characteristics are most important. A film having the best combination of these characteristics will then be chosen.

FILM CHARACTERISTICS

A knowledge of film properties can either be empirical or it can be based upon a sound technical background. For a wide range of work and ever changing circumstances, a reasonably thorough, technically accurate knowledge is preferred to a limited, loose understanding of film characteristics.

Considerable information is available on the characteristics of film, including characteristic c u r v e s, wedge spectrograms, time-gamma and time-temperature tables, resolving power values, speed ratings, and other factors. Much of the information is immediately usable, but a greater portion is limited in practicality. But being limited in direct practical application does not detract from the general value of the data. There is no better way to learn the functional properties of photographic films than by becoming conversant with the terminology and procedures of the professional sensitometrist.

It is recognized by the people engaged in sensitometric laboratories, especially those who have to correlate laboratory findings with practical camera exposures, that reproducibility of results is accomplished only when the conditions of exposure, development, and other factors do not vary. It is actually difficult for two independent workers conducting sensitometric studies on the same emulsions to produce identical results even though their instruments and techniques are similar. Naturally the gap between laboratory testing and practice is greater than the difference between two laboratory workers. Therefore it is not surprising to find differences between published data and actual results.

DATA LIMITATIONS

We should not lose sight of the need for knowing the exceptions and limitations in applying film data. Technical knowledge is helpful in teaching the relative differences among various products, and in giving an insight into the magnitude and rate of change of a given property when another property is changed.

The latter point can be made clear by an example: Negative graininess increases with the extent of development. The extent of development can be expressed in terms of gamma, so we can attempt to establish a simple relation between the increase of graininess and gamma.

Suppose that with a given film and developer we found the increase in graininess (within certain limits) to be constant for any two constant intervals of developing time. But in another instance, using a different developer, we discovered that this specific relation failed to hold. It would be impossible, then, to frame a general statement such as "graininess of photographic images increases at a constant rate with constant increases in gamma."

However, if we worked on an empirical basis and, after gaining our initial experience, used a film and developer that did comply with the above statement, we would be likely to assume this knowledge for other films and developers. Upon referring to published data, the folly of the assumption would become obvious, and our thinking on this particular point could be straightened out, even though the actual gamma values or actual graininess magnitudes were not known to us.

We can conclude that technical knowledge concerning films is useful

To capture the soft quality of children, a panchromatic film is best. Hasselblad 1000F with Gevapan 30 film exposed for 1/50 of a second at f/4.5. (Photo: Anders Sten)

Candid photography demands a high-speed film since a fast shutter and fairly large depth of field enable the photographer to work less obtrusively. Zeiss Ikon Tenax Automatic camera with 50mm Zeiss Tessar f/2.8 lens. Tri-X film exposed f/5.6 for 1/125 of a second. (Photo: Hedwid Elser)

if correctly interpreted and misleading if its limitations are not recognized.

FILM SPEED

The first consideration in classifying films is that of speed or sensitivity. No other film property has occupied the minds of photographers so much as that of speed. This property has always been recognized as the determining factor in exposure. Because of the desirability of short exposure times, even under adverse lighting conditions, there has been great demand for and immediate acceptance of high-speed films.

Unfortunately the designation of film speed by a simple, single number has not proved easy. Numerous criteria have been proposed, based on various methods and using varying portions of the characteristic curve as a testing area. The trouble here is that the curves for various films are just that—*curves*. They are not straight-line relationships; the shape of the curve has as much influence on the results obtained by various speed-measurement systems as the actual exposure level used.

For example, the obsolete Scheiner system used a point far down on the toe of the curve, while the Weston system used a point well up on the straight line. Two films having equal Scheiner speeds would have very different Weston ratings, depending on how long and sweeping the toe of the curve was for one film, or how short and abrupt it was for another.

The ASA and BSI systems use a more complex relationship based on part of the toe and part of the straight line. This results in a speed rating fairly consistent with the results obtained in picture taking. But ASA numbers will not translate accurately into either Scheiner or Weston numbers.

The important thing to recognize about film speed is that no value, whatever the criterion, is an absolute specification of an inherent film property. Speed ratings, when employed in connection with exposure guides and tables or exposure meters, can be successfully adapted to one's particular equipment, technique of development, and personal preferences.

Thus it is important to assign speed ratings to films which represent, as closely as possible, the relation in sensitivity of one film to another. If a worker accustoms himself to a given film and through experience learns how to successfully use an exposure guide or photoelectric meter with the film, he then experiences no difficulty in changing to another listed film.

EFFECT OF DEVELOPER

On the other hand, should a different camera be used, or a change in developers seem advisable, it is very possible that speed ratings formerly employed will have to be adjusted to meet the new conditions. Once the new conditions are met, the relative speeds of the various films to be employed are indicated as before by the relations of the speed numbers.

When new equipment is used, its influence on a previously established method of exposure calculation must be learned by trial. A series of test exposures, a one-half lens stop under and over the calculated value, will indicate whether or not revision of the method is required.

However, if there is a change in the type of developer, it is usually sufficient to know whether the effective film speed is now greater or less than before.

Some developers yield a relatively lower film speed which is usually the result of a compromise to improve some other property, such as grain structure. Table 1 gives a partial list of developers used in 35 mm photography to yield low graininess. Some of the developers cause no change in emulsion speed; others cause some loss in effective speed.

Subject matter has an effect on the apparent speed of the film. For instance, a very harshly lit scene, with deep shadows and brilliant highlights, will use up the entire latitude (straight-line part) of the curve. To photograph such a scene, exposure must be accurate and a bit on the full side; we cannot overrate the film on such subject matter.

On the other hand, a snow scene shot on a cloudy day, with no shadows of any importance, will probably appear a bit dense on the negative and can easily and safely be "underexposed" as much as two stops without harm. This does not mean that the speed of the film is greater with snow scenes—it just means that when we do not need the full latitude of the film, we can safely use less exposure.

CONTRAST AND GRADATION

The extent to which a film increases in density upon increasing exposure is determined by its contrast properties. It is not uncommon to speak of films as being flat, average, or of high-contrast working characteristics. In other words, it is generally well known that there is an inherent tendency for films to exhibit low, high, or normal contrast under any given circumstances.

It is equally well known that the final contrast of a negative is controlled to a great extent by the degree of development. That is, short development times yield less contrast, in most instances, than do long periods of development.

Of course the degree of development cannot be associated directly with time of development as a singular controlling factor. The conditions surrounding the exposure of the negative and its development play important parts in the resulting negative contrast. But the significance of these latter factors is not widely appreciated. The time of development is popularly thought of as the chief, if not the only, factor that governs the degree of development.

Apart from exposure and development conditions, negative contrast is definitely a function of the emulsion characteristics. The nature of the film contrast determines the suitability of a certain film for a given type of work. For example, it would be possible to have a commercial panchromatic film of sufficiently high speed for portraiture and of suitable color sensitivity. However, it would be undesirable for portrait work because of its high contrast properties.

While the contrast available depends to some extent on the degree of development, it also depends on a quality of the emulsion itself, known as gamma-infinity (symbol $\gamma\infty$), and this is simply the maximum gamma, or development contrast, that a given emulsion can attain. (See article *Gamma*.)

Some emulsions cannot be developed beyond a gamma of approximately 1.2. These are called "soft-working" films. In practice they are developed to gammas between 0.5 and 0.7. On the other hand, there are special photomechanical emulsions that can reach gammas as high as 7.0. They are used entirely for line work.

There are wide variations in gradation among films. Photographers should study the types of film gradation to form a clear idea of the tendencies of certain films to

---

Table 1

Higher emulsion speed
Ethol Type T
Ethol UFG
Kodak D-76
DuPont 6-D
Ilford ID-11
Gevaert G.206
Ferrania R-18
Acufine

Normal to slight loss in speed
Ethol TEC
Kodak D-23
Ansco 17
FR X-22 and X-33B

Marked loss in speed
All paraphenylene-diamine developers including Sease 3 and Edwal Super-20

Table 2.	RESOLVING POWER OF FILM EMULSIONS
Ansco Films	
Triple S Pan	*50-60 lines per mm.*
Superpan Press	
Ultra Speed Pan	
Superpan Portrait	
Triple S Ortho	
Versapan	*60-75 lines per mm.*
Commercial	
Commercial Ortho	
DuPont Films	
Safety Positive	*70 lines per mm.*
Fine-Grain Safety Positive	*90 lines per mm.*
Kodak Films And Plates	
Plus-X 35 mm and Bantam	*95 lines per mm.*
Plus-X Roll and Pack	*95 lines per mm.*
Verichrome Pan, Roll and Pack	*95 lines per mm.*
Safety Positive 35 mm	*100 lines per mm.*
High Contrast Safety Positive 35 mm	*165 lines per mm.*
Direct Positive Pan	*95 lines per mm.*
High Contrast Copy 35 mm	*175 lines per mm.*

produce steep shadow contrast or soft shadow contrast; or steep or soft highlight contrast; or steep, normal, or soft middle-tone contrast.

The actual negative gradation is affected by the character of the subject lighting, the lens and camera, the extent and nature of the film development, and other factors. Any effort to incorporate all possible effects which have a bearing on film gradation would be futile, since the curve would still represent but a single situation.

Modern films are capable of rendering an exceptionally wide range of brightness values. Seldom is the full density scale of a film utilized in practice, and one should make no such effort, since the negative transmission range would far exceed the exposure range of even the softest paper. The capability of modern films to record a wide range of brightness is useful, in an indirect sense, by permitting large variations in exposure without much depreciation of negative quality.

COLOR SENSITIVITY

When we speak of a photographic emulsion as "light-sensitive," we mean that after exposure to light and development a deposit of silver will form. This general statement will be found extremely qualitative, for if in one case our exposing light is provided by a blue mercury lamp, and in another case by an orange neon light, the extent of the gray deposit will be found to differ. The extent of difference will change with different films to which the test is applied. "Color sensitivity" defines this difference in response to radiations of unlike wavelengths.

It is unfortunate that the expression "color sensitivity" became deeply rooted in the minds of practical photographers before it was realized that the term is not all-inclusive. A better term would be "wavelength sensitivity," which in turn could be divided into the inherent emulsion sensitivity and the conferred sensitivity.

The breakdown is necessary because natural emulsions are sensitive only within the limits of ultra-violet, blue, and blue-green rays. To make them sensitive to radiations beyond these limits, certain types of dyes are added. This conferred sensitivity by means of dyes can go outside the visible spectrum, and it is for this reason that it is inadvisable to refer to the property as color sensitivity, when it applies to infra-red and ultraviolet radiations as well.

Modern films are available in a widely varied range of nonsensitized

Table 3.	PANCHROMATIC				ORTHO				SPECIAL
	XF	F	M	S	XF	F	M	S	
Portraits—Men	7	5	6	4	2	1	3		
Portraits—Women	2	1	3		5	4	6		
Portraits—Children	1	3	5		2	4	6		
Landscapes—Dull	6	4	5		3	1	2		
Landscapes—Bright	6	4	3		5	2	1		
Landscapes—Snow	3	2	1		4	5	6		
Landscapes—Distant									Infrared, 1
Still Life	5	2	1		6	4	3		
Candid	1	3			2	4			
Architecture—Outdoors	3	1	2		6	4	5		
Architecture—Indoors	1	2	3						
Speed shots—Outdoors	1	3			2	4			
Speed shots—Indoors	1	3			2	4			
Copies—Line B & W								2	Process, 1
Copies—Line Color				2				3	Process Pan, 1
Copies—Half-tone B & W				3				2	Commercial, 1
Copies—Half-tone Color		3	2	1					

In this table we grade the films according to their desirability for various uses. The film marked 1 is the first choice, 2 the second, 3 the third, etc. The speed classification used here is deliberately rather flexible, but corresponds roughly to the following list:

XF—Extra Fast	ASA 250—1000
F—Fast	ASA 125—250
M—Medium	ASA 64—125
S—Slow	Less than ASA 50

and sensitized emulsions. There are still emulsions which depend wholly upon the natural characteristics of silver halides for their wavelength response. These films are sometimes called "color-blind" and are listed in Tables 4, 6, and 7 as "blue-sensitive." Films with such emulsions have definite uses, and the lack of extended wavelength sensitivity, in most cases, is a virtue and not a shortcoming.

On the other hand, emulsions are available having sensitivities to all regions of the visible spectrum and beyond. Moreover there are variations in the relative sensitivity to different spectral regions for emulsions of similar type. That is, emulsions sensitive within the spectral limits from, say, 3200 A to 6450 A differ in sensitivity between these limits.

SENSITIVITY CLASSIFICATIONS

Because of the variety of films available, some attempts have been made to set up simple classification systems. The problem is quite complicated and it is questionable if any entirely satisfactory classification system can be devised. Not only must the limits of spectral sensitivity be considered, but the magnitudes of the sensitivity for various wavelengths as well. This is complicated by the fact that data on spectral sensitivity is not useful unless applicable to definite sources of radiation.

In other words, the effective spectral sensitivity of a film differs according to the wavelength energy distribution of the radiation source (color of light). Perhaps if these were the only factors to be considered, a simple film classification system would be possible.

However, the practical rendition of colors in terms of values of gray is also influenced by the gradation of the emulsion for each wavelength region. This is tenable because the density separation or contrast in a negative for two subject colors depends not only upon the respective relative sensitivity of the film for the two colors, but depends as well upon the steepness of the gradation of the emulsion in the particular spectral regions.

This factor of variation in con-

Table 4.	35 mm FILMS		
FILM	**TYPE**	**ASA SPEED**	**PREFERRED USES**
Adox Films			
KB-14	Pan	40	*General, big enlargements*
KB-17	Pan	80	*General*
KB-21	Pan	125	*Candid, sports, etc.*
Agfa Films			
Isopan IFF	Pan	16	*Copying, large blow-ups*
Isopan IF	Pan	40	*General use*
Isopan ISS	Pan	100	*Sports, news, etc.*
Isopan Ultra	Pan	250	*Candid, artificial light*
Isopan Record	Pan	1000	*Available light, news, etc.*
Ansco Films			
Super Hypan	Pan	500	*All around, candid, news*
Gevaert Films			
Gevapan 27	Pan	64	*General, big enlargements*
Gevapan 30	Pan	125	*General*
Gevapan 33	Pan	250	*News, sports, etc.*
Gevapan 36	Pan	500	*Candid, available light*
Dia-Direct	Pan	25	*Reversal film for slides*
Infra-R	I-R	—	*Special*
Ilford Films			
Pan F	Pan	50	*Copying, big enlargements*
FP3 Series II	Pan	125	*General photography*
HP3	Pan	400	*Sports, action, etc.*
HPS	Pan	800	*Available light, candid, news*
Kodak Films			
Tri-X Pan	Pan	400	*Candid, available light*
Plus-X Pan	Pan	160	*General*
Panatomic-X	Pan	40	*Copying, big enlargements*
Infrared	I-R	—	*Special*
High-Contrast Copy	Pan	64 T	*Microfilming*
Direct Pos. Pan.	Pan	80	*Reversal film for slides*
Fine-Grain Pos.	Blue Sens.	—	*Positive prints, line copy*

trast (when an emulsion is exposed to different regions of the spectrum) is especially familiar to color photographers who sometimes find it necessary to develop negatives exposed through filters of different color for varied times in order to get a similarity to the original scene in the contrast of the final negatives.

Early panchromatic emulsions had fairly low red sensitivity in comparison to their green and blue sensitivities. As improved sensitizers were developed, the red sensitivity of emulsions increased and eventually the pendulum swung too far; the red sensitivity overbalanced the blue, producing pictures which had color values as distorted as those of the early films, but in the opposite direction. Faces were pale and washed out, skies dark, and little clouds stood out like thunderheads.

In modern emulsions the sensitivity is fairly uniform for all colors. There are variations between emulsions of different manufacturers and also between emulsions from a single manufacturer. Usually these can be deduced by checking the filter factors, specifically that for the red (A or number 25) filter. If its factor is about four, the emulsion may be considered a "high-red" type (Kodak Type C). If about seven or eight, then the emulsion is a normal pan (Kodak Type B). If the factor for the A filter is over ten, it may be considered a "low-red" or old-style pan emulsion (Kodak Type A).

Table 5. ROLL FILMS

FILM	TYPE	ASA SPEED	PREFERRED USES
Agfa Films			
Isopan IFF	Pan	16	*Fine-grain, big blow-ups*
Isopan IF	Pan	40	*General use*
Isopan ISS	Pan	100	*General use, sports, news*
Isopan Ultra	Pan	250	*Artificial light, sports*
Isopan Record	Pan	650	*Available light*
Ansco Films			
All-Weather Pan	Pan	125	*General, snapshots, etc.*
Super Hypan	Pan	500	*News, sports, candid, available light*
Superpan Press	Pan	200	*Filmpacks only, for news, etc.*
Gevaert Films			
Gevapan 27	Pan	64	*General*
Gevapan 30	Pan	125	*Sports, news, etc.*
Gevapan 33	Pan	250	*Artificial light*
Gevapan 36	Pan	500	*Candid, available light*
Dia-Direct	Pan	25	*Reversal film for slides*
Infra-R	I-R	—	*Special*
Ilford Films			
FP-3	Pan	125	*General*
HP-3	Pan	400	*Sports, news*
HPS	Pan	800	*Candid, news, available light*
Kodak Films			
Verichrome Pan	Pan	125	*General*
Panatomic-X	Pan	40	*Fine grain, big blow-ups*
Plus-X Professional	Pan	160	*Portrait, fashion, commercial*
Tri-X Pan	Pan	400	*News, sports, etc.*
Royal-X Pan	Pan	1250	*Candid, available light, etc.*

Table 7. PLATES

PLATE	TYPE	ASA SPEED	PREFERRED USES
Gevaert			
Gevapan 30	Pan	125	*General, copying, etc.*
Gevapan 33	Pan	250	*News, rush work, etc.*
Gevapan 36	Pan	500	*Flash, available light*
Gevachrome 32	Ortho	200	*Portraits, etc.*
Replica 23	Ortho	24	*Copying*
Diapositive Normal	Blue Sens.	—	*Lantern slides, transparencies*
Diapositive Contrast	Blue Sens.	—	*Lantern slides, transparencies*
Ilford			
Lantern	Blue Sens.	—	*Available in a number of grades and two speeds for camera use and for contact printing*
FP4	Pan	160	*Fine grain, copying, big blow-ups*
HP3	Pan	400	*General use*
HPS	Pan	800	*Candid, available light, news*
Kodak			
33	Blue Sens.	50	*Copying, commercial*
Process	Blue Sens.	—	*Line copying*
Lantern Slide	Blue Sens.	—	*Several grades for normal and high-contrast slides*
Super Ortho Press	Ortho	125	*Press and portraits*
50	Ortho	64	*Copying and commercial*
Tri-X Pan Type B	Pan	320	*Separation negatives, etc.*
Separation Negatives	Pan	125	*Separation negatives, etc.*
Panchromatic	Pan	32	*Copying, colored paintings, etc.*
Super Panchro Press	Pan	200	*Flash, available light, etc.*

As mentioned, few Type C or Type A pan emulsions are made today, all Kodak and Ansco films being essentially of the normal pan (or Type B) sensitizing. One Kodak emulsion of the Type C class is still manufactured, but as a special purpose material, coated on glass plates only.

LATITUDE

The latitude of a film is its ability to give satisfactory results over a range of exposure times. It is latitude, for instance, which permits the use of inexpensive box cameras during all seasons of the year and during any hour of the day. Box cameras usually have but one exposure time and usually only one aperture, yet satisfactory pictures are made with them even though daylight variations of one to 1000 occur. In other words, films have the ability to give satisfactory results in spite of exposure inconsistencies.

Latitude actually, when used in the above sense, depends as much upon the subject as it does upon the film. The film has an inherent ability to record a limited number of brightness values. When this limit is surpassed, the latitude of the film is exceeded. Now if the subject is of such a nature that the brightness scale matches or exceeds the recording limits of the film, then the latitude's value is one, meaning that only one exposure is possible and that variations from this exposure lead to inferior results. On the other hand, if the subject-brightness scale is low, then the film exposure can vary through an appreciable range without much influence upon the final result.

There are many factors to be considered in the exposure of a negative. To reduce the entire matter to a simple relation between brightness scale in the subject and density scale of the negative is pure folly. Nevertheless, the quality of latitude in a film exists. The difficulty is in defining what it is in a quantitative manner so that the definition will be applicable.

Latitude depends not only on the length of the straight-line part of the film's characteristic curve but also on its slope; this is a direct measure of development contrast or gamma. In general, for a given film, the latitude will be greater at low gamma than at high gamma which provides a good argument against overdevelopment. More specific information on this point will be found in the article *Gamma*.

GRAININESS

Negative graininess is perhaps the most controversial factor in photography. The reasons for this are: 1) a lack of knowledge as to what graininess is, 2) what factors contribute to it, 3) how it is measured, and 4) the necessity for rigidly controlling all factors before graininess comparisons can be made.

Graininess is a film property. It can be measured both subjectively and objectively, but the measuring criteria are not too well established nor universally applicable. Graininess is a property which must be considered with other film properties, because a maximum of film speed, a lack of gradation properties, a high order of sharpness, and other attributes cannot be had at the same time with a minimum of graininess. The graininess of a negative depends greatly upon the conditions of exposure and the nature and extent of development, as well as upon many other variables.

However, when the requirements at hand demand low graininess, one should not depend upon these influences to assure satisfactory results. The inherent graininess of an emulsion exerts the real limiting factor, and no amount of control of other factors will alter the situation.

SHARPNESS AND RESOLVING POWER

The ability of an emulsion to render fine detail is defined as its resolving power. This is a property that is measured by laboratory methods using ruled gratings which are photographed and subsequently examined under a microscope to determine the maximum number of lines which the emulsion is capable of rendering. So long as the lines can be recognized under the microscope as separate and distinct images against a background of different density, the requirements for measuring the resolution are met.

Table 6. SHEET FILMS

FILM	TYPE	ASA SPEED	PREFERRED USES
Agfa Films			
Isopan IFF	Pan	16	*Copying, fine-grain, blow-ups*
Isopan IP	Pan	100	*Portraiture, general*
Isopan Ultra	Pan	250	*News, artificial light*
Isopan Record	Pan	650	*Available light, candid*
Ansco Films			
Commercial Ortho	Ortho	50	*Copying, commercial*
Super Hy-Ortho	Ortho	250	*Portraits, commercial*
Superpan Portrait	Pan	100	*Portraits, commercial*
Versapan	Pan	100	*Commercial, copying, etc.*
Triple-S Pan	Pan	400	*News, artificial light*
Superpan Press	Pan	200	*News, rapid processing*
Super Hypan	Pan	500	*Sports, available light*
DuPont Films			
Cronar Commercial	Blue Sens.	100	*Copying, etc.*
Cronar XF Pan	Pan	125	*General, portraits, etc.*
Cronar High-Speed Pan	Pan	320	*Press, sports, etc.*
Cronar Arrow Pan	Pan	320	*Flash, sports, etc.*
Cronar Press	Pan	400	*Candid, available light, etc.*
Gevaert Films			
Gevapan 30	Pan	125	*General*
Gevapan 33	Pan	250	*News, sports, etc.*
Gevapan 36	Pan	500	*Press, available light*
Gevachrome 32	Ortho	200	*Portraits, retouching*
Ilford Films			
N5.30	Blue Sens.	—	*Copying, line work, etc.*
Commercial Ortho	Ortho	80	*Commercial, copying, etc.*
Hyperchromatic	Ortho	400	*Portraiture, etc.*
FP3	Pan	125	*General, copying, etc.*
HP3	Pan	400	*News, etc.*
HPS	Pan	800	*Candid, available light*
Kodak Films			
Commercial	Blue Sens.	50	*Copying, commercial*
Commercial Ortho	Ortho	80	*Copying, commercial*
Super Speed Ortho Portrait	Ortho	125	*Portraits*
Royal Ortho	Ortho	400	*News, portraits, etc.*
Contrast Process Ortho	Ortho	—	*Line copying*
Super-XX Pan	Pan	200	*General, separation negatives*
Panatomic-X	Pan	64	*Big enlargements, copying, etc.*
Portrait Pan	Pan	125	*Portraits, commercial*
Contrast Process Pan	Pan	80	*Line copying, colored drawings*
Tri-X Pan	Pan	400	*News, commercial, portraits*
Super Panchro Press Type B	Pan	250	*News, flash, portraits*
Royal Pan	Pan	400	*News, portraits*
Royal-X Pan	Pan	1250	*Available light, press, etc.*
Infrared	I-R	—	*Special*

However, the ease with which the readings can be made varies from film to film. Two films which resolve the same number of lines per unit distance may differ widely in the ease with which the lines can be seen.

This sharpness characteristic of a film is known as acutance and is not always directly related to the resolving power. It appears to be a separate property and is affected by coating thickness as well as by the actual composition of the emulsion. Exact measurement of acutance is not easy and most manufacturers simply rate films for acutance as low, moderate, or high.

Resolving power is usually expressed as "lines per millimeter." The highest speed emulsions will record up to 50 lines per millimeter, whereas the highest resolving powers are found in slow films, especially prepared emulsions which have been made to record as many as 500 lines per millimeter. In dealing with such small dimensions, it is clear that the ultimate resolution of image detail will be arrived at only if focusing, exposure, and development are perfect.

For example, slight movement of the camera or subject during exposure upsets the resolution entirely. Inaccurate focusing is bound to be reflected in the fineness of the resolution. People with good vision can resolve 150 lines per inch at most. This is equivalent to about six lines per millimeter. With accuracy of vision as the limiting factor, it is no wonder that the full resolving power of a film is seldom realized.

Table 2 gives the resolving power values for several popular films used for various purposes. Such tables can be used as guides in selecting films when resolution of detail is the prime requisite, as is the case when the negative image is to be substantially enlarged.

RECOMMENDATIONS

It should be emphatically understood that there is seldom one best film for any given set of conditions. Personal taste is frequently the deciding element in making a choice. Numerous occasions arise where the requirements can be met by several films, even though the films may

be very different in certain respects.

Many photographers doing reasonably limited types of work cling to one film for all purposes simply because it is convenient. The photographer who uses but one film can become unusually familiar with the exposure required to give the result he is seeking. He knows the developing requirements and is able to use a single developer for all his work.

PORTRAITURE

Before selecting a film for portraiture, one must decide what is to be expected in the final results. If strong, virile portraits are desired, the film selection will be away from

the higher-speed panchromatic films in favor of a medium-speed pan film of brilliant contrast or an orthochromatic film.

The portraits of men which are described as "character studies" are most frequently made on orthochromatic films. Such films render red skin colors darker than do panchromatic films, and variations of the natural pigmentation are exaggerated. This is especially true if the ortho film has a brilliant gradation.

The question is often asked, why ortho films for portraiture at all, if they are known to bring out or even exaggerate facial blemishes? The answer is that this is a professional procedure, and professionals always retouch their portraits. They prefer ortho film because it does render these little blemishes crisply and clearly for the retoucher to work on.

Portraits of men intended for certain purposes (publicity, newspaper reproduction, etc.) can well be made on pan films. Men require flattering just as much as women in many instances, and these films are preferred over ortho films in such cases.

Women like to look younger than they are. It is a rare woman who wishes to face the reality of her complexion, age, and beauty. Therefore nearly all portraits of women are made on panchromatic films. This practice is not absolutely

necessary, of course, for ortho films have their place in portraiture of women. A woman with a very light skin, almost void of pigmentation or color, is much better photographed on an ortho film than on a pan film. Pan films tend to flatten out skin texture and, when no texture or color is present, to render the flesh tones artificially. If a woman has gray or green eyes, a light complexion, and dark hair, the best film is an orthotype.

In making portraits of children, high speed is a prime requisite. This factor is even more important than color sensitivity or gradation. Children cannot be made to hold still for even a short period. Therefore, a fast film is needed unless a lot of light is used.

LANDSCAPES

Orthochromatic or pan films can be used with landscapes; under most conditions a filter is used. The best filters for landscape work are the Aero-1, K-2, or occasionally the G (number 15). For dramatic cloud effects the red (A or number 25) filter is effective. These filters must be used on panchromatic films, of course, though picture taking on ortho film is possible with the Aero-2 or K-2.

To secure an "ortho" rendition when only pan film is available, a filter can be used. Since ortho film is sensitive to blue and green, and not to red, the obvious filter to simulate an ortho rendering is a blue-green, such as the Wratten numbers 44, 64, or 65, which are not usually available mounted in glass, but can be secured on special order in gelatin. To simulate the effect of a noncolor-sensitized or "color-blind" film, a deep blue filter

Left: *While using pan films, clouds can be emphasized by exposing through a yellow, orange, or red filter. Isopan F exposed for ¼ of a second at f/11 with an orange filter.* (Photo: A. C. Wopsley)

Below: *Panchromatic or ortho films can both be used for scenic photographs. Changes in the film's color response can be easily altered with the use of filters. Adox KB-14 exposed for 1/10 of a second at f/16.* (Photo: Laura Gilpin)

such as the Wratten C-5 (number 47 or number 47B) may be used.

INFRARED

The atmosphere is full of tiny particles of moisture which scatter and inter-reflect the light to form the phenomenon of haze. But since the red portion of the light is not scattered so much as the blue, it is possible to cut through this haze with infrared film. For this reason many photographers use infrared film for distant landscapes, and mountain scenery, or for any other situation where the presence of haze would adversely affect results.

Infrared film is not recommended where there is considerable fore-ground, unless you wish a night effect. For a dramatic shot of a nearby object, such as a figure against a black sky, the photographer will find that he can obtain a quite satisfactory shot on a pan film with an orange or red filter combined with a little under-exposure.

STILL LIFE

In the making of still-life photographs, speed is of no importance. An emulsion of the commercial panchromatic type or a slow portrait pan is fast enough. Panchromatic films are employed most frequently, because in still-life photography the subjects are usually colorful.

A favorite film of many photographers for still-life photography is commercial ortho used without a filter. When using this film (or pan film) the colors of the subject should be studied to determine just how each color is to be rendered before a final selection is made of the emulsion and filter. The color reproduction will have a considerable influence on the effectiveness of the composition.

It should be pointed out that red objects are often rendered satisfactorily on an ortho emulsion. The reason is that pigments and dyes are not pure in hue. Green, for instance, reflects practically all the colors in the spectrum, the predominantly green reflection giving the characteristic color to the object only. When photographing this color, we are therefore able to get a passable reproduction on even a blue-sensitive film.

The same holds true with other colors. Reds and blues have a dominant reflection in those particular regions, yet the red will often have a strong blue reflection and the blue a strong reflection in the red end of the spectrum.

In selecting an emulsion for still life, avoid the high-speed emulsions. The subject will not move, so there is no necessity for high speed. Never use a fast film when a slower one will do. The slower film will always have some qualities which make it superior to the fast film and, by giving a little more exposure, an improvement can be effected in the final result.

In making architectural pictures, the slower pan films are commonly employed, but a high percentage of

Left: *Nearly all portraits of women should be made on panchromatic film since it flatters most complexions. Leica IIIF with 50mm Summitar f/2 lens. Plus-X film exposed for 1/60 of a second at f/2.* (Photo: Michael L. Edelson)

Right: *Because the camera must catch the excitement and drama of events as they happen, it is necessary that the news photographer use a high-speed film. This is true even though a flash may be employed. Here the quick working photographer caught the hysteria of the crowd as a woman was about to be trampled. Royal Pan exposed for 1/125 of a second at f/11 with flash.* (Photo: Dan Techonchuk)

For portraits of men where a strong, virile rendering is sought, use a slower panchromatic film with higher contrast or an ortho film. Panatomic-X film in Rolleiflex exposed f/4 at 1/60 of a second. (Photo: T/Sgt. Gene Delmar Spradling / Ninth Interservice Photography Contest)

They are preferably developed in special formulas, but in an emergency the familiar D-72 diluted one-to-one is often used. The process pan emulsions can be used on black-and-white as well as color copies.

In half-tone copy work, where the object shows all tones (a photograph or painting), use a film of less contrast than the process emulsions or the negative will be too hard. On black-and-white half-tone work any slow film such as the commercial films can be employed, while for colored originals the slow panchromatic emulsions are preferable. (See article on *Copying and Close-up Photography.*)

SPECIAL APPLICATIONS

Table 4 lists a few films which do not come into use in general photography very often.

Positive Film. As its name implies, this film is used for the making of positives or transparencies. Though only listed under 35 mm film, it is also supplied in sheet film in standard sizes. It is used for making black-and-white positives for projection in regular 2×2 projectors, or in large sizes for display purposes. Because it is slow and may be handled under the regular bromide safelight, positive film is often used in the camera for making copies. Positive film has a short exposure scale, a long density scale, fine grain, and properties which promote easy handling. Positives are sometimes made on this film and then, from these positives, duplicate negatives are made. Occasionally a duplicate negative is made on positive film using the reversal procedure.

AUTOPOSITIVE AND REVERSAL FILMS

There are two special types of film which are used where a direct positive image is required without an intermediate negative. These are the Autopositive films and the Direct Positive Pan films, both made by Kodak. They differ in two ways.

First of all, there is a contrast difference between the two types of film. The Autopositive film is of very high contrast and is intended mainly for duplicating line images and other purposes in photomechanical work. The Direct Positive

professional photographers prefer the ortho emulsions. With the pan films they too often get a "washed-out" look if the subject contains too many reds. If pan films are used, one should consider the effect of a filter. Filters are often advisable for contrast. If a brilliant result is desired, such as for an outdoor shot, commercial pan film or commercial ortho film is used.

Indoors the preference would be for the softer effect obtained with a slow portrait pan emulsion. Avoid the use of high-speed emulsions because of their relatively higher graininess and lower resolving power.

COPIES

Copy work is specialized and the films designed for this work are seldom used for any other purpose. If a copy is made of a line drawing or printed material, a process film is employed. The ordinary process film is used if the original is simply black-and-white, while process pan film is used for a colored original. These films are slow, but develop to a very high contrast.

film is a 35 mm film of normal gradation, and is used to produce direct positive slides for projection of any subject, either line or halftone.

The second difference is in the sensitizing of these two films. Autopositive is essentially color-blind, although it has green sensitivity. Exposure is made through a yellow filter and no other special treatment is required to produce a direct positive image; it is developed in the ordinary way.

It has, however, one special characteristic. An unexposed sheet of film will develop black. Exposure to yellow light produces a *lighter* result; thus if it is exposed to a positive in yellow light, another positive image will result. If, however, the film is first given an over-all exposure to yellow light, and is then exposed to white light, the last exposure restores the density that was washed out by the yellow-light exposure, and thus produces a positive from a negative. This peculiarity is used a good deal in photoengraving for combination work. It is also possible that the ingenious amateur might find some interesting uses for this effect.

Kodak Direct Positive Pan, on the other hand, is a fully panchromatic, medium-speed emulsion, which must be developed through a complete reversal procedure in order to secure the direct positive image. This involves developing as a negative, bleaching, and redeveloping the remaining silver to form the positive image. Special kits for this process are available.

PLATES

Though this article is about film, the word "film" is taken in its broadest sense, meaning the photographic negative. In speaking of the photographic negative we cannot omit reference to plate emulsions.

Except for the basic structural difference, plates and films are very much alike. Their emulsions are similar and all previous remarks on films will apply equally as well to plates. By consulting Table 7, however, one sees that the majority of plates are designed for some commercial purpose. There are many special emulsions for copying be-

cause such work requires an image which will not expand or shrink.

Plates were at one time commonly used by professional photographers and by some amateurs. Although films are light, unbreakable, and easily filed and stored, plates still offer some distinct advantages of their own. Plates dry rapidly and this is of importance when prints must be turned out in the shortest possible time. The professional retouchers prefer plates because there is no give to the support when working with their knife or pencil. Plates do not shrink; for this reason they are often used in astronomical photography, photoengraving, and other phases of photography where extreme accuracy is essential.

☐

Since there is more ultraviolet light present at high altitudes, mountain photographs usually suffer from excessive haze. This can be partially eliminated by using an ultraviolet filter. Rolleiflex with Isopan F exposed at f/11 for 1/100 of a second. (Photo: Hans Plattner)

FILTERS

WILLARD D. MORGAN
General Editor, "Encyclopedia of Photography"

[Many amateur photographers think filters are to be used only to emphasize clouds in black-and-white pictures. But filters have many more uses, and it is just as important to know when not to use a filter. This article outlines the theory of filter use and gives the necessary practical data.]

• *Also see: Color Filters for Color Films; Color: Making Color Separation Negatives; Exposure; Films, When and How to Use Them.*

TO THE BEGINNER A FILTER IS A little disk of colored glass which in some mysterious way "brings out the clouds" in black-and-white pictures. Thus a yellow filter will enhance

Series of photographs showing the use of filters. Upper left: *No filter;* upper right: *K-2 filter;* lower left: *G filter;* lower right: *A filter.*

the rendition of fluffy white clouds against a blue sky, while a blue filter will wash them out. But no filter can put clouds against an overcast grey sky, and if the clouds happen to be big black thunderheads, you don't need a filter at all.

To understand how a filter works, let's go back in the history of film manufacture. The first films were "color-blind"—they were sensitive to blue and violet and to little else. They did have some ultraviolet sensitivity (all films do), but since the average lens is made of glass which has little transmission in the ultraviolet ranges, this was not very important.

If a film is sensitive only to blue and violet, all other colors will photograph black—and this includes red apples, yellow bananas, mahogany furniture, and red lips. Luckily most natural objects have some reflectance other than the color of light which they appear to match; nature's colors are seldom unmixed. Fairly acceptable pictures were possible because of this, though lips,

freckles, and other objects were usually too dark.

Since the first films were sensitive to blue, blue objects photographed white. Thus a white cloud on a blue sky became a white cloud on a white sky. Later manufacturers found that by adding certain dyes to the emulsion, additional sensitivity was obtained in the green range. In some cases sensitivity extended all the way to the yellow line between green and red. These films were named "orthochromatic" meaning "correct colored."

To call them "correct" was something of an exaggeration, of course, since the films still had no usable sensitivity in the red range. But they represented a considerable improvement over the earlier films, especially for taking landscapes and portraits. However, while there was sensitivity to green, there was still an excessive sensitivity to the blue end of the spectrum. Since the blue sensitivity of the film could not be diminished, a way was devised to keep too much blue light from

reaching the emulsion.

THE FIRST FILTERS

All that was needed was to place a piece of pale yellow glass over the lens to cut down the transmission of blue rays, while not noticeably affecting the green or yellow. These yellow glasses were originally marketed under the name "ray screens," but eventually acquired the name of "color filters" or "light filters."

Since ortho films were sensitive only to blue and green, there was no particular need for any filters other than yellow ones. A blue filter would merely turn the film back to "color-blind" rendition; a red filter was of no use at all, since the film still had no red sensitivity.

Further research in color-sensitizing dyes led to the making of emulsions that were sensitive to red also. Since the proper name, "orthochromatic," had already been pre-empted by the green-sensitive film, the new film was called "panchromatic"—all-colored. This was a reasonably accurate name as the film had *some* sensitivity to all colors but was not *equally* sensitive to all.

Even today's greatly improved panchromatic films have some inequality in their spectral sensitivity —they are too sensitive to blue and not sufficiently sensitive to red. In making these films, the green and red sensitivities are added by separate dyes. The same dye used for ortho sensitization is used to gain the green sensitivity, then another dye is added to get red sensitivity. These dyes don't produce a sharply limited range of sensitivity but may either overlap or fall slightly short of each other. The result will be a peak or a dip in the middle of the spectrum.

As films have improved, these irregularities have been corrected, and today's "Type B" panchromatic is almost evenly sensitive throughout the spectrum. In fact the film sees things much as the eye does. Thus if we want our black-and-white pictures to look like the subject in terms of tonal rendition—we could get along without any filters most of the time, as many photographers do. But a true rendition of relationships is not always wanted.

CHOOSING THE FILTER

Consider a still life such as a red apple on a bed of green leaves. If correctly rendered, both the red and the green will be about the same tone—and technically that is correct.

But suppose you think of red as a bright color and of green as dull —you'd want the apple lighter than the leaves. Or if you think of apples as rich red objects, and green leaves as light and delicate, you would want the apple darker than the leaves. By using filters, you can have the effect you want.

The trick is to give the apple more exposure than the leaves, if you want it lighter, or to give the apple less exposure than the leaves, if you want it darker. You could do this by shadowing, or with spotlights. Or you could do it the easy way, by using a filter to take advantage of the color differences.

Which filter should be used? We've seen that we can darken blue objects and lighten red and green ones with a yellow filter. Thus a filter of the complementary color to an object will darken the image of that object in the final print.

All filter colors are shades of just six basic colors. Divide the spectrum into three even parts, and it will consist predominantly of blue, green and red. The complement of any color is what is left of the spectrum after that color has been removed. Thus the complement to blue is green plus red, which appears yellow. The complement of green is blue plus red, which is magenta. The complement of red is blue plus green, which is called cyan.

Suppose you want to lighten a color. You can't do it directly, but you must go around the back way and darken all the complementary colors in the scene. Suppose you want to lighten a yellow (green plus red): you must darken the blue. This is done by using a complementary filter to the blue, the yellow filter. So, for a rule of thumb, to lighten a color use a filter of the same color.

To create the effect you want in still life use the correct filter. If you

Photograph taken without filter, above. *The same subject,* below, *with the same lighting, photographed through the Tiffen Polaroid Rotoscreen.*

want a light red apple on dark green leaves, use a red filter. If you want a dark red apple on light green leaves, use a green filter. This applies only to black-and-white work, because in color photography the final picture would take on the cast of the filter in use.

Chart 1 is a good starting point, but you'll have to learn by experience when not to follow it literally. This is not because the table is wrong, but because some colors are not what they seem to be. Green foliage actually reflects a red light, so you can't make green leaves come out completely black with a red filter. In fact, if you use a deep red filter and infrared film, the foliage will come out snow white due to high infrared reflectance, and not because the instructions are incorrect.

Some artificial colors, such as the dyes in fabrics, have even more erroneous reflectances. The worst are the blues and blue-greens, all of which have considerable red reflectance, making it difficult to correctly show the fabric tone in black-and-white.

Most of the time you want an object to appear just a bit darker or lighter than normal. You generally need a medium-yellow K-2 filter; a light-green X-2; an orange-red, number 23; or medium-red, Wratten A, number 25.

When in doubt as to the probable result of using a given filter, look at the subject through the filter. The Kodak Master Photoguide has a simple cardboard device with small pieces of various filter gelatins mounted in it which give you a quick check on the filter required. Its use avoids handling the actual filters too much, which might result in scratching or fingermarking them.

For many subjects, experience will have shown the most desirable filter; Chart 2 lists filter suggestions for use with panchromatic film and the most common subjects. These are only suggestions, but they do provide a starting point for the choice of a filter.

EXPOSURE AND FILTER FACTORS

Filters work by removing a certain colored part of the light which would ordinarily reach the film. As a result, using a filter actually cuts down on the exposure of our film. It would seem that the filter would affect only certain objects in the picture, and since we want to reduce the exposure of these objects, we are not really affecting the exposure of the entire picture. However, the entire picture is modified.

There are three important points: First, we generally do not wish to have the filtered objects go completely black. Second, natural objects reflect light of colors other than their dominant color, so the filter is affecting the entire scene, not just the selected object. Third, filter dyes are not perfect, so the filter has some light absorption outside the basic absorption band. This is variable, being least with yellow filters and most with blue and green

Chart 1

FILM AND FILTER COMBINATIONS FOR PHOTOGRAPHING COLORS IN BLACK-AND-WHITE

To photograph as black on			Color of Original	To photograph as white on		
Blue-sensitive Material	Ortho Material	Pan-chromatic Material		Blue-sensitive Material	Ortho Material	Pan-chromatic Material
(Kodak Wratten Filters)				(Kodak Wratten Filters)		
Not recomm.	Yellow (No. 8) Green (No. 58)	Green (No. 58)	Magenta	None	Blue (No. 47) Magenta (No. 30)	Red (No. 25) Magenta (No. 30) Blue (No. 47)
None	None or green (No. 58)	Green (No. 58) Blue (No. 47)	Red	Not recomm.	Not recomm.	Red (No. 25)
None	Blue (No. 47) Magenta (No. 30)	Blue (No. 47)	Yellow	Not recomm.	Yellow (No. 8) Green (No. 58)	Yellow (No. 8) Green (No. 58) Red (No. 25)
None	Blue (No. 47) Magenta (No. 30)	Red (No. 25) Blue (No. 47) Magenta (No. 30)	Green	Not recomm.	Yellow (No. 8) Green (No. 58)	Green (No. 58)
Not recomm.	Not recomm.	Red (No. 25)	Cyan	None	None Green (No. 58) Blue (No. 47) Magenta (No. 30)	Green (No. 58) Blue (No. 47)
Not recomm.	Yellow (No. 8) Orange (No. 16) Green (No. 58)	Green (No. 58) Red (No. 25)	Blue-Violet	None	Blue (No. 47) Magenta (No. 30)	Blue (No. 47)

NOTE: *These are not the only filters which can be used to produce the desired effects. Experience will show which variations can be used with certain hues of the original colors.*

ones. In all cases, however, some light of all colors is lost when using a filter.

The result is that when you use a filter you must increase the exposure to compensate for reducing the amount of light reaching the film. Just how much we have to increase the exposure depends on a number of things.

Type of Filter. A deep-red filter will absorb more light than a pale-yellow one, both because it removes more of the spectrum (two areas instead of one) and because the dye is less efficient.

Film Sensitivity. If the filter removes the color of light to which the film is most sensitive, it will have more effect on the exposure than if it absorbs the light to which the film has little or no sensitivity. In the case of a color-blind film (which is sensitive only to blue and has no green or red sensitivity), if we use a deep-yellow filter which removes most of the blue, we will have to increase the exposure considerably. If we use a pale-blue filter, it removes red and green. But the film isn't sensitive to these colors anyway, so the exposure will hardly have to be increased. As an exaggerated case, if using a red filter (which removes all the blue from the light) with a film sensitive only to blue, such a filter is just about equivalent to a lens cap. No reasonable amount of exposure will produce an image.

Today nearly all modern pan films are Type B sensitizing. Thus the filter factors for various manufacturers' films will be similar, and the few exceptions usually will be listed in the instruction sheet which comes with the film. Some orthochromatic sheet films are still used for special purposes; again, they are similar from one manufacturer to another.

Light Sources. Light varies in color content, depending on the source. Daylight is richer in blue than in red. Tungsten light has much more red and much less blue. Both sources of light fluctuate. Daylight is bluer at midday, redder at sunrise and sunset. Photoflood bulbs have more blue, less red, but still do not begin to approach the high blue

Photographs taken with and without a Pola-Screen, showing how undesired reflections may be eliminated.

Chart 2

FILTERS FOR TYPICAL SUBJECT MATTER USING PANCHROMATIC FILMS

SUBJECT	EFFECT DESIRED	SUGGESTED FILTER
Clouds against blue sky	Natural	K2
	Darkened	G
Blue sky as background for other subjects	Spectacular	A
	Almost black	29(F)
	Night	A plus Pola-Screen, A or 29(F) with Infrared Material
Marine scenes when sky is blue	Natural	K2
	Dark water	G
Sunsets	Natural	None or K2
	Increased brilliance	G or A
	Addition of haze for atmospheric effects	47(C5)
	Very slight addition of haze	None
Distant landscapes	Natural	K2
	Haze reduction	G
	Greater haze reduction	A or 29(F)
	Haze elimination	A or 29(F) with Infrared Material
Nearby foliage	Natural	K2 or X1
	Light	58(B)
Outdoor portraits against sky	Natural	X1, K2, or Pola-Screen
Flowers, blossoms, & foliage	Natural	K2 or X1
Red, "bronze," orange, and similar colors	Lighter to show detail	A
Dark blue, purple, and similar colors	Lighter to show detail	None or 47(C5)
Foliage plants	Lighter to show detail	58(B)
Architectural, stone, wood, fabrics, sand, snow, when sunlit and under blue sky	Natural	K2
	Enhanced texture rendering	G or A

In this picture a green-yellow filter is used to delineate the balloon against the background of the sky. Notice also how the clouds stand out. Contarex 35 mm camera with slow pan film exposed at f/11 for 1/125 of a second. (Photo: Werner Slahler)

Actually, photographers rarely use anything but pan films, eliminating the film problem as a variable. As for the light sources, we can consider that they fall, for photographic purposes, into just two classes—daylight and tungsten.

Most of the time you need just two numbers for any filter—its daylight factor and its tungsten factor. If ortho film is used occasionally, you'll have to have a second pair of factors for filters used with this film. In general, you will find Chart 3 contains just about all the useful filter factors likely to be needed.

HOW TO USE FILTER FACTORS

The numbers given in Chart 3 are multipliers; they represent the amount the exposure must be increased when a given filter is used. In all cases the unfiltered exposure is multiplied by the factor to get the exposure through the filter. There are three ways of doing this, depending on whether we wish to change the time of exposure, the f-stop, or the nominal film speed.

To use the first method, changing the time of exposure, suppose we have a meter reading of 1/50 of a second at f/11, and the filter factor is 2; then the time (1/50 of a second) must be multiplied by 2, the aperture remaining unchanged: $2 \times 1/50 = 1/25$ of a second.

In the second method, the shutter speed stays constant and the aperture is enlarged instead. Remember that each full lens stop inceases the exposure 100 percent, or, doubles it. The full stops on an American or modern foreign camera are 22, 16, 11, 8, 5.6, 4, 2.8, 2, 1.8, 1.0. If you have an older German or French camera, you may find the series is 25, 18, 12.5, 9, 6.3, 4.5, 3.2, 2.2, 1.6, 1.1. Again, each stop gives twice the exposure of the preceding one. So, if the basic exposure is 1/50 of a second at f/11, we simply move one space to the right to double the exposure and get 1/50 of a second at f/8.

Since each lens stop doubles or halves the exposure, this method is most convenient with simple or large factors, but not very easy to use where the factor is fractional. Thus

proportion of daylight.

EXPOSURE AND LIGHT TYPES

To be effective, a yellow filter requires the presence of a certain percentage of blue in the light. With incandescent light, which contains less blue and more red to begin with, the filter has considerably less effect— that is, it removes a smaller part of the total light and therefore will require a smaller increase in exposure.

All of this seems to make the problem much more complicated than it is in practice. If we take a single filter, we can see that the problem reduces itself to finding out how much the exposure must be increased for a given film in a given light. As far as the film is concerned, we can simply assume that there are three kinds—color-blind, ortho, and panchromatic.

with a filter factor of 8, remember that opening one stop doubles the exposure, two stops multiplies by 4 (2×2) and three stops multiplies by 8 ($2 \times 2 \times 2$). So at the same basic exposure, 1/50 at $f/.11$, if a filter with a factor of 8 is used, the corrected exposure will be 1/50 of a second at $f/4$.

FILTER FACTOR AND EXPOSURE METER

In the third method, the filter factor is applied to the film-speed setting of the exposure meter, and after this no calculations are required. Remembering that the filter factor must indicate increased exposure, the nominal speed of the film is effectively decreased and you divide the normal film speed by the filter factor. Thus if we have a film with a speed rating of ASA 80, and the filter factor is 2, you must set the meter to a film speed of $80 \div 2 = 40$. This will have the effect of doubling the indicated exposure.

This is a handy method when we have a filter with an odd factor, say 2.5. If the film has a basic speed of 100, dividing by 2.5 gives us a new setting of 40. This is much easier than multiplying, say, 1/50 of a second by 2.5 which would give us $2.5 \times 50 = 1/20$ second, a practical result for some cameras but not for others.

Remember in using this system that you haven't altered the actual speed of the film nor given the meter any new powers to judge exposure of colored objects. You

are merely using the meter dial to eliminate some figuring. However, you can use this system only with known filter factors. It is not possible to put a filter over the meter-cell window and take the resulting decrease in exposure reading as a measure of the filter factor, because the factor depends partly on the

sensitivity of the film. The meter cell does not respond to color in the same manner as any specific film type.

To avoid accidents, remember that the film-speed settings used with this method hold good only so long as you use that specific filter and light source. Be sure to reset your meter to the normal film speed as soon as you take the filter off the camera.

Remember, also, that published filter factors are based on laboratory tests of representative samples of films and filters, and on a specific light source. Your results may vary from the norm, but usually the variation will be within the latitude of the film. For precise work, you may have to shoot a few tests with and without a given filter to establish a working factor for your particular use.

Chart 3. FILTER FACTORS

FILTER LETTER	COLOR OF FILTER	No.	NON-COLOR-SENS.		ORTHO-CHROMATIC		PAN B	
			Sun	Tung.	Sun	Tung.	Sun	Tung.
Aero-1	Light yellow	3	4	3	2	1.5	1.5	
	Yellow	4	8	5	2	1.5	1.5	1.5
K1	Light yellow	6	4	3	2	1.5	1.5	1.5
K2	Yellow	8	12	10	2.5	2	2	1.5
K3	Yellow	9	20	16	2.5	2	2	1.5
CK-3	Yellow						2	1.5
X1	Light green	11					4	3
Minus-Blue	Yellow	12			3	2.5	2	1.5
X-2	Green	13					5	4
G	Deep yellow	15			5	3	3	2
	Red	23A					6	3
L	Blue	50					20	40
A	Red	25					8	4
B	Green	58			8	5	8	8
CS	Blue	47	2.5	2.5	3	4	5	10
F	Deep red	29					16	8
N	Green	61					10	10
C4	Blue	49	6	6	10	12	12	25
Pola-Screen	Gray	For darkened sky effects use a factor of 2.5 (in addition to the exposure increase required for side lighting), or increase the exposure four times as compared to the exposure for the same subject with frontlighting and without a Pola-Screen.						

Leitz Three-Filter Turret for the Visoflex II and IIa. For use with the Leitz E43 filters or with an adapter ring and series VI filter.

Chart 4. FILTER RECOMMENDATIONS FOR COMMERCIAL SUBJECTS		
(With Type B panchromatic films unless otherwise specified)		
Subject	**Effect Desired**	**Suggested Filters**
ARCHITECTURE Light-colored buildings against blue sky	Separation between building and sky	*K2*
	Greater contrast between building and sky	*G*
	Dark sky	*A*
	Darker sky with any of above filters	*Pola-Screen*
Red brick buildings	Lightening of tone to show texture	*G*
Reflections from roofs and windows	To subdue	*Pola-Screen*
AUTOMOBILES Dark colors	Lightening of tone to show shape and detail	*Filter similar to color of car*
Lettering on trucks, buses	Contrast to increase legibility	*Complementary filter*
Reflections from lacquered surfaces	To subdue	*Pola-Screen*
COLORED CHINA, GLASS, PLASTICS, POTTERY, TILE, MOSAICS	Natural rendering	*K2 or X1*
	Contrast to show pattern or indicate color contrast	*Complementary filter*
Reflections	To subdue	*Pola-Screens at lens and lights*
FABRICS, CLOTHING, TAPESTRIES, UPHOLSTERED FURNITURE	Natural rendering	*K2 or X1*
	Contrast to show pattern or indicate color contrast	*Complementary filter*
Dark colors	Lightening of tone to show texture	*Filter similar to color of material*
FURNITURE Red woods, as mahogany and rosewood	Best rendering of wood grain	*A*
Yellow woods and others, as maple, walnut, oak	Best rendering of wood grain	*G with Commercial Ortho Film*
Wood furniture with other colors, as in a room setting	Best grain with good rendering of other colors	*K2 or G*
LEATHER, LINOLEUM, WALLPAPER	Natural rendering	*K2 or X1*
	Contrast to show pattern or indicate color contrast	*Complementary filter*
Colored leather with chromium	Lightening of leather so image of metal detail will print	*Filter similar to color of leather*
Reflections from linoleum	Subdue reflections which obscure pattern	*Pola-Screen*
PACKAGING Colored boxes	To separate light reds from other colors	*X1 or K2*
	To make lettering more readable, or to separate various colored parts of package design	*Complementary filter*
	Penetration of colored acetate sheeting to show material or detail within	*Filter similar to color of sheeting*
	To subdue reflections from Kodapak or other clear sheeting	*Pola-Screen*

EXPOSURE AND TONE RENDITION

Since no filter cuts off the light completely in the band that it is supposed to suppress, all practical filters have some light "leakage." Therefore it is possible to increase or decrease the effect of a filter by control of the exposure. Overexposure will cause more leakage and, to some extent, will neutralize the effect of the filter. Underexposure drops the leakage below the threshold point of the film and tends to exaggerate the effect of the filter.

This can be effectively utilized when you have only a medium-yellow filter and want a dramatic cloud effect. By underexposing about one stop or less, an effect very close to that produced by a light-red filter is obtained. A deep-yellow filter can be used to obtain a subtle darkening of the sky by a slight overexposure which will moderate the effect of the filter.

FILTER MANUFACTURE

A filter is more than a simple piece of colored glass. The color must be accurately controlled, especially a closely graded set of yellow filters. The glass must be of good optical quality, as flat as possible, and nearly plane-parallel. It makes little sense to put a piece of third-rate colored glass over a precision-made lens and expect to get sharp pictures.

There are three possible ways of making a filter. One is to color the glass during manufacture by adding metallic salts to it while it is in the melted state. After the glass has been poured out into rough sheets, it is cut into pieces and these are ground like lenses until they are flat and their opposite faces are parallel.

However, only a limited range of colors is possible from metallic pigments, and even these colors are not pure. It is also difficult to duplicate the strength of the color precisely from one batch to the next. The usual method of correction is to adjust the depth of color by grinding the finished filter to a greater or lesser thickness. Slight errors in color will do little damage, but poor

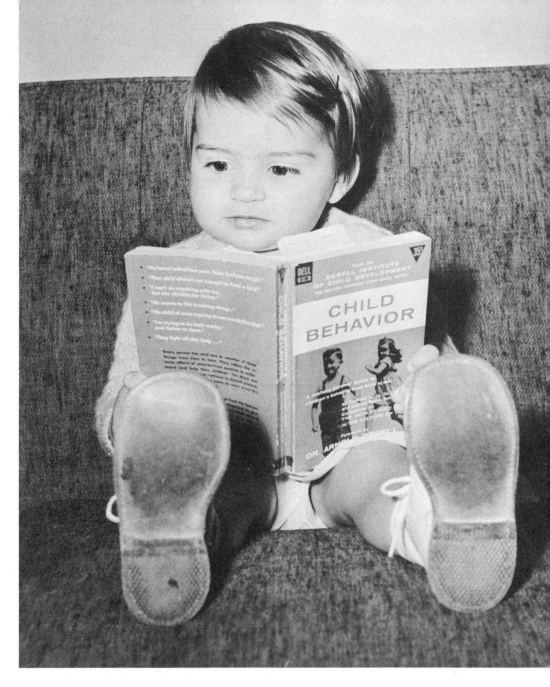

grinding can seriously upset the sharpness of the lens. It is very difficult to grind a thin plate of glass perfectly flat, and true "optical flats" are often as much as one-half inch thick. But a very thin filter will upset the corrections of a lens less than a thicker one of the same quality. Among the economical solid-glass filters, a thinner one is likely to be better than a thicker one, although it may not be perfectly flat.

The second method of making filters is to cast sheets of colored gelatin in which various dyes are dissolved. These can be made quite accurately for thickness and color; there are hundreds of dyes available, making the range of colors nearly unlimited. The finished gelatin filter is quite fragile and easily damaged, but it is also inexpensive. For permanent filters, colored gelatin is cemented between glass plates, producing a filter which is easily cleaned. The quality of glass used determines the effect the filter will have on the performance of the camera lens. Wratten filters are cemented in three different types of glass, depending on their intended use.

A glass: Hand-surfaced optical flats, approximately half an inch thick. These are used for precision work, with lenses having focal lengths of ten inches or more.

B glass: Optical glass of good quality and flatness, varying in thickness according to the size and intended use of the filter. B glass filters are used in still photography for amateur, professional and commercial work, and motion-picture work, with lenses shorter than a ten-inch focal length.

C glass: Plate glass of good quality, but not flat nor parallel; intended for use only in optical instruments which do not form an image, or in the path of a light beam such as the illuminator of a microscope.

The third method of making a filter is to cement two plates of clear glass together with a colored cement. This can produce filters of a wide variety of color and of good quality.

For practical work there is little difference between the various filters. Solid-glass filters are probably the most permanent and, when only a few standard colors are needed, are excellent. Gelatin filters, and cemented filters of all kinds, provide the widest range of color but are somewhat more fragile. A shock which would not affect a solid-glass filter may cause damage to the cement bond of a cemented filter. Also, since the coloring materials of gelatin and cemented filters are dyes, they vary somewhat in stability and may fade.

SPECIAL EFFECTS

You may want to disregard all rules and use filters to produce effects that are out of the ordinary. Take the example of the red apple and green leaves. For emotional purposes you may want to make the apple a sinister black, on nearly white leaves. It'll take a deep-green filter, some underexposure, and probably a bit of dodging in the enlarger to do it. Want a white apple on black leaves? Use a deep-red filter such as the F (Wratten number 29). Again, you'll probably have to dodge the print. How about

a white apple on white leaves? Try infrared film and a deep-red filter such as the F, or an even deeper red like the Wratten 70 or 87 (the latter looks black because it transmits no visible light).

For atmospheric effect in landscapes, such as "early morning" scenes covered with mist, the old color-blind film has never been surpassed. But special film is not necessary, just slip a blue filter (Wratten C-5, number 47) over the lens and you'll get exactly the same effect. It will have a fairly large factor and slow down the film considerably. But a really high-speed pan film used with a C-5 filter will probably end up being faster than any color-blind film you can buy.

On the other hand, if you want to eliminate the haze, treat it like any other blue object and use a yellow or red filter with pan film. In extreme cases, use infrared film. Note carefully, this refers to blue haze, not to white fog or mist. Only infrared film may eliminate atmospheric haze.

POLARIZING FILTERS

The Pola-Screen or polarizing filter distinguishes between light rays vibrating in one direction and light rays vibrating at right angles to that direction. It transmits one and rejects the other but has no effect on color rendition.

Under normal circumstances, light rays vibrate in all directions, and most objects look exactly the same through a polarizing filter as they do without it. But if two filters of this kind are used, and one is rotated so its light-stopping characteristic is at right angles to the other, the effect is obvious. Light is restricted to rays vibrating one way by the first filter and these cannot pass through the second filter. The result from combining these two filters is a complete blackout.

This effect has one practical application. Remember that light which has been polarized (that is, filtered

Striking effects can be achieved by the creative and imaginative use of filters. A red filter was used here to produce a dark, dramatic mood. Rolleiflex with medium-speed film exposed for 1/15 of a second at f/8. (Photo: R. F. Rhoads, Jr.)

Sometimes the scene you may want to photograph is too bright for the modern, high-speed film in your camera. Here the light intensity can be reduced by using a neutral-density filter. (Photo: Wolf Shlegel)

so it vibrates in only one plane) will be depolarized, or turned back into ordinary light, when it is reflected from a rough or random surface. It maintains its polarized quality when reflected from metal or glass.

To photograph a shiny metal or glass object, we put a Pola-Screen over the light and another one over the camera lens. The light is polarized by the first filter with the second filter oriented to block all these polarized rays. The light reflected from the rough parts of the set-up and from its surroundings is depolarized, and so it is transmitted by the second filter. But reflections from the shiny metal parts retain their polarization and are rejected by the second filter.

What you get is a picture of the metal object with reflections elimi-

nated. You can, by correctly orienting the second filter, retain some reflections if desired.

You don't always have to use two filters. Light is sometimes naturally polarized, as when it is reflected from a glass pane, or from shiny paint (but not when it is reflected from polished metal). To eliminate reflections from windows, water, or the finish of a car, use a single Pola-Screen over the camera lens. Similarly, blue-sky light is polarized by being scattered from water droplets. A dark sky effect can often be obtained by properly orienting a single polarizing filter over the camera lens. (This is the only way to get a darkened sky with color films, where a yellow filter cannot be used.) This effect is strongest in the quadrant of the sky at right angles to the direction of the sun and is most effective in side-lighted scenes.

The polarizing filter divides the light into two parts, rejecting one and transmitting the other. Thus only half the light is transmitted and the filter would be expected to have a factor of 2. However, a small amount of absorption in the glass and cement must be taken into account, so the actual factor of most polarizers is 2.5.

For stronger sky effects, the polarizer can be combined with a yellow filter. Here the factor is obtained by multiplying the factors of the two filters. Thus if the yellow filter has a factor of 2, and the polarizer a factor of 2.5, the com-bined factor is $2 \times 2.5 = 5$. (This applies only to a combination where one filter is neutral in color; it cannot be applied to combinations of two different colored filters.)

In using the polarizer, the result can be visualized by looking through the filter itself and rotating it slowly until the desired effect is secured. The filter is then attached to the camera in the same position. Some polarizers have a small viewing filter in a handle or extension oriented in the same way as the main polarizer. The filter is placed over the lens and the handle swung into various positions while you watch the scene through the small filter. When the desired effect is seen, it will be the same in the camera.

INFRARED FILTERS

Infrared films are rather peculiarly sensitized. Their sensitivity covers two regions, with a wide gap between. The first region is the usual blue sensitivity, just like any color-blind film. This is the basic sensitivity or the silver halide emulsion. The second region begins in the far red and extends into the invisible infrared.

If an infrared film is used without filter, the infrared portion will be drowned out by the exposure due to the visible blue light. In order to secure true infrared rendition, a filter must be used. For most uses, any filter which eliminates the blue sensitivity of the film will do. It may be a very deep yellow such as the Wratten number 15 G filter or it may be a medium or deep red such as the Wratten A, number 25 or F, number 29 filters.

No specific factor can be given for these filters, because exposure meters do not measure infrared, and there is no basic exposure to which the factor can be applied. The instruction sheet for the film usually lists some typical exposures with an infrared filter included. Since all the above filters transmit freely in the red, they will have about the same exposure factor and the exposure will be the same with any of them.

Since the infrared sensitivity of the film starts in the visible red, there will be some effect from any visible red light, even when one of the filters is used. For some special kinds of work, it may be necessary to make a picture entirely by infrared for which Kodak makes a number of special filters.

Kodak Wratten filter number	Transmission begins at
70**	660mµ*
89A	700
88	710
88A	730
87	760
87C	800

* The Greek letter µ represents microns; one micron = .001 mm. The abbreviation mµ stands for millimicrons; 1 millimicron = .000001 mm.

** Transmits some visible red light between 660 and 700 mµ.

Because of the large amount of red in ordinary tungsten illumination, it is sometimes best to use a green filter in order to restore natural tones. This is particularly true of portraiture. Contarex 35 mm camera with Sonnar 250mm lens. (Photo: Margaret Menet)

The problem of excessive haze is often encountered in aerial views such as this shot of the Ras Tanura marine terminal in Saudi Arabia. Here an ultraviolet filter cuts down the effect of the haze. (Photo: Standard Oil)

While exposure indexes and filter factors cannot be given for infrared film in daylight because the proportion of infrared in daylight is highly variable, the percentage of infrared in tungsten light is fairly constant. Usually the meter setting given by the film manufacturer includes the filter, generally a Wratten number 25 A filter. In general, it is best for the photographer to make tests under his own working conditions, and to expose accordingly.

In using infrared film and filters, it must be remembered that most lenses are not corrected for this work and will have a rather large focus shift. It is usually recommended that the photographer focus sharply without the filter and then, before the picture is taken, rack the lens out an additional distance (away from the film) of about 1/200 of its focal length. Some lenses have an auxiliary focus mark (indicated by a small R) indicating the distance.

NEUTRAL DENSITY FILTERS

The neutral density filter is gray in color and has no effect on the color rendition of the scene. It is intended to reduce the amount of light entering the camera and serves the same purpose as stopping down the lens. It is used primarily with very fast films, outdoors, where an exposure of, say, $f/32$ is called for and the lens cannot be stopped down that far. It is sometimes used by movie cameramen where for artistic reasons a short depth of field may be required in a given shot. Rather than stop down and get too much depth of field, a neutral filter is used with the lens wide open.

Some cameramen believe that neutral filters have a softening effect

Sometimes with fill-in flash, the highlights of the subject's face will blend with the light sky. This can be avoided by using a medium-yellow filter to separate the tones. Twin-lens reflex with slow pan film exposed at f/8 for 1/100 of a second. (Photo: Ullmann)

FISHEYE (SUPER-WIDE-ANGLE) CAMERAS

The so-called "fisheye" lens, designed by Nippon Kogaku for the Nikon F single-lens reflex, is a super-wide-angle lens having a focal length of 8 mm and a maximum aperture of f/8. On the 35 mm frame for which it is designed, it produces a circular image having an angle of view of the subject of a full 180 degrees. The lens has nine elements and a built-in filter turret with six filters. Because the rear of the lens extends far into the camera, the reflex mirror cannot be used and must be locked up into position before the lens is inserted.

For use with the "fisheye" lens, a special finder mounts on top of the winding crank of the camera. The finder is similar to a rifle sight, showing just the center of the picture in a small ring. The limits of the picture cannot be shown, but the user can easily judge the field of view since whatever is in front of the camera will be in the picture. Because of its short focal length, no focusing is required; everything is sharp from a few inches to infinity.

Some interesting results can be obtained with such a lens, though the perspective of the picture is necessarily distorted. If the camera is placed flat on its back on the floor, in the middle of the room, it will photograph the ceiling and all four walls, down to the baseboards. Held in normal position, just two negatives will encompass the entire

Nikon Fisheye Nikkor 180-degree super-wide-angle lens for 35 mm photography. 8 mm focal length, f/8. For use with Nikon F automatic reflex.

on the image contrast. This is not true, since the filter is as perfectly neutral as it can be made. The only effect it can have is to reduce the amount of light reaching the film.

The factor of a neutral filter is sometimes indicated right on the filter mount, or the neutral filter may be marked directly in density. This is easily translated into a factor if one simply remembers that each density increment of 0.3 is equal to 50 percent transmission or a factor of 2. A filter having a density of 0.6 is equal to 25 percent transmission and will have a factor of 4.

Density	Factor
.30	2 X
.60	4 X
.90	8 X
1.00	10 X
1.20	16 X
1.50	32 X

Or you can look at it this way: a .30 neutral filter is equal to one lens stop; a .60, two stops; a .90, three stops; a 1.20, four stops; a 1.50, five stops.

Figure 1. Angles of view for a conventional lens range from 50 to 160 degrees.

horizon. Close-ups of people at a distance of a few inches produce sharp, but severely distorted results.

PRINCIPLE OF THE FISHEYE LENS

The idea of a 180-degree wide-angle lens originally came from a study of the operating principle of the fish's eye. It is generally known that when passing out of a dense medium (water) into a lighter medium (air), light rays are so refracted that a 180-degree angle is compressed into about 97 degrees. A pinhole camera filled with water and covered by a glass slab was used by R. W. Wood in 1919 to simulate this effect.

In 1924, Robin Hill conceived the idea of replacing the water with a portion of a glass sphere above the lens of the camera, and thus produced the first practical 180-degree wide-angle lens. This lens was known as the Hill Sky lens, and was used for meteorological survey work.

Figure 1 shows a conventional lens at various view angles from 50 degrees, which is about normal, to 160 degrees, which is about the limit of a conventional wide-angle lens. One of the difficulties with normal lens construction in this case is that even with very short focal lengths, the size of the picture increases rapidly with the angle after passing 150 degrees. For a 180-degree picture with a conventional lens, the film would have to be infinitely large. Such a film size is, of course, out of the question.

In the Hill lens, the first element is a negative spherical one, which bends the lateral rays quite sharply while having little or no effect on the central ones. Thus the lens

compresses an angle of 180 degrees into about 90 degrees. This lens serves to redirect the light rays so that a conventional lens, placed behind it, can pick them up and focus them on the film. The two rear elements of the lens perform the task of focusing the image on the film, and also of correcting the aberrations in the whole system. Figure 2 shows the construction of the Hill lens: A is the front negative element; B is the diaphragm, which also contains provision for inserting filters; and C is the remaining section of the lens, having two elements properly curved and selected to produce the desired focal length (in terms of distance to film) and corrections.

The resulting lens had a diameter of about two and a quarter inches, and its actual working aperture was $f/22$. At $f/22$, it had enormous depth of field, which could be increased still further by stopping down. The lens was used on a specially built 3¼ × 4¼ camera.

The Nikon Fisheye lens works on the same principle but is considerably more complicated. Its front element is nearly three inches in diameter, and it has a total of nine glass elements for superior correction. This makes it possible to increase its aperture to $f/8$, which is remarkably fast for a lens of this type.

Actually, those who are interested in lens design recognize that these lenses are basically telephoto lenses, reversed back for front. The conventional telephoto has a positive element in front and a negative element in the rear, producing a narrower angle of view than a normal lens requiring the same bellows extension. The Hill lens and the Nikon Fisheye, on the other hand, have the negative element in front with the positive in the rear, producing a wider angle of view than a normal lens of the same extension.

RECTIFICATION OF IMAGES

As mentioned, the image of the fisheye lens is considerably compressed at the edges and uncompressed in the center. The image is nonrectilinear, useful mainly for trick effects and for survey work,

Kinoptik 1.9mm f/1.9 Super Tegea for 16 mm motion pictures. 197-degree angle of view. From Karl Heitz, Inc., New York City.

where mathematical methods can be applied to determine the true size and distance of objects at various distances from the center.

For those who wish to employ the lens in ultrawide-angle interior work, the image as received on the negative is too distorted to be useful. However, selected parts of the image may be restored to normal rectilinear condition by the simple expedient of enlarging the negative back through the same fisheye lens

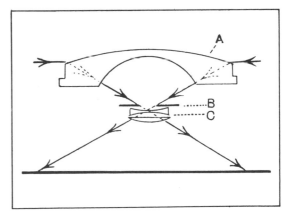

Figure 2. Construction of the Hill lens. A, front negative element; B, diaphragm; C, remaining section of the lens. Light rays from the horizon strike A, pass through the opening at B, and reach the regular photographic lens C at an acceptable angle.

that took it. The whole picture cannot, of course, be projected at once (it would extend beyond the walls of the darkroom), but sections of the image can be printed as desired.

Areas near the edges of the round negative can be restored to straightness, and parallel lines which appear as arcs on the negative will again be parallel. By successively enlarging portions around the edges of the negative made with the camera pointing up at the sky, we can produce a series of pictures which will join together into a continuous panorama of the entire horizon.

The fisheye lens thus provides the imaginative photographer with a means of producing new and different perspective effects, and also of securing pictures under conditions that would otherwise be impossible.

Photography can chronicle the disappearing scene. To insure that the chronicle is seen in later years requires attention to the details of fixing and washing of both the negatives and prints.

FIXING

IRA B. CURRENT
Photo & Repro Division, General Aniline & Film Corporation, Binghamton, New York

[Many photographers fail to realize the importance of the fixing process. It is in the fixing tray, just as much as in the developer tray, that a print or film's future is made or broken. An expert here discusses the many factors involved in fixing, such as composition of the solution, agitation, temperature, and degree of exhaustion. He also gives formulas for hardening and nonhardening baths and a detailed account of defects due to improper fixing and how to eliminate them.]

• *Also see: Beginner's Guide to Developing and Printing; Development, Fixing and Drying; Development, Formulas.*

IN THE LIGHT-SENSITIVE SILVER-halide photographic processes, a fixing step which completely removes the undeveloped silver halides is necessary following development to form the silver image. If the unexposed and undeveloped halides are left in the film or paper, they are very susceptible to print-out reduction when exposed to the ambient light necessary for display and viewings. Also, the chemical nature of the residual halides is such that they react readily with many of the substances in the air to form silver, silver sulfide, or other compounds of silver.

When this occurs, the photographic image is ruined by a build-up of stain densities in the areas not occupied fully by the developed image. In time, if the fixing step or later washing steps are not complete, these reactions cause an attack on the silver image itself, resulting in yellowing and fading, particularly if the fixing step or the later washing step are not properly carried out. The term "fixing" implies the removal of the silver halides by their reaction with a fixing agent that yields a soluble compound, a "silver complex," and second, the removal of this soluble compound from the film or paper by washing with water.

There are some photographic processes in which the unexposed and undeveloped silver halides are rendered insensitive to light, contamination, etc., and are not removed by fixing and washing. The term "stabilization" is generally applied to these processes, and they usually find application in the fields of industrial or recording photography, rather than in artistic photography. "Stabilized" photographic records are usually not as permanent as those that have been fixed and washed.

CHEMICALS

There are several chemicals that are capable of reacting with the silver halides to form soluble silver complexes, but the ones most commonly used are the sodium and ammonium thiosulfates. Sodium thiosulfate is available in the anhydrous form ($Na_2S_2O_3$, molecular weight, 158.13) or crystalline form ($Na_2S_2O_3 \cdot 5H_2O$, molecular weight, 248.2), and is commonly known as "hypo."

When the anhydrous form is dissolved in water, heat is given off, so that the resulting solution is hotter than the water was prior to adding the chemical. While a greater quantity of active chemical is available in a given volume or weight of anhydrous hypo, it has a tendency to cake when stored. It dissolves in water more slowly than the crystalline form.

In view of this, crystalline forms of hypo are more commonly used. These crystalline forms are more stable, are free flowing, and are more easily dissolved in water than the anhydrous forms. When crystalline hypo is dissolved in water, the final solution is cooler than the water was before addition of the chemical.

Ammonium thiosulfate [$(NH_4)_2S_2O_3$, molecular weight, 148.21] is usually available in a 60-percent solution. The silver halides react with ammonium thiosulfate, more readily than with sodium thiosulfate, and the fixing time is thus reduced when the ammonium salt is employed.

RATE OF FIXING

The reaction between sodium thiosulfate and silver bromide, to take a single halide as an example, may be represented as follows:

$$3\,AgBr + 4Na_2S_2O_3 \rightarrow Na_5Ag_3(S_2O_3)_4 + 3NaBr$$

This is only one equation of a series involved in the formation of soluble silver complexes. The rate of fixing is governed by several factors. The first of these is the make-up of the halides in the emulsion. Silver chloride fixes at a faster rate than does silver bromide, which, in turn, fixes at a faster rate than does silver iodide. The presence of silver iodide in the emulsion, even if proportionately lower than the silver bromide or silver chloride, tends to slow down the rate of fixation of the combination. Accumulation of iodide in the fixing bath also will lower the rate of fixation of a film or paper that does not contain any silver iodide.

The thickness of the emulsion also has a considerable effect on the rate of fixation, with the thinner emulsions fixing considerably faster than thicker ones, if other factors such as halide composition remain the same. The amount of surface presented for chemical reaction by the silver-halide emulsion grains also has an effect. If these crystals are small or are characterized as having fine "grain," a greater surface is presented, and the rate of fixing is faster.

Concentration. The rate of fixation is also affected by the concentration of the thiosulfate solution. In practical applications where the films or papers have been developed prior to fixation, the clearing time as an indication of rate of fixation decreases as the concentration of the solution is increased. The limiting factor in concentration of solution is the solubility of the salt itself, and the other factors influencing stability of the solution—its acidity and the necessary hardening and buffering chemicals required in the formula. At low temperatures, there may be a slight decrease in fixing rate as the concentration of thiosulfate nears the maximum possible, but this is usually of little significance. (See Figure 1.)

Temperature. As would be expected, the rate of fixing is also influenced by the temperature of the fixing solution, the rate being higher at higher temperatures. However, limiting factors in practice are the effects of higher temperatures on the swelling of the gelatin, which may become excessive. This, in turn, may favor reticulation and result in excessive drying time, scratching, or other damage to the image. Also, the film or paper may become too tacky during the drying phase. The fixing bath itself is also more readily decomposed at higher temperatures. Therefore, the recommended temperature for ordinary fixing baths should be between 65 F and 70 F (exceptions are processing procedures where higher temperatures are required, and which involve special formulations).

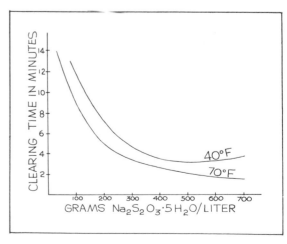

Figure 1.

Agitation. Agitation has a pronounced effect on the fixing time with constant replacement of the fixing solution over the surface of the film or paper providing more rapid and complete diffusion of the reaction products. The effect of agitation is considerably more pronounced for lower concentrations of sodium thiosulfate. Lack of agitation of prints in a tray during fixation is liable to result in irregularities that become very pronounced as the improperly fixed prints start to stain or fade with age. These irregularities are most apt to occur where the prints come into contact with one another in the solution.

Exhaustion. When a fixing bath is used to fix film or prints, the products formed in the reaction between the thiosulfate and the silver halides accumulate in the solution as the thiosulfate is consumed. Also, the developer, or rinse or stop-bath solution carried over with the films or prints tends to dilute the solution so that it is less effective. When the concentration of thiosulfate is high, these effects are not observed as quickly as when the original thiosulfate concentration is low. When the reaction products increase, and the concentration of thiosulfate is decreased, the time required for complete fixation, i.e., formation of soluble silver complexes, is increased.

Further causes of deterioration of the fixing bath are the contamination of the solution with the alkaline developer carried over from the development step, and the frothing caused by the presence of gelatin particles and surfactants incorporated in the emulsion at the time of manufacture. Also, in the case of films, some of the sensitizing and antihalation dyes may be bleached into the solution and later deposited on paper fibres or in the film gelatin layers, causing subsequent discoloration as the pH is changed on subjecting the print or negative to the vicissitudes of atmosphere.

Two-bath procedure. To obtain the highest print or film-fixing capacity, to insure adequate fixation in the minimum of time, and to insure that the photographic negatives or prints processed in the solution do not fade or discolor on aging, a two-bath fixing procedure is recommended (see *Faded Photographs*). In this procedure, the prints or films are first introduced into a fixing bath that has been used to a partial degree of exhaustion.

To start with, a fresh fixer may serve as both fixer number one, and as fixer number two. When number two is partly exhausted it becomes bath number one. The prints are allowed to remain in the first bath for one half of the total time, and then they are transferred to a fresh bath, number two.

Fixing is completed in this bath, and the prints are then transferred to the wash water. This second bath is utilized until it is partially exhausted, and then it is substituted for the first bath, which, in turn, is discarded. A new second bath is provided to take the place of the partially used one. This procedure increases the fixing capacity of a given volume of fixer solution by about four times that of a fixer used as a single solution.

Clearing time. The "clearing time," or the time it takes a film to lose its milky appearance in the fixing bath, is an indication of the time required for fixing. When the milkiness disappears it may be assumed that most of the insoluble halides have been converted into soluble silver-thiosulfate complexes that can be washed out of the film. However, due to the difficulty of visually judging the clearing time under many darkroom or other working conditions, it is best to multiply the observed clearing time by two to determine the total fixing time, and to insure that fixing is indeed complete.

It is not easy to detect the clearing time of photographic papers, however, and in many cases there is no visual indication that the fixing reaction is taking place. Thus, more care may be required to insure that papers are adequately fixed. This is all the more important in view of the fact that the paper fibres and baryta layers, if any, tend to "mordant" or adhere to the silver complexes that are formed, particularly as the fixer is exhausted to some degree. The presence of these complexes after the prints have been "washed" hastens the fading reaction that is likely to occur as the prints age.

Formulation. A solution of sodium thiosulfate alone can be used to fix films or papers for the limited life of the solution under cool temperature conditions if there is little stress placed on the requirement that the negatives or prints be properly hardened. However, after a short period of youth, such a solution will contain a considerable quantity of oxidized developer that is carried over from the previous processing bath.

Also, a considerable quantity of this developer is retained in the swollen gelatin layer, and continues to act for some time after the negatives or prints have been transferred to the fixer. The developer in the film or paper layers will tend to cause staining, or dichroic fog, and therefore acid is ordinarily added to a fixing bath in order to neutralize the developer.

ACIDITY

The acidity or pH of the fixing bath is important, for, in addition to neutralizing the alkali of the carried-over developer, it governs to a great extent the effect of the hardening agents and the swelling of the emulsion or noncurl gelatin back coating. This, in turn, affects the rate of diffusion of the fixing chemicals into and out of the gelatin layers. A buffer is added to maintain reserve acidity over the neutralization caused by developer carryover.

The correct pH is associated with the isoelectric point of the gelatin, which in most cases is in the vicinity of a pH of 4.8. The useful pH range of the fixing bath is usually slightly below the isoelectric point. When the pH is above the isoelectric point, the gelatin starts to show a greater degree of swelling, and the action of the hardening agents is reduced so that the emulsion tends to be soft and tacky. This condition permits easy abrasion or scratching, and, in the case of paper prints, may give trouble as the prints are dried, by their adhering to the dryer belt or the drying rack cloth.

In the case of roller-transport processors, in which the films are exposed to the processing solutions for shorter times at higher temperatures than those employed ordinarily in tank or tray processing, the effect of gelatin swelling and hardening plays an important part. With this type of processing, the degree of softening (or hardening) in the development stage is controlled to some extent by the formula of the developer.

Hardening of the emulsion should be sufficient to prevent excessive swelling, tackiness, and damage to the film prior to fixing. The added thickness of the swollen gelatin layers may interfere with the proper mechanical transport of the films. Excessive swelling also permits a high water load during fixing and washing. This may exceed the ability of the washing unit to remove

soluble complexes, and that of the drying unit to remove the water in the time allotted to this operation. Yet, higher pH fixing favors more rapid removal of silver complexes in washing. Therefore the pH range for the fixing stage must be adjusted to keep the fixing and washing rate as high as possible without excessive swelling and tackiness.

The effects of acidity are carried over into the washing step even in ordinary processing, where it has been demonstrated that excess acidity has a retarding effect on the rate of removal of the silver complexes from the paper or film. The use of a neutralizing bath such as sodium sulfite (two percent) or sodium carbonate (one percent) after the first removal of hypo by rinsing, and prior to final washing, effectively hastens the washing rate. Alkalies, such as carbonate, however, tend to cause gelatin to swell,

and this may make their use for this purpose unsatisfactory in some instances.

Buffer. Acid solutions of thiosulfate tend to decompose to form sodium sulfite and sulfur, or to "sulfurize." Since it is desirable that the life of the fixing bath extend over a reasonable period of time and use, a reserve of acidity must be maintained. The degree of acidity, or pH, should be kept within fairly narrow limits to insure best hardening and minimum swelling of the gelatin. Therefore, sodium sulfite, one of the decomposition products of sulfurization, is added to the fixer as a stabilizer. Control of acidity is usually provided by acetic acid, or one of the other mild organic acids, such as citric acid.

Another method of buffering is to add to the solution an acid which is itself highly buffered. The acid generally employed is boric acid; used alone it would not have sufficient acidity to produce the required pH in the fixing bath, but in combination with the acetic acid, it provides a reserve acidity which maintains the pH of the solution practically constant. The result of this is that the usual sludge of aluminum sulfite, which appears in an ordinary acid-hardening fixing bath when the pH rises above normal, is not formed in this buffered solution. Thus the bath remains clear and useful throughout the active fixing life of its basic hypo concentration.

While the boric-acid-buffered fixing bath may be used for both films and papers, it is generally best not to use it for papers. The reason is simply that since it is not possible to tell when papers are completely fixed by their appearance alone, it is well to have some other sign of exhaustion of the fixing bath; this is provided by the "sludging" which takes place somewhat before the actual exhaustion point of the fixing bath in use and provides a margin of safety.

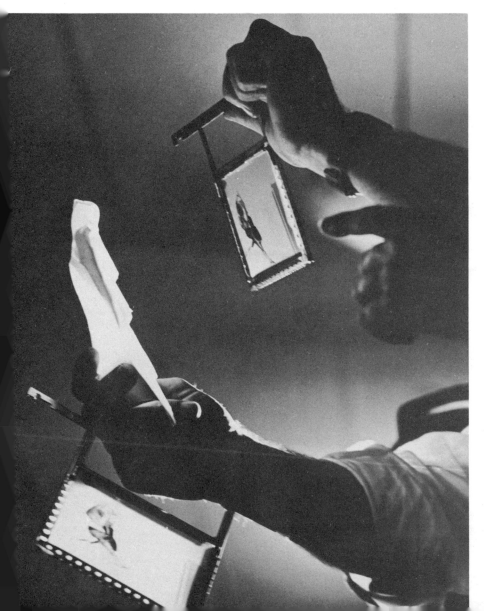

While negatives can be viewed before fixing has been completed, they should be returned to the fixing solution until any residual milkiness, indicating unfixed silver halides, has disappeared from the films.

HARDENERS

In order to prevent excessive swelling or softening of the gelatin layers of films and papers, a hardening agent is necessary to complete the fixing bath formula. The most common fixers are those that utilize potassium alum as the hardening agent. Maximum hardening is provided by potassium alum when the bath is maintained at a pH range of about 4.0 to 4.5.

Chrome alum has also been used as a hardener, but while the hardening properties of an acid fixing bath containing chrome alum are usually superior to those of one containing potassium alum when the solutions are fresh, the hardening properties of the chrome alum bath are rapidly lost on standing. Chrome alum fixers are no longer recommended.

Chrome-alum fixers definitely should not be used for paper prints; with exhaustion, or with use at higher than normal temperatures, a light green stain or sedimentation of chromium hydroxide may occur.

This may be difficult to remove from paper. The occurrence of this stain, if uniform, is not objectionable on film; it may be removed in a five percent solution of potassium citrate (at a temperature below 68 F, as citrate tends to swell gelatin).

Potassium alum and chrome alum are classified as "permanent" hardeners because they tan or modify the gelatin, so that even though the excess hardening chemicals are removed by washing, the gelatin layer will be prevented from excessive swelling or softening. Thus, films or papers that have been properly treated in a potassium-alum fixing bath in good working order can well withstand the physical effects of subsequent washing and drying.

Another class of "hardeners" are those whose action is only temporary; the gelatin is prevented from swelling only in the presence of the salt. When it is removed with subsequent washing, the gelatin takes on water and swells as before. Typical of this class of hardener is sodium sulfate, which is sometimes added to processing baths to control excessive swelling at high temperatures.

TYPICAL FORMULAS

There are several formulas for fixing baths, but the following are representative of those in most common use (proprietary prepared fixers contain modifications to insure better solution, better keeping properties, etc., but they are in essence similar to those given):

ACID HARDENING FIXER
Solution 1
Water (125 F or 52 C)
    16 ounces   500.0 cc
Sodium thiosulfate (crystal)
    8 ounces   240.0 grams
Solution 2
Water (125 F or 52 C)
    5 ounces   150.0 cc
Sodium sulfite (anhydrous)
    ½ ounce   15.0 grams
Acetic acid, 28%
    1½ ounces   45.0 cc
Boric acid
    ¼ ounce   7.5 grams
Potassium alum
    ½ ounce   15.0 grams

Add the second solution to the first and add water to make a total volume of one liter (32 ounces). The chemicals should be dissolved thoroughly in the order given, and should be stirred rapidly while the second solution is added to the first. (Glacial acetic acid may be diluted to 28 percent by adding three parts of acid to eight parts of water.)

The above fixer will fix approximately 15—8 × 10 prints per liter of solution when used as a single bath, or up to 60—8 × 10 prints per liter if a two-bath system is used. It is also suitable for films.

However, for films, some prefer the more stable bath employing boric acid as a supplementary buffer. It is preferable, here, because it prevents sludging; sludge has a tendency to deposit on films even before it becomes visible in the bath, and once deposited, is difficult to remove.

Clearing of films as they become fixed can be judged by viewing them against a dark background (such as that provided by the solution in the dark tank). This viewing makes it easy to see any milkiness resulting from unfixed silver halides.

ACID HARDENING
FIXING BATH
For Films, Plates, and Papers

Water (125 F or 52 C)
  20 ounces 600.0 cc
Sodium thiosulfate (hypo)
  8 ounces 240.0 grams
Sodium sulfite, desiccated
  ½ ounce 15.0 grams
Acetic acid (28% pure)
  1½ fl. oz. 48.0 cc
Boric acid, crystals
  ¼ ounce 7.5 grams
Potassium alum
  ½ ounce 15.0 grams
Add cold water to make
  32 ounces 1.0 liter

Crystalline boric acid should be used as specified. Powdered boric acid dissolves only with great difficulty, and its use should be avoided.

Dissolve the hypo in the specified volume of water (about 125 F or 52 C) and then add the remaining chemicals in the order given, taking care that each chemical is dissolved before adding the next. Then dilute with water to the required volume. Films or plates should be fixed properly in ten minutes (cleared in five minutes) in a freshly prepared bath. The bath need not be discarded until the fixing time (twice the time to clear) becomes excessive, that is, over 20 minutes. The solution remains clear and hardens well throughout its useful life. About 20 to 25 8×10 films or plates (or their equivalent in other sizes) may be fixed per 32 ounces (1 liter).

This bath has the advantage over the older types of fixing baths, which do not contain boric acid, in that it gives much better hardening and has less tendency to precipitate

A frequent criticism of the photographic process is that the resulting photographs may not be permanent. Proper fixing and washing is the best assurance that pictures will survive the ravages of time, and portray the life of years gone by.

a sludge of aluminum sulfite throughout its useful life.

A chrome-alum fixing bath tans or hardens gelatin to a greater extent than a fixing bath containing potassium alum and may therefore be useful in hot weather.

A chrome-alum bath, unless used fresh, rapidly loses its hardening properties after standing a short time either with or without use. This is due to the sodium sulfite which, although necessary to prevent decomposition of the hypo, reacts with the chrome alum, gradually rendering it useless as a hardening agent.

Pictures with large expanses of sky will be ruined if fixing is not complete. Uneven areas of unfixed silver halide will show in the print. On the other hand, irregular densities such as those in the rock formations will mask the effects of uneven fixation.

CHROME-ALUM FIXER
Solution 1

Water (125 F or 52 C)

    20 ounces   625 cc

Sodium thiosulfate

    8 ounces   240 grams

Sodium sulfite, anhydrous

    ½ ounce   15 grams

Water to make

    24 ounces   750 cc

Solution 2

Water   8 ounces   250 cc

Potassium chrome alum

    ½ ounce   15 grams

Sulfuric acid, CP

    $1/_{16}$ ounce   2 cc

Slowly pour the second solution into the first while rapidly stirring the first. Do not dissolve the chrome alum at a temperature higher than 150 F (66 C).

While a chrome-alum bath does not readily precipitate a sludge through carry-over of developer, once the sludging starts it is excessive, and the scum formed is very difficult to remove if allowed to dry on a film.

A hardening-type fixer may sometimes be undesirable for some specific reason, such as in toning, where hardening might influence the rate of toning or the quality of toned image. A nonhardening fixer may be indicated in some tinting or coloring applications. If, for any reason, a nonhardening fixer is desired, the following formula can be used. The temperature of the developer, rinse bath, fixer, and wash water should be kept below 65 F.

NONHARDENING FIXER

Sodium thiosulfate

    ½ pound   240 grams

Potassium metabisulfite

    1½ ounces   45 grams

Water to make

    1 quart   1 liter

The metabisulfite should be added only when the thiosulfate solution is cool.

There is an increasing use of ammonium-thiosulfate fixers, particularly in proprietary formulas sold in liquid form. Due to the greater concentration that can be made of ammonium thiosulfate in water, the higher fixing rate of these solutions when diluted, the economy of manufacture where dry salts are not involved, and the ease of dilution for use, this type of fixer is often desirable.

Faster fixation is often necessary, especially in newspaper work, and also in processing machines where the put-through time is limited by the design of the machine. Ammonium thiosulfate fixes films much more rapidly than does ordinary hypo, but as mentioned, it is unstable, not easily stored, and difficult to obtain in the dry form. For this reason, the usual rapid fixer produces the ammonium thiosulfate directly in the bath by combination of sodium thiosulfate and ammonium chloride.

The following rapid fixing bath is recommended for use in the machine-processing of negative films. It can also be used for papers, but has no advantage over other formulas which do not contain ammonium chloride. With papers it should invariably be used in conjunction with an acid stop bath; otherwise, if the bath becomes alkaline, dichroic fog is apt to be produced.

The advantages of this formula are: 1) The time to clear most negative films is less, and 2) the fixation life is about 50 percent greater than that of the usual sodium-thiosulfate fixing bath.

RAPID FIXING BATH
For Negative Films

Water (125 F or 52 C)

    20 ounces   600.0 cc

Sodium thiosulfate (hypo)

    12 ounces   360.0 grams

Ammonium chloride

    1 oz. 290 grains   50.0 grams

Sodium sulfite, desiccated

    ½ ounce   15.0 grams

Acetic acid (28% pure)

    1½ ounces   47.0 cc

Boric acid crystals

    ¼ ounce   7.5 grams

Potassium alum

    ½ ounce   15.0 grams

Cold water to make

    32 ounces   1.0 liter

When compounding this formula, the ammonium chloride should be added to the hypo solution and not to the final fixing bath; otherwise a sludge may form.

Caution: With rapid fixing baths, do not prolong the fixing time for fine-grained film or plate emulsions or for any other paper prints. Otherwise the image may have a tendency to bleach, especially at temperatures higher than 68 F (20 C). This caution is particularly important for warm-tone papers.

There has been some question as to the relative permanence of images fixed in ammonium thiosulfate as compared to those fixed with ordinary hypo. Recent studies indicate that there is no important difference in image permanence whichever salt is used. The essential part of the reaction is carried out by the thiosulfate, and whether it be sodium or ammonium seems to make no difference at all.

As mentioned, a number of organic chemicals have been proposed as substitutes for hypo in specialized work. Of the list given, only mercaptoacetic acid is sufficiently economical and available to be considered for this purpose. It is unlikely, however, that it will replace hypo in ordinary photography. It does have the advantage of permitting the combination of development and fixing in the form of a monobath (though this can be done with hypo, too, under certain conditions; for further information on monobaths, their design and use, see the article *Monobaths).*

MAINTENANCE OF FIXERS

As a fixing bath is used, it is diluted with developer. The alkali of the developer reacts with the acid and reduces the acid reserve which leads to loss of hardening, sludging of the solution, discoloration, and a tendency to stain film or prints. This may occur prior to the actual exhaustion of the thiosulfate in the solution. The alum is only slightly consumed in the hardening process.

However, the bath should not be "revived" with the addition of more acid, since it is difficult to estimate the optimum amount relative to the sulfite remaining in the bath. In l a r g e laboratories, where the amounts of components in the fixing bath can be controlled by laboratory analysis of the solution, "recovery" of the silver can be accomplished on a continuous basis by removing the silver by means of electrolysis.

In some installations the used solutions are continuously circulated through an electrolytic recovery system, and the fixer is "rejuvenated" by making up the shortages in the chemical components that have been exhausted through use. The silver is deposited electrolytically on a cathode made of a material such as stainless steel. Recovery is only practical in large installations where substantial volumes of hypo are used.

On the other hand, even relatively small laboratories can recover the silver from exhausted fixers, where no attempt is to be made to revive the solution itself. Silver can be precipitated from exhausted fixing solutions by the addition of sodium sulfide which precipitates the silver as silver sulfide. This is allowed to settle, the supernatant liquid decanted off, and the sulfide sludge, moist or dried, sent to a silver refinery.

SLUDGING

Sludging, the white milkiness that is most likely aluminum sulfite, may occur immediately after the addition of the hardener to the solution during the mixing operation,

or it may occur some time after the solution is in use. In the first instance, it may be caused by too little acid in the hardener, or too rapid addition of the hardener to the remainder of the solution. It may disappear on standing for a few hours, and then reprecipitate or settle out as a sludge.

In the second case, sludging may occur when excess developer is carried over into the fixing bath to neutralize the acid. This sludge may also be caused when sodium bisulfite or potassium metabisulfite are substituted for acetic acid in the fixing bath. These acid salts are satisfactory for use in nonhardening acid fixing baths, but they are not suitable for use in acid fixing baths that contain alum. Sludging can also be caused by improper mixing. It is important that the acid be added after the sodium sulfite, and before the alum in the order indicated in the formula.

A more yellow-colored sludge or milkiness may be caused by insufficient sodium sulfite in the solution, which permits decomposition of the thiosulfate by the acid. This type of sludge can also be caused by an excessive amount of acid, which will counteract the correct amount of preservative leading to decomposition. Temperatures that are above about 85 F will have a tendency to sulfurize fixing baths, even though

they have the proper proportions of chemicals. Improper mixing will also cause this type of sludge.

An acid fixing bath containing acetic acid has a tendency to precipitate aluminum sulfite, or to sludge, after a certain amount of developer has been carried into it by the film or paper. This sludging is minimized by the addition of about one ounce of boric acid to each gallon of fixing solution containing potassium alum. Boric acid does not inhibit sludging in a chrome-alum fixer.

STAINING

A white stain may be caused by hypo that crystallizes out when the film is drying. Such staining is the result of insufficient washing; and it can usually be removed by further washing of the film. But, if it is not removed by further washing, it is likely that a deposit of aluminum sulfite has settled on the surface of the film. Such a stain can then be removed by soaking the film for a few minutes in a solution containing two ounces of sodium carbonate dissolved in a quart of water, after which the film should be thoroughly washed.

A yellow stain is most likely caused by finely divided or colloidal sulfur that has been precipitated in the fixing bath or in the gelatin of the film. It is due to decomposition of thiosulfate by acid in the presence of too much acid, or too little sulfite. It can also be caused by subjecting the fixing bath to a temperature higher than 85 F. Such a stain can be removed by first hardening the film in the following:

FORMALIN HARDENER

Formalin (40% formaldehyde solution)		
	1/3 ounce	10 cc
Sodium carbonate		
	92 grains	6 grams
Water to make		
	32 ounces	1 liter

To insure adequate fixation, prints should be "leafed" from the bottom of the pile in the solution to the top, for the recommended time. Failure to do this does not permit circulation of the fixer, particularly near the centers of the prints, and these areas most likely will not be adequately fixed.

Film should be left in the hardener for three minutes. After hardening, it is immersed in a ten-percent solution of sodium sulfite, at a temperature of 120 F, until the stain disappears, after which it is washed thoroughly.

A yellow or brownish-yellow stain may also be caused by insufficient fixing which leaves undissolved silver complexes that are reduced on aging.

A yellowish-green stain, or dichroic fog, can be caused by using an exhausted fixing bath or one containing insufficient acid. The stain will appear yellowish-green in reflected light, and reddish-pink by transmitted light. This is usually caused by carried-over developer continuing to reduce the silver halides in the emulsion while they are being fixed by the thiosulfate. This trouble can be prevented by using a bath that is not exhausted or neutralized by developer, by using an acid shortstop bath between developing and fixing, by rinsing the film thoroughly between developing and fixing, and by carefully agitating the film during fixing—especially during the first few minutes of immersion.

BLISTERS

The neutralization of an alkali carbonate by acid produces carbon-dioxide gas. If this reaction takes place in the emulsion layer of the film or paper, small bubbles of the

Photography during the winter months, particularly if fixing bath and wash water temperatures are low, may call for special attention to agitation in the fixer, and for extension of washing time with good agitation.

gas are apt to form within the gelatin and rupture it. This usually occurs when the film is transferred directly from the developer into an acid stop bath, or acid fixing bath without agitation, and the gelatin is excessively soft or has not had a chance to be hardened. It is less likely to occur if the temperatures of the solutions are below 75 F. Also the use of developers with large amounts of carbonate in the formula may cause the film to blister more than in a formula with low carbonate.

FIZEAU GRAVURE PROCESS

The publication in 1839 of Daguerre's process for permanently capturing a camera-obscura image on a silvered copper plate created great interest, particularly in France. One writer said, "Paris has caught the Daguerreotype fever and cameras are to be seen on the balconies of houses, on the boulevards, before the monuments, everywhere."

Daguerreotypy, as the new art was called, was limited to single original pictures, a defect which promptly gave rise to experiments on multiplication of copies, particularly on paper.

Printing from copper plates etched with acid, where the engraver's tool had cut through a resistant coating down to the metal, had been practiced since the sixteenth century. So acid etching of daguerreotype plates was attempted in the hope of getting a differential etch between the mercury and silver which made up the gradations of the picture. The results were not satisfactory because the depth of etching which could be obtained before the acid attacked the whole surface was insufficient for printing-press purposes.

In 1844, Hippolyte Fizeau, who had been responsible for the gold-toning of daguerreotypes as a means of preserving their delicate surfaces, displayed to the members of the French Academy a series of paper prints "made by transformation of a daguerreotype plate to an engraving plate without engraving or retouching by an artist." (See Figure 1.)

Fizeau's Method. Fizeau's method was quite complex. The daguerreotype plate was lightly etched with a mixture of nitric and hydrochloric acid, then treated with ammonia to remove insoluble silver chloride from the silver portion of the image. Sometimes these steps were repeated to get greater initial contrast in depth of etching. The etched plate was next coated with boiled linseed oil and the surface carefully wiped so that the oil remained only in the depressions.

Gold was then electroplated onto the clean surface and the oil removed from the depressions by caustic potash. Fizeau now had a plate which could be etched to reasonable depth with nitric acid, for the acid would attack the silver in the depressions but not the gold-plated surfaces.

The earliest examples of Fizeau's work, done in 1841-42, lack half tones and detail, but by 1843 he had overcome this fault through "graining" the plate with resin dust before the final etching. Some of Fizeau's prints from etched daguerreotype plates resemble aquatint engravings. Figure 2 is a "grained" print made by Fizeau for distribution to members of the French Academy at the close of his lecture in 1844.

Below: Figure 2. *Fizeau described his prints as made from "printing plates engraved by chemical agents without any recourse to the work of an artist." Note the spottiness resulting from the graining of the daguerreotype with resin dust. Original size, 2¾ × 3½ inches.*

FLASHLAMP CHARACTERISTICS

DR. GILBERT H. REILING
Photolamp Department, General Electric Co., Cleveland, Ohio

[To master the techniques of flash photography, the cameraman should understand the characteristics of flashlamps. In this article an expert covers flashlamp construction, time-intensity characteristics, light characteristics, color, reflectors, firing and timing, and guide numbers.]
• *Also see: Flash Photography; Lighting Sources for Color; Lighting with Multiflash.*

A WIDE VARIETY OF FLASHLAMPS are available today not only to assist

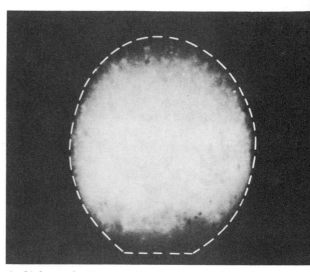

A high-speed photograph of the light from a burning photoflash lamp. (Photo: T.H. Rautenberg, Jr., and P. D. Johnson / General Electric Company)

the photographer in picture taking at night but to supplement daylight as well. Flashlamps ("flashlamp" is the term used in this article for what is commonly called "flashbulb") provide the additional light needed to correctly expose the photographic emulsion; they are particularly helpful in controlling contrast (flash-fill) and depth of field.

In most cases, five factors are responsible for the density obtained when the emulsion is exposed to light: the sensitivity of the emulsion; the efficiency of the optical system; the color of the subject; intensity and direction of the light; and the exposure time. Many of the emulsion properties, such as speed and exposure latitude, have been improved so that correct densities now can be obtained with much less exposure than was required in the past.

Since exposure is a product of light flux entering the camera and exposure time, the photographer can now employ higher shutter speeds to obtain greater sharpness in action pictures. Also, the intensity of light falling on the subject can be greatly increased, if needed, by decreasing the distance between subject and illumination source.

The illumination of the subject is nearly inversely proportional to the square of the distance from source to subject. It is the lamp-to-subject distance, not the camera-to-subject

distance, which affects the exposure. In fact it is possible to duplicate the illumination from sunlight, with much less intense illumination, if artificial sources are placed close to the subject.

Expendable flashlamps developed by lamp manufacturers provide the photographer with an intense light which is universally available, with lamps being sold wherever film is sold. Flashlamps provide an inexpensive convenient light source, easily portable and very dependable.

DEVELOPMENT OF THE FLASHLAMP

In 1930 the General Electric Company introduced in this country a photoflash lamp called the number 20 which consisted of a 260-cubic-centimeter bulb with 65 milligrams of aluminum foil in pure oxygen gas at one fourth of an atmosphere. To ignite the lamp, a small filament of tungsten was heated by electricity. This filament was covered with primer which would flash and ignite the foil. The light output from this lamp was 45,000 lumen-seconds. If these lamps were placed near one another, the heat from one lamp, when flashed, would cause the others to flash. Modern flashlamps are not so susceptible to sympathetic flashing as the older types.

Typical blue photoflash lamps. From left: AG-1B, M2B-M3B-M5B, 5, 6, 11, 22, 50.

During the decade following 1930, flashlamp size was reduced, improvements were made in the ignition, and synchronization of the peak light intensity to the camera shutter was introduced. Along with the number 20, types 10, 11, 16, 75, and several others were manufactured. In these lamps, instead of large sheets of aluminum foil, lamp manufacturers employed aluminum wire or aluminum-magnesium wire.

All these lamps operate on the same principle: A fine tungsten filament about $1/1000$ of an inch in diameter is heated by a small electric current to a temperature high enough to ignite the primer mixture on the supports at the end of the filament. The burning, flying primer then ignites the wire or foil. The radiant energy (light) emitted from the lamp is from the heat of combustion of the metal foil and oxygen which occurs when the temperature is sufficiently high. After burning, which usually lasts a fraction of a second, the deposit left on the bulb is a harmless white aluminum oxide.

After 1940 several lamp manufacturers used shredded foil instead of wire or sheet foil. Two improvements were necessary to obtain control over the metal combustion process: a more efficient lamp for emitting light, due to the additional openings in the foil; and a higher flame temperature in the bulb. About this time the number 5 photoflash lamp was marketed, marking the beginning of the miniature lamp types; the SM type lamps were introduced in 1941. The SM-type flashlamp does not use foil but obtains light from the primer paste itself. It was designed primarily for box cameras and has an unusually fast flash, $1/200$ of a second, which stops most camera or subject movement.

In 1953 General Electric marketed the M2 miniature lamp, approximately one fourth the volume of the number 5, which incorporated a pinless base. Later came the M5 and M25 flashlamps. In these lamps, zirconium foil was used for the first time. Zirconium burns with a higher flame temperature, thereby producing more light per unit volume and

Cross-section view of the AG-1 lamp.

FOIL AND OXYGEN GAS

COATING OF LACQUER

TUNGSTEN FILAMENT

PRIMER BEADS

SUPPORT BEAD

LEAK DETECTOR

OUTER ELECTRODES

0.5 INCHES

making possible the reduction of flashlamp size.

In 1958 General Electric introduced a small flashbulb of all-glass construction and called it the AG-1 lamp. As certain flashlamp types such as 7, 16, and 30 became obsolete, they were removed from the market to make room for improved lamp types.

FLASHLAMP CHARACTERISTICS

A number of radiation and time characteristics should be known to appraise the flashlamp as a photographic light source:

1. The total quantity of light emitted—that is, the average luminous flux multiplied by the time of the flash. This is given in lumen-seconds which, in turn, are related to photographic effectiveness.

2. The maximum luminous flux of radiation (peak intensity), generally measured in millions of lumens.

3. The time-intensity relationship —that is, the time from the start of the current through the filament to the start and peak of the flash.

4. The spectral distribution of the radiation.

5. The total time duration of the flash above a certain intensity. Usually this quantity is called the time duration of half-peak of the radiation. It is the time at which the light has an intensity greater than one half the peak intensity.

Obviously a close relation is needed between the time and intensity of the flashlamp and the opening and closing of the shutter. Originally the lamps were used to take pictures by opening the shutter, flashing the lamp to expose the film, and closing the shutter. This is called the open-flash technique, as the shutter of the camera is not synchronized with the flashlamp. For photographing subjects and objects not in motion, this method is satisfactory.

Normally, the photographer requires the camera shutter and flash of the lamp to be synchronized. The flashlamp has a planned time delay between the starting of the current and the peak of the flash. By general agreement between lamp manufacturers and camera manufacturers, a specific time has been established for various lamps between the start of the current flow and the peak flash of the lamp. A typical time delay is 20 milliseconds.

CONSTRUCTION OF THE LAMP

In principle a photoflash lamp is patterned after a common incandescent lamp, but instead of being able to emit continuous radiation, it is designed to produce a burst of intense light and heat. Unlike the older, open magnesium-powder systems, this light is nearly instantaneous and the subject seldom has time to respond by blinking his eyes or moving.

All flashlamps contain oxygen in quantities from less than one atmosphere (14.7 pounds per square inch) to as much as six atmospheres of pressure. Enclosed in the lamp are several milligrams of aluminum or zirconium foil shredded into one rectangular piece several inches long, less than $1/1000$ of an inch thick, and approximately $1/1000$ of an inch wide. The foil is carefully fluffed to be uniformly distributed and fill the bulb completely. Each lamp type has a specific mass of foil to obtain the light output for which it was designed.

Figure 1. *Spectrum of a typical No. 5 photoflash lamp.*

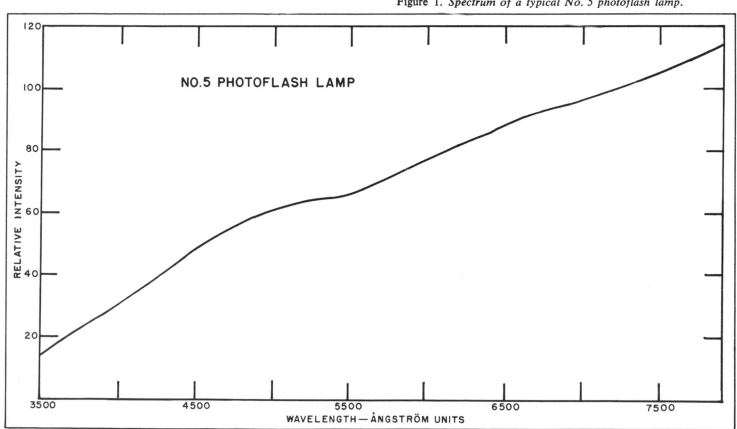

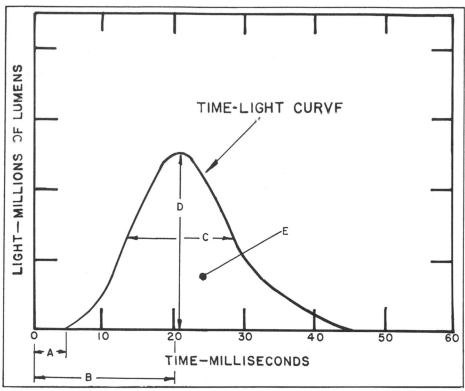

Figure 1a. *A time-intensity curve of a photoflash lamp showing: A, contact time of the camera; B, time to reach light peak; C, half width of light; D, peak light in lumens; E, total light proportional to area under the curve.*

of zirconium-metal powder and potassium-perchlorate oxidizer. The oxidizer propels the burning incandescent zirconium into the foil charge. Due to the intermittent contacts and the frequent use of weak batteries, the energy available to fire the lamp is often about $1/1000$ of a watt-second.

The manufacturer attempts to avoid stray electrostatic charges from igniting the lamp inadvertently. Nevertheless, the photographer should avoid unnecessary handling of the lamps until they are to be used, to prevent scratching the lacquer and to avoid unplanned ignition.

IGNITING THE FOIL

The incandescent ejected particles, or the flame itself from the zirconium-oxidizer paste, ignite the foil of the lamp by raising part of it to combustion temperature. The flame burns with a continuous visible radiation and fills the entire lamp. It appears that, to a large extent, the flame temperature (which is the controlling factor of light yield) is limited by the boiling point of the metal oxide formed in combustion.

This oxide is the white powder remaining after flashing. Since the radiation originates from the heat of combustion, the color of the light

Depending on the condition of the electrical source, the primer in the lamp is normally ignited in about $1/1000$ of a second after the electric current is applied. In simple cameras the current is provided by small batteries in the flashing circuit and synchronized with the camera by contacts in the shutter mechanism. The electric current flows through the lead-in wires and heats the filament which ignites the primer.

It is the position and composition of the primer paste which determines the time of ignition of the main foil. Usually primer is composed

Figure 2. *Time delay-light emission curve for a number 5 flashlamp.*

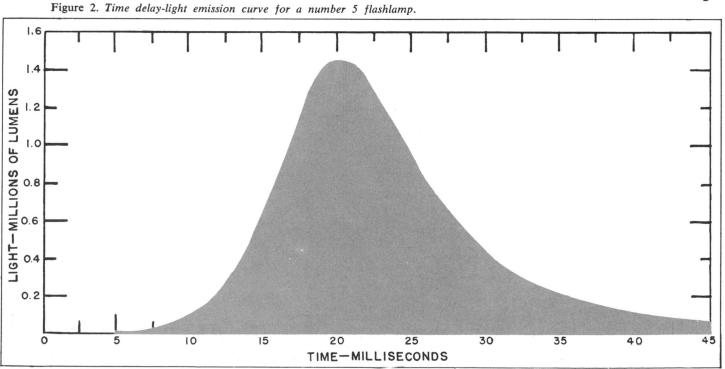

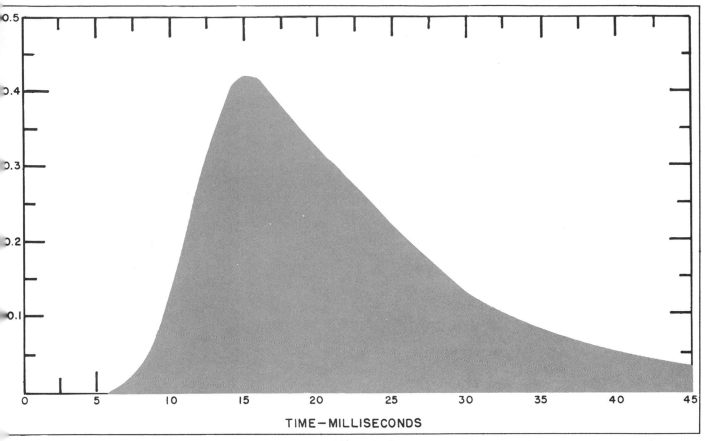

TIME—MILLISECONDS

Figure 3. *Time-intensity curve for the zirconium foil AG-1 lamp.*

changes only a few hundred degrees Kelvin throughout the flash. The highest color temperature is at the peak of light output.

Several lamp manufacturers use a cobalt salt to indicate when a lamp has leaked and admits air containing moisture. (The normally blue spot turns a pink color when exposed to moisture.) Lamps with air leaks should not be used, since they will not ignite or, if ignited, will have the improper time to peak. Occasionally a defective bulb will burst when fired because of increased pressure due to the additional air and moisture or because of cracks in the bulb. But the lacquer coating on the outside tends to prevent this bulb explosion.

Lamps are always lacquered on the outside and often on the inside to prevent bursting of the glass when struck with the flying incandescent particles. Often this lacquer will look discolored after the lamp is flashed. The phenomenon occurs after the burst of light has been substantially emitted and has no effect on the exposure time or the quality of the picture.

TIME-INTENSITY CHARACTERISTICS

A time-light curve of a flash-lamp shows the intensity at any time after the lamp is ignited. In order to understand and use the characteristics of flashlamps, it is necessary to study these curves and the nomenclature photographers use with the curve. Figure 1a. shows a typical curve. The time required for the light to start after the shutter is moved is known as the initiation time (A). From the start of the sequence, the light requires a definite time to reach the peak intensity (B), and this is known as the time-to-peak. On the ordinate of the curve, the light intensity is measured in millions of lumens; peak light in lumens is illustrated by (D). In order to know the exposure time, it is necessary to know the total lumen-seconds, represented by the area under the curve (E).

Typical time-light curves are shown in Figures 2, 3, 4, and 5. Figure 2 shows a curve representative of the number 5 lamp. Lamps are designed to operate best with shutters which are synchronized for

the particular class of lamp. Class F has a fast-narrow peak illustrated in Figure 5. Class M has a normal peak of about 20 milliseconds; lamps numbered 5 (25), M2, or AG-1 fall into this category. The S class has a slow peak, such as the number 50. Class FP, illustrated in Figure 4, is primarily for focal-plane shutters and includes number 6 flashlamps.

Certain manufacturers of simple cameras prefer a lamp which reaches peak in a short time, since it allows for an unsophisticated shutter mechanism. Manufacturers found that such a lamp would conveniently have a narrow half-width in light output. This lamp has the same physical size as the number 5 with a single contact bayonet base, but it is different from all other flashlamps in that it contains no wire or foil filling.

Light is produced when a primer paste applied to the leads and filament of the lamp is ignited in oxygen. Its electrical characteristics are similar to other lamps; however, the time-to-peak of the lamp has been made to equal the time re-

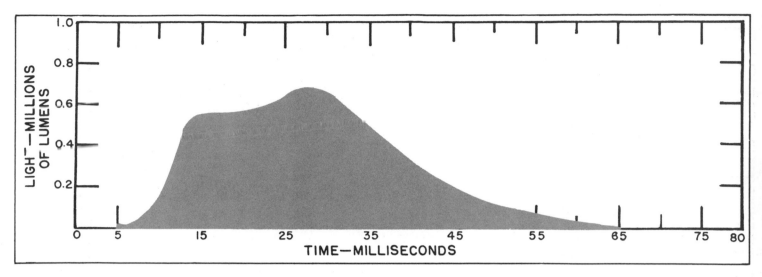

quired for the average between-the-lens shutter to open after tripping. The lamp requires only five milliseconds, instead of the usual 20 milliseconds, to reach peak intensity.

Thus if the lamp circuit is completed at the instant the shutter is tripped, the lamp reaches peak intensity at the same instant that the shutter is wide open. The light output need not be high, since it is concentrated in a few thousandths of a second. The photographic effectiveness is comparable to that of the longer duration lamps.

For example, approximately 75 percent of the total light from the SM lamp is radiated in five milliseconds in comparison to about 35 percent of the light from the number 5 lamp. Since the flash is over very quickly, the lamp itself may be used to stop motion, the stopping power being at least as good as a $1/100$ of a second shutter speed. Because of the very short duration and comparatively low output, the flash is said to be less blinding than other lamps.

A synchronizer designed for lamps peaking at 20 milliseconds cannot be used with an SM-type lamp unless adjustments are made in the unit. On several makes of cameras which do not have F settings but do have X settings (for electronic flash), the photographer can use SM bulbs by using the X setting and a speed of $1/100$ of a second or less.

FOCAL-PLANE SHUTTER LAMPS

Special lamps have been developed for use with a focal-plane shutter. Such a shutter consists of a curtain with a fixed or variable slit that moves across the focal plane of the camera just in front of the plate or film. Thus each portion of the negative material is exposed for a short time as the slit passes across the aperture.

While a given part of the emulsion may be exposed for as little as $1/1000$ of a second, the total duration of slit travel may be as long as $1/30$ of a second. As this curtain generally moves with acceleration, the last part of the plate passed over is exposed for a shorter time than the first part. Many focal-plane shutters are operated to minimize this variation in the time of the exposure of the two edges of the plate.

Since a time varying from 13 to 30 milliseconds is required for the curtain to pass across the film, the photoflash lamp should give an intensity of approximately constant value for the same period. For use with the shutter that moves with an accelerated motion, it is desirable that the intensity increase slightly during the time of the flash to compensate for the shorter exposure on the trailing part of the film frame. In addition, the lamps should reach a high intensity in a definite time

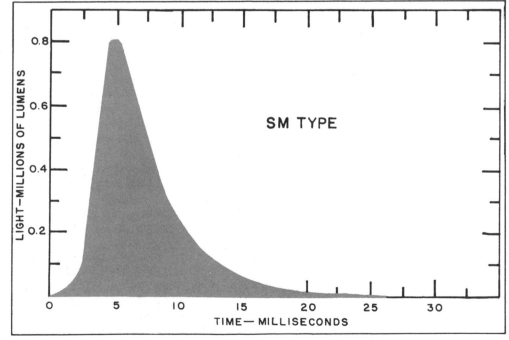

Figure 5. *Light curve for an SM-type lamp. The fast flash is for use primarily with box cameras.*

Left: Figure 4. *Time-intensity curve for a lamp designed to synchronize with small focal-plane shutter cameras.*

after ignition to make possible synchronization between the starting of the flash and starting of the curtain.

By making a lamp containing two selected sizes of shredded foil in the proper proportions, it is possible to control the time-intensity of the lamp, permitting its use with a focal-plane shutter. Figure 4 shows a curve of the number 6 lamp. Larger focal-plane cameras require the use of the number 31 lamp.

It is not always necessary to use FP lamps with focal-plane cameras. At lower shutter speeds, all flashlamps can be used with late-model 35 mm focal-plane cameras.

LIGHT CHARACTERISTICS

When a lamp is flashed, the radiation of light useful to the photographer is that which has the property of evoking a chemical change in the emulsion, that is, the actinic radiation. Since each emulsion has a different sensitivity to radiation, there was a serious question as to which physical units should be used for measuring the output of the lamp. After consultation with those

working on the measurement of the characteristics of the photoflash lamp, it was decided early in the history of photography to use the lumen, a unit of flux employed by physicists to convert radiant energy into visible energy or brightness.

Two reasons can be given for this choice. In the first place, if a photographic unit were used, it would require a new standard and it would apply only to a single emulsion, and a correction factor would have to be used for other types of emulsion. In the second place, the photographer examines his subjects and the final picture with light, that is, by visual observation. It is logical, therefore, that a unit of light be used. For these reasons, the quantity of the light radiated is given in lumen-seconds and the maximum luminous flux is given in lumens. A lumen is 0.00146 watts of radiant flux or light flow at 5500 Ångströms wavelength or its equivalent in producing a brightness sensation.

The total light output (lumen-seconds) of a lamp is significant only when the whole flash is used, as for instance, with an open flash or with shutter settings of $1/50$ of a second or longer. For high-speed

synchronization, $1/100$ of a second or less, only a portion of the light is used. Flashlamp specifications are shown in Table 1. The designation "B" refers to lamps which properly expose daylight color film (effective color temperature, 6000 Kelvin).

PHOTOFLASH-LAMP SPECTRUM

A photograph depends not only upon the intensity of light, but also upon its quality or character given by the energy distribution in the spectrum, that is, by the energy radiated at different wavelengths or in different colors. White light is composed of many colors blended together. Other colors are determined by a wavelength or a band of wavelengths. For instance, red light covers the wavelength region from 6300 to 7600 Ångström units, green light from 4900 to 5500 Ångströms.

The subjects most often photographed are opaque and therefore are seen by the light reflected from them. If an object reflects all the colors or wavelengths equally, it appears white; if it absorbs part of the light (spectrum) and reflects others, it appears the color of the reflected portion.

Since the amount of reflected light is dependent directly on the amount

Table 1. *Characteristics of photoflash lamps.*

CHARACTERISTICS OF PHOTOFLASH LAMPS

LAMP DESIGNATION	CLASS	FLASHING VOLTAGE RANGE	APPROX. TIME TO FULL PEAK (MILLISECONDS)	FLASH DURATION AT ½ PEAK (MILLISECONDS)	APPROX. LUMEN-SECONDS	APPROX. PEAK LUMENS	BASE
AG-1	M	3 TO 45	14	15	7,000	400,000	GLASS GROOVE
AG-1B	M	3 TO 45	14	15	5,500	330,000	GLASS GROOVE
M2	M	3 TO 45	14	9	7,000	700,000	MIN. NO PIN
M2B	M	3 TO 45	14	9	3,800	380,000	MIN. NO PIN
M3B	M	3 TO 45	17.5	14	8,500	530,000	MIN. NO PIN
M25B	M	3 TO 45	15	14	8,500	530,000	MIN. NO PIN
	M	3 TO 45	20	14	16,000	1,000,000	MIN. NO PIN
M5B	M	3 TO 45	20	14	8,500	530,000	MIN. NO PIN
NO. SM	F	3 TO 45	5	5	4,800	810,000	S.C. BAY.
NO. 5	M	3 TO 45	20	13	20,000	1,450,000	S.C. BAY.
NO. 5B	M	3 TO 45	20	13	9,400	680,000	S.C. BAY.
NO. 6	FP	3 TO 45	. . .	27	19,000	680,000	S.C. BAY.
NO. 6B	FB	3 TO 45	. . .	27	9,000	320,000	S.C. BAY
NO. 8	M	3 TO 45	20	10	10,000	950,000	S.C. BAY.
NO. 11	M	3 TO 45	20	13	33,000	2,000,000	MEDIUM
NO. 22	M	3 TO 125	20	14	70,000	4,200,000	MEDIUM
NO. 22B	M	3 TO 125	20	14	32,000	1,900,000	MEDIUM
NO. 31	FP	3 TO 45	. . . .	60	81,000	1,400,000	MEDIUM
NO. 50	S	3 TO 125	30	17	100,000	5,000,000	MEDIUM
NO. 50B	S	3 TO 125	30	17	43,000	2,300,000	MEDIUM

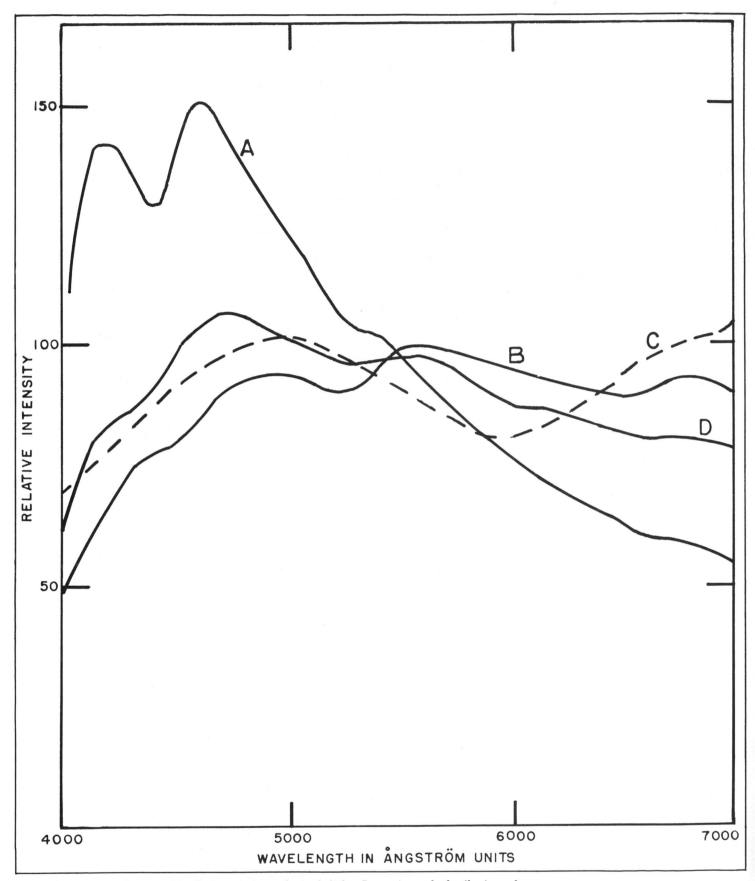

Above: Figure 6. *Distribution of energy from skylight. Curve A, north sky (horizontal plane); curve B, direct sunlight; curve C, No. 5B blue photoflash lamp; curve D, entire overcast sky.*

COLOR TEMPERATURE OF SOME PHOTOGRAPHIC SOURCES

SOURCE	COLOR °K – TEMPERATURE
DIRECT SUNLIGHT *	5,600
TOTAL OVERCAST SKY *	6,800
SUNLIGHT PLUS LIGHT FROM CLEAR SKY	6,500
CLEAR BLUE SKY	26,000
120 V, 500 WATT GENERAL SERVICE TUNGSTEN LAMP	2,960
DXK 650 WATT MOVIE FLOOD	3,400
SM PHOTOFLASH LAMP	3,300
CLEAR NO. 5 PHOTOFLASH	3,900
BLUE NO. 5 PHOTOFLASH	6,000
ECT STUDIO – 500 WATT	3,200
EBW STUDIO – 500 WATT (BLUE)	4,800

*COLOR TEMPERATURE FROM A.H. TAYLOR AND A.P. KERR
JOUR. OPT. SOC. AM., 31, 1, (1941)

Above: Table 2. *Color temperature of some photographic sources.*

received, the object has its true color only when observed by light which contains equal portions of all wavelengths of the spectrum. For instance, a mercury-vapor lamp lacks red radiation, so a red object appears black under such a lamp. Sunlight has its own spectrum which varies with the time of day. Certain photographic emulsions record radiation not visible to the eye but reflected from the subject, thus adding another factor to the quality of the final image.

Various methods are used to describe the spectral character of different light sources. One such is to plot a curve showing the intensity of radiation versus the wavelength. Figure 1 shows this kind of curve for a clear No. 5 flashlamp. Other clear (aluminum-foil-filled) flashlamps have a similar spectrum: a great amount of infrared with the peak radiation lying in the near-infrared (long-wavelength) region.

Another method is to give the color temperature of the source. The color temperature of a source is defined as the temperature at which it is necessary to operate a black-body (perfect radiator) so that the emitted light is color-matched approximately with that of the source considered. Generally color temperature is applied to the matching of visible radiation. Thus when a tungsten filament is said to have a color temperature of 3200 Kelvin, it means the light from the tungsten lamp has the same color as that from a blackbody operated at 3200 Kelvin.

The concept of color temperature is best assignable to sources of continuous radiation which have a spectral distribution not greatly different from that of a blackbody. When such sources are at the same color temperature, they have nearly the same relative spectral distribution. Color temperatures of sources often used in photography are listed in Table 2. Since the spectral distribution of the visible radiation from flashlamps is similar to that of a blackbody, the assignment of

Table 3. *Guide numbers for AG-1, AG-1B, and No. 5 photoflash lamps for front-shutter cameras.*

FRONT SHUTTER CAMERAS

CLEAR FLASHLAMPS
AG-1 WITH 2" POLISHED REFLECTOR *

WITH "M" SYNCHRONIZATION···USE ANY SHUTTER SPEED.
"X" OR "F" SYNCHRONIZATION···USE 1/30TH OR SLOWER.

TUNGSTEN FILM SPEED	16	20	25	32 40 50	64 80 100	125 160 200	250 320 400	500 640 800	1000 1250 1600
1/30 OR SLOWER	55	60	70	90	120	180	240	360	480
1/50 & 1/60	44	50	55	70	100	140	200	280	400
1/100 & 1/125	38	42	48	60	85	120	170	240	340
1/200 & 1/250	28	32	34	44	60	90	120	180	240
1/400 & 1/500	22	26	28	36	50	70	100	140	200

*FOR DIFFUSE OR FOLDING FAN REFLECTOR MULTIPLY GUIDE NO. BY .7.

BLUE FLASHLAMPS
AG-1B WITH 2" POLISHED REFLECTOR *

WITH "M" SYNCHRONIZATION···USE ANY SHUTTER SPEED
"X" OR "F" SYNCHRONIZATION···USE 1/30TH OR SLOWER

DAYLIGHT FILM SPEED	10	12	25	32	64	100	160	200
1/30 OR SLOWER	40	44	65	70	100	130	160	180
1/50 & 1/60	30	32	48	55	75	95	120	130
1/100 & 1/125	26	28	40	46	65	80	100	120
1/200 & 1/250	20	22	32	36	50	65	80	90
1/400 & 1/500	15	16	24	26	38	48	60	65

*FOR DIFFUSE OR FOLDING FAN REFLECTOR MULTIPLY GUIDE NO. BY .7.

NO. 5 - WITH 4" TO 6" POLISHED REFLECTOR

WITH "M" SYNCHRONIZATION···USE ANY SHUTTER SPEED
"X" OR "F" SYNCHRONIZATION···USE 1/30TH OR SLOWER

TUNGSTEN FILM SPEED	16	20	25	32 40 50	64 80 100	125 160 200	250 320 400	500 640 800	1000 1250 1600
1/30 OR SLOWER	110	120	130	170	240	340	480	700	950
1/50 & 1/60	95	100	120	150	200	300	420	600	850
1/100 & 1/125	80	90	100	130	180	260	360	500	750
1/200 & 1/250	70	80	90	110	160	220	320	440	600
1/400 & 1/500	55	60	70	90	120	180	240	360	480

*FOR DIFFUSE OR FOLDING FAN REFLECTOR MULTIPLY GUIDE NO. BY .7.

color temperature to the lamp has meaning.

FLASHLAMPS FOR INFRARED FILM

A study of the spectral distribution of radiation from a flashlamp shows that it is rich in infrared. The lamp may be used with infrared film and any of the standard infrared filters on either lamps, reflector, or camera lens. Also, flashlamps may be purchased which are coated with a resin that transmits principally the infrared portion of the spectrum.

Two lamp-types are available, the 5R and the 22R. Since infrared-flashlamp photographs can be made with most cameras and flash-gun attachments, there are many special uses for this branch of photography, including candid camera photographs and news photographs during wartime blackouts.

FLASHLAMPS FOR COLOR FILM

Films for color photography need light sources of a specific color temperature for true color reproduction. In general, four types of film are available from manufacturers: one balanced for daylight, one for clear flashlamps, one balanced for photoflood lamps, and one balanced for professional studio lamps. Manufacturers of color film also supply filter information to enable photographers to produce effective color temperature with the flashlamp light within the film latitude.

Many color film flashlamp combinations need no additional filters. For example, Kodachrome II daylight film requires no filter when used with blue flashlamps. While it is easy for the photographer to make good flash photographs on color film, he must be careful with his exposure calculations since color film requires a specific amount and color of light for best color rendition.

A flashlamp used to supplement daylight for taking pictures with daylight color film must radiate a bluer light (i.e., have a higher color temperature) than the regular (clear) flashlamps. This high-color temperature has been obtained by coating the lamps with a blue lacquer; flashlamp radiation with this corrective blue-lacquer filter matches the average color of skylight.

The color of skylight is dependent on the position of the sun and the condition of the atmosphere, so it is impossible to show an intensity distribution of universal skylight. Figure 6 shows the various energy distributions versus the wavelength of light in the visible region. The preferred average skylight is from an overcast sky with some north light added.

Blue lamp lacquer, Figure 7, has a transmission such that the light from the photoflash lamps is of the proper color to balance pictures with daylight-type color film. The difficulty in obtaining the proper transmission through blue lacquer lies in getting transmission of the yellow-green part of the spectrum properly balanced with that at the ends of the spectrum. A typical photoflash lamp emits a curve which, while it is not perfect, has a creditable performance. It is this relative radiation output which is referred to as a color temperature of 6000 Kelvin. Of course, blue flashlamps should not be used with indoor film, which is balanced for artificial light.

Blue-plastic flash shields are also available to cover the regular photoflash lamp. These flash shields generally do not give the finely corrected color available from blue flashlamps.

REFLECTORS

Light can be increased several times by using an efficient reflector behind the flashlamp. Since flashlamps have been decreased in size, a reflector can be made smaller and remain efficient. In general large reflectors are more efficient than small ones, but the size of the light source, the reflectivity of the reflector, and the position of the source determine the effectiveness of the reflector.

Before the advent of the miniature lamps, there were few reflectors designed to concentrate light on the subject. Wasteful and inefficient use of the radiation resulted from spreading the light over a larger angle than that viewed by the camera lens.

Since the "normal" camera lens covers an angle of not more than 70 degrees, the reflector should concentrate as much light as possible within this angle. For uniform density across the negative, however, the minimum intensity of the light must be more than half the maximum intensity falling on the picture area. Thus the reflector must direct the light from the lamp over the

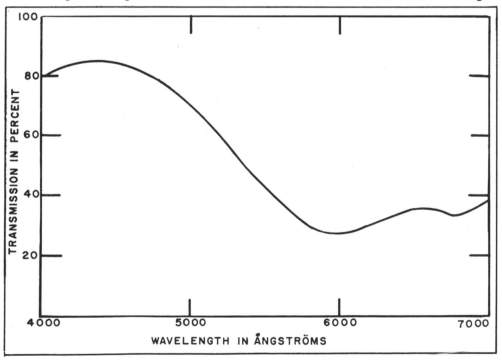

Figure 7. *Transmission in percent of visible light through the blue lacquer used on photoflash lamps.*

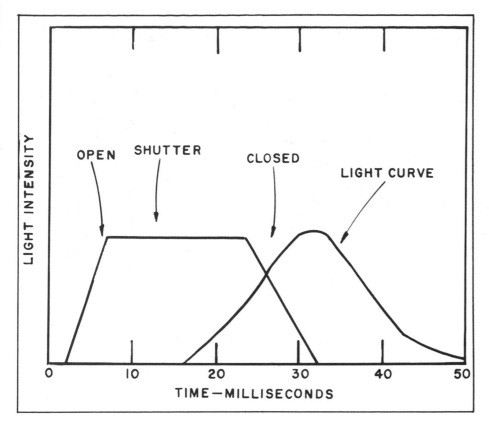

Figure 8. *Sketch showing improper synchronization of camera shutter and light radiation from flashlamp.*

increases, their internal resistance becomes larger, thus limiting the current. This deterioration is more rapid when current is being drawn from the batteries, but occurs even when they are not being used. High temperature also causes batteries to deteriorate. Even if the flash equipment is used intermittently, batteries should be changed periodically.

In 1962 General Electric introduced a new filament wire made of a tungsten-rhenium alloy. This wire has a higher than normal resistance and is more effective in igniting lamps on weakened batteries.

Unknown to the photographer, the lamp can flash but, if the synchronization is improper due to weak batteries, wrong exposure will result. Figure 8 shows a shutter open but with the light output too late (occurring while the shutter is closing), resulting in improper exposure.

Many flash guns use a battery capacitor (B-C) arrangement to flash the lamps. These units give consistent results since the energy to flash the lamp is great. Many B-C flash attachments contain a lamp to test the complete circuit when the flashlamp is in the socket.

GUIDE NUMBERS

Exposure times with photoflash lamps depend, among other things, upon the efficiency of the reflector used, and vary with the surroundings and with the density of the negatives desired. Tables 3 and 4 show guide numbers obtained by taking a great number of pictures under what were considered average conditions—in medium-sized rooms with fairly light walls and with the lamp in a standard polished reflector.

Exposure can be determined from guide numbers listed for any lamp and any film speed, by dividing the guide number by the distance from lamp to subject. First, find the guide number. This number is generally furnished with the film and with the flashlamp. Second, measure the distance of the subject from the

area covered by the lens in such a way that the variation in the intensity is less than two.

A reflector simply redirects the light from the flashlamp and, in the case of the small AG-1 lamp, a two-inch reflector diameter is quite satisfactory. These reflectors give a beam intensity of two to ten times more than an open bulb. Usually the reflectors are curved toward the source and have spherical, parabolic, or conical surfaces. An efficient collection of light and a uniform distribution of light over the picture-taking area are needed no matter what the surface configuration of the reflector. Although generally not important, the surface reflectivity of the reflector may shift the color of the light.

FIRING AND TIMING

Lamps can be flashed on batteries of from 3 to 30 volts. A few of the large flashlamps—numbers 22, 22B, 50, 50B—can be flashed on 115 volts, since they contain an internal fuse which shuts off the current before it becomes excessive.

Probably the principal cause of flash failure is weak or defective batteries. A weak battery will either burn out the filament without igniting the lamp or fail to fire it at all. Another cause of improper firing or timing is flash-gun circuit failure. Additional circuit resistance can arise from defective contacts, excessive contact bounce, or corrosion of the socket. If the camera has been idle, it is well to work the shutter a few times to clean the contacts before loading the film or the lamp.

In simple camera-flash attachments, resistance is very often due to a weak or corroded spring in the switch or battery case. If several lamps are used in series, it is well to provide a minimum of three volts per lamp, though actually the lamps require very little energy ($^1/_{1000}$ of a watt-second) to be ignited. Test lamps are available from lamp manufacturers to check both the battery and the flash-gun circuit. Normally, about 0.3 to 2.0 amperes are needed to ignite the lamp. For the best synchronization, a 2.0 ampere minimum current is recommended.

As the circuit resistance increases from zero to five ohms, the time lag in firing goes from less than a millisecond to ten milliseconds or more. As the age of batteries

FOCAL PLANE SHUTTER

AG-1 WITH 2" POLISHED REFLECTOR*

TUNGSTEN FILM SPEED	16	20	25	32 40 50	64 80 100	125 160 200	250 320 400	500 640 800	1000 1250 1600
1/30 OR SLOWER	55	60	70	90	120	180	240	360	480
1/100 & 1/125	36	40	44	55	80	110	160	220	320
1/200 & 1/250	26	28	32	40	55	80	110	160	220
1/400 & 1/500	18	20	22	28	40	55	80	110	150
1/1000 & 1/1250	12	13	15	19	26	38	55	75	100

AG-1B WITH 2" POLISHED REFLECTOR*

DAYLIGHT FILM SPEED	10	12	25	32	64	100	160	200
1/30 OR SLOWER	40	44	65	70	100	130	160	180
1/100 & 1/125	26	28	40	46	65	80	100	120
1/200 & 1/250	19	20	30	34	48	60	75	85
1/400 & 1/500	13	14	20	24	32	40	50	60
1/1000 & 1/1250	9	10	14	16	22	28	36	40

NO.6-WITH 4"TO6" POLISHED REFLECTOR*

TUNGSTEN FILM SPEED	16	20	25	32 40 50	64 80 100	125 160 200	250 320 400	500 640 800	1000 1250 1600
1/30 OR SLOWER	110	120	130	170	240	340	480	700	950
1/100 & 1/125	55	60	70	90	120	180	240	360	480
1/200 & 1/250	40	46	50	65	90	130	180	260	360
1/400 & 1/500	28	32	34	44	60	90	120	180	240
1/1000 & 1/1250	20	22	26	32	44	65	90	130	180

*FOR DIFFUSE OR FOLDING FAN REFLECTOR MULTIPLY GUIDE NO. BY .7.

Table 4. *Guide numbers for AG-1, AG-1B, and No. 6 flashlamps for use with focal-plane shutters.*

Data from film manufacturers can be used as a guide for obtaining the ideal exposure with specific equipment. When a subject is near light walls having a high reflection factor, the camera aperture usually can be closed one stop. On the other hand, if the picture is being taken in a large auditorium or outdoors where there is no reflection from walls, the aperture usually should be opened one stop. Since fan-type folding reflectors, which are not very deep in contour, may have low efficiency, it may be necessary to increase the exposure above those indicated.

The guide number can be calculated by using the total lumens (L) given by the flashlamp manufacturer, the time of exposure (t), the reflector factor (M), and the tungsten exposure index (S) of the film listed by film manufacturers. The following equation is then used:

$$G = \sqrt{.005\ LtMS}$$

Remember if the shutter speed is inaccurate, a correction factor must be made in "Lt," since the total light (in lumen-seconds) will be more or less than expected. This can be true, for instance, when using a lamp with the improper time-to-peak, or using short exposure times.

FLASH SAFETY

Since flashlamps are fragile, they should be handled with care. Lamps which have come loose from the package should be examined for cracks, since a damaged lamp may shatter when flashed. While flashlamps are safety-coated, it is recommended that a shield be used over the reflector. Never flash a lamp in an explosive atmosphere.

Lamps should be flashed only on batteries, unless the carton specifically states they are designed for 125-volt line voltage. Once in a while a defective flash gun will be found with the electrical circuit closed; thus the lamp will ignite when it is inserted in the socket. To avoid this mishap, use test lamps available from lamp manufacturers.

flashlamp. Third, divide the guide number by the distance, in feet, and the result is the *f*-stop. This guide number is associated with a given shutter speed.

$$\frac{\text{Guide Number}}{\text{Distance}} = f\text{-stop}$$

(lamp to subject)

Since these guide numbers are only guides, a photographer may make his own for his particular camera equipment. One way of doing this is to set the camera exactly ten feet from the subject. Next take pictures at various *f*-numbers, one stop apart, using specific film. After processing, pick the *f*-number which made the best photograph. Then use the following equation:

$$\text{Guide Number} = f\text{-number} \times \text{distance}$$

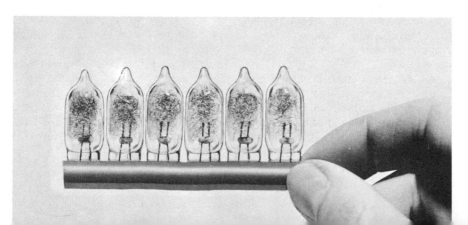

Smallest popular flashlamp, the AG-1.

CONSTRUCTION   **MICHAEL L. EDELSON**

At one time, many photographers felt that a winding road was essential to the success of any photographic landscape. Taking a fresh approach to an old idea, this picture features a "road" of men, which starts in the lower right and fluidly curves up into the upper left. By itself, this bare line could never be considered flowing. But in contrast to the sharp angles of the construction material, it acquires an element of grace. The contrast created by strong sidelighting is essential to the composition's strength.

FLASH PHOTOGRAPHY

DON MOHLER
Director of Technical Photography, General Electric Photolamp Department, Cleveland, Ohio
[Photography with flashlamps is one of the most widely used and practical methods of taking pictures. Basic techniques for using single and multiple flash are explained in this article, and open flash, bounce lighting, exposure, reflectors, cameras, and daylight flash are described.]

• *Also see: Electronic-Flash Lighting and Exposure; Flashlamp Characteristics; Lighting Sources for Color; News Photography.*

FLASH IS USED TO GET PICTURES IN any surroundings, regardless of prevailing illumination or the lack of it—to balance lighting, to give lighting direction, to gain control of illumination and exposure.

Flashbulbs are used in flash holders, flash guns, or in flash attachments equipped with a reflector. When these are fixed to the camera there is no problem of aiming the light: it points where the camera points. This serves the purpose if flash photography is used simply to make quick and easy record pictures of people, places, and events. To this end, flash on the camera is the best guarantee of a picture every time for amateurs as well as for newspaper photographers. But lighting will be monotonously flat.

How much light you get and how well it covers the scene depends on the reflector as well as on the bulb. Well-designed, good-sized, polished reflectors will concentrate eight times

Flashlamps or electronic flash often are used in studio set-ups when working with animals or children who may have to be "caught" with a fast shutter. The set-up may be arranged using photoflood bulbs to set the exposure and position the lighting. The models then may be placed in the scene after flashlamps have been substituted for the photofloods. The fast flash will catch just the right moment wanted for the photo. This soft-lighting effect was achieved with the use of two electronic-flash units. (Photo: Larry Keighley)

as much light in a forward direction as will the bare bulb without a reflector. Satin-finished and folding-fan reflectors generally give four times as much light as a bare bulb. They spread the light more, so aiming is not critical and there is enough coverage for use with lenses of moderately wide angle. Reflectors that are made quite small and shallow for portability and convenience may put only twice as much light into the picture as would a bare bulb.

There are some 30 types and sizes of flashbulbs available. Three sizes—midget, miniature, and subminiature—account for 90 percent of flash use. Two types, clear bulbs for black-and-white photography and blue bulbs for daylight color films, are available in all sizes. One type and size, best suited to the photographer's equipment, method, subject matter, and desired results, is generally selected and standardized by the amateur photographer for all work.

EQUIPMENT

Equipment too is standardized: one flash holder, one camera, one lens, one film. Complicated subject matter should not be attempted at first. Mastery of elementary flash technique depends upon standardization of all possible variables, and with this foundation variations for special purposes can be attempted later.

The basic tools for flash photography, whether with flashbulbs or with electronic flash, are: 1) Adjustable camera with built-in synchronization; 2) Flash holder; 3) Three-foot extension cord; 4) Data guides; and 5) Tripod.

Flash camera. A fully adjustable camera is essential to serious photography, with its control of focus, aperture, and shutter speed. This is as true of a camera used for flash photography as of one used for other purposes. To use flash at all shutter speeds, a synchronizer is necessary. This is usually a timing-switch mechanism built as an integral part of the camera shutter. The device sends current to the flash so that the shutter is open during the few thousandths of a second

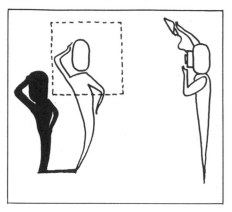

High positioning of flash throws shadow down and out of picture area.

when the flash is at full output.

For shutters at, in, or near the camera lens, this is called "M" synch. For focal-plane-shutter cameras, this is called focal-plane synch. "X" or "F" synch is limited to slow shutter speeds with flash and is usually found on simple, nonadjustable cameras.

Flash holders. The flash holder preferably should have a removable or folding reflector so that bare bulbs can be flashed to reduce the light when working very close, to weaken the forward light when not too much flash is wanted in combination with existing lighting indoors, or to gain the brilliancy of small highlights and sharply edged shadows characteristic of bare-bulb photography. Bare flashbulbs should be covered or enclosed in clear plastic as protection against the slight possibility of a weak or damaged bulb shattering when flashed. Another highly desirable feature of some flash holders is an "open-flash" button which allows bulbs to be fired manually and independently of the camera.

Extension cord. The three-foot extension cord is essential to flash control. With the flash holder connected to one end of this wire and the camera to the other, the flash can be fired at arm's length from the camera. It can be used high, low, or to the side. It can be aimed far or near, or can be directed to the floor, ceiling, or side walls for indirect, bounced-light effects.

Flash data. Exposure data for all shutter speeds, flashbulbs, and films is available from lamp manufac-

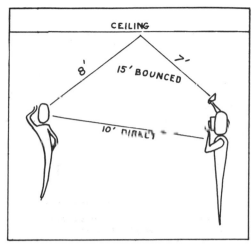

Above: *Bounce flash directed halfway between camera and subject.*

Below: *Bounce flash aimed just above the subject.*

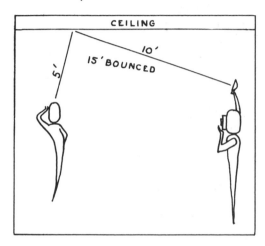

turers. Sufficient information cannot be obtained from the abbreviated data on lamp packages or from the instruction sheets packed with films. The particular information needed for any combination of camera, lamp, reflector, film, synchronization, and shutter speed can be taken from the data booklet, which is updated periodically as products change or new products are introduced.

Tripod. A tripod is essential to all serious photography. With flash it allows you to aim, frame, focus, set, and anchor the camera. The photographer then can concentrate on controlling the lighting effect and directing or watching the subject.

MALFUNCTION

Photoflash lamps ordinarily function with great reliability and uniformity. When they do not, it is a relatively simple matter to find and correct the trouble. Except in the rare case of an imperfect or damaged bulb, trouble will be due to weak batteries or poor electrical connections.

With the flash holder off the camera, check the batteries. This and all other tests can be made with a small clear filament test lamp available in sizes to fit all photoflash sockets. It should light up or give a quick blink of light on strong batteries when a bit of wire is touched across the flash holder-outlet terminals. If it does not light, check the flash holder itself for weak physical contact at the battery ends, or for corrosion. Tighten or clean the damaged part.

Next check cords and connectors. If the test lamp blinks weakly or not at all, look for loose or broken parts between flash holder and camera. Finally check the camera itself. With the flash holder connected, test lamps should light or blink when the shutter is operated.

EXPOSURE

The amount of flash light on the subject depends upon the distance between flash source and subject. At distances of seven to ten feet, small flashbulbs give illumination fully equal to direct sunlight. Since light intensity varies with the distance between light source and subject, an adjustable camera is needed so that uniform exposure can be had over a range of flash-to-subject distances.

The bedrock of elementary and advanced flash techniques is pinpoint exposure control. The constant point of reference is the exposure guide number. Five of the nine variables involved in optimum exposure are accounted for in each exposure guide number. To find the correct number in a table of guides, make cross reference to the data for the flashbulb, reflector factor, speed rating of the film, type of synchronization, and shutter speed employed.

Having located this guide number, use it to find the correct stop for all lamp-to-subject distances. For instance, if using a number M5 flashbulb, three- to six-inch polished reflector, film rated ASA 40, M synchronization, shutter speed of $1/_{200}$ of a second, the exposure guide number is 110. Dividing this by ten, for a ten-foot flash-to-subject distance, gives 11 for an indicated stop of $f/11$. By dividing the guide number by five for a five-foot distance, the stop is $f/22$. At 55 feet, $f/2$.

EXPOSURE CORRECTION

The lamp-to-subject distance becomes more and more critical as a factor in exposure the closer you get to the subject. An error of plus or minus ten inches in measuring distance at five feet lamp-to-subject distance makes a difference of a half stop in either direction. With a guide number of 110, for instance, the indicated correct opening at five feet is $f/22$; at 5.8 feet $f/19$, halfway between $f/22$ and $f/16$; at 4.1 feet $f/27$, halfway between $f/22$ and $f/32$. To put it another way, there's a spread of one full stop in the 20 inches between 4.1 feet and 5.8 feet.

Lamp-to-subject distance should be measured exactly. When the distance is less than seven feet, a tape should be used to measure it down to inches. If you use flash quite near the camera, you can measure the distance by focusing the camera sharply on the subject and reading the focusing scale.

Once the camera is set at the correct f-stop according to the guide number, three more variables—

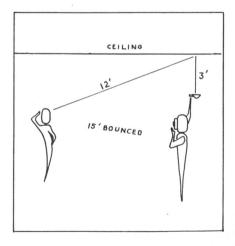

If the bounce flash is aimed directly overhead, open up the diaphragm another stop.

surroundings, subject matter, and results desired—must be taken into account in pinpoint exposure control.

In small highly reflective surroundings, such as a bathroom, as much as one half stop less exposure than is indicated by the guide would give better results. In large or dark-walled surroundings, such as an auditorium or gymnasium, or outdoors at night, a half to a full stop more than indicated exposure might be necessary. A very light subject, such as a white kitten, calls for a bit less exposure than a dark one, such as a dirty engine.

And finally exposure is varied according to the results desired. Exposure might be increased somewhat to play safe, rather than risk a too-thin negative. On the other hand, for optimum print quality and considerable enlargement, the best exposure might be the minimum that would barely capture detail in the shadow areas.

To compensate for all these on-the-scene variables, the serious photographer will bracket his exposures by making one picture at the indicated correct stop, one at a half to a full stop less, and one at a half to a full stop more. The method used depends on whether he is exposing transparency material, where small adjustments make noticeable differences, or exposing negative material, where there is some room for final adjustment when making the print.

One last correction. At flash-to-subject distances of seven feet or less, underexposure will result even though allowances have been made for all nine variables listed above. This is because the lens-to-film distance is increasing as the camera is focused closer, thus upsetting the true *f*-stop value toward the underexposed side. Also the relative amount of light reflected into the picture area by walls, ceiling, and surroundings will be less as the light source is moved close to the subject.

Rather than calculate the necessary allowance for close use, the practical answer of many working photographers is to bring the flash one foot closer to the subject than calculated. This makes a quick, reliable correction. For what nor-

This photo of the fuzzy colt would have been less effective without flash fill-in, which makes each hair of his coat stand out. Without flash, this side of the animal would have been in heavy shadow. (Photo: Zeiss Ikon)

mally would be a seven-foot shot, the flash would be used at six feet; on a five-foot shot, set the flash at four feet. If the flash is anchored on the camera, calculate the *f*-stop by adding one foot to the true flash-to-subject distance before dividing the guide number.

GUIDE, APERTURE, DISTANCE

Two thirds of the value of an exposure guide number is wasted if it is used only to determine the calculated *f*-stop at various dis-

tances. There are other uses for the relationship of guide number (G), aperture (A), and distance of flash to subject (D).

Dividing G by the largest aperture on the camera gives the maximum shooting distance, wide open. Or if a given stop is selected to control depth of field, then dividing G by this A will tell exactly what D should be for normal lighting.

Also $G = A \times D$. If a series of test pictures are flashed from the same ten-foot distance, starting at

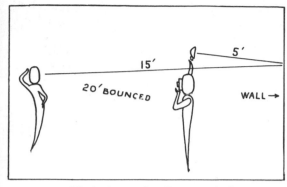

Flash bounced off a vertical surface.

one *f*-stop less than the published guide number indicates and continuing at half-stop increments up to one full stop more than the indicated aperture, the results will show the best exposure for the individual reflector, shutter action, and synchronization. Multiplying the D of ten feet by the A used on this shot gives the G best suited to the combination. If this is different from the published G, divide one by the other to get a personalized correction factor applicable to all other guide numbers.

For example, in testing a guide number of 80, suppose the best personalized exposure guide calculated by the above method was 63. (63÷80=0.78.) Multiply all other published guide numbers for bulbs of the same physical size, shutter speeds, or film speeds by 0.78 to correct them for use with that specific tested equipment.

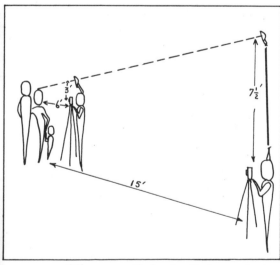

Off-camera flash should be used one half as far above camera as camera-to-subject distance.

SHADOW AND GLARE CONTROL

The best position for the flash is rarely at the camera, aimed straight ahead. A three-foot connecting cord between flash and camera unshackles the flash. The camera is operated with one hand, preferably from a tripod, the flash aimed with the other.

When taking a straight-on picture, use the flash high and to one side to throw background shadows low and to the other side. Use flash nearly touching the camera lens, and the picture will be almost shadowless. Use it low to throw the shadow high behind the subject for an unusual, sometimes grotesque, effect. With two or more people in the picture, the safest position for the flash is high, directly above the camera lens. By this method no face in the group will be shadowed by the others.

When light is directed straight at a smooth, polished surface such as glass, metal, or wood paneling, a hot spot of glare is reflected. A shift of position, placing the surface at an angle to the light, avoids reflection into the lens. Often overlooked is the glare from a clear window located behind the principal subject, or from eyeglasses. If subjects with glasses are directed to turn their heads slightly, the glare will be deflected. If they must face squarely into the camera, a flash high and to one side will eliminate the glare.

DEEP SUBJECTS

A properly aimed flash is practically the only solution to photographing scenes where objects near and far must be included, such as groups, interior views, high vertical subjects, and people seated at long tables. The light should be elevated and aimed at, or over, the far part of the scene. The center beam will light the furthest parts, while weak spilled light from the edge of the reflector will light the near parts. Exposure should be set for a point about two thirds into the scene.

If one part of a subject is much darker than another, for instance, the groom in formal black and the bride in white satin, aim the light at the groom and away from the bride.

BOUNCE LIGHT

Subject contrast can be flattened by bouncing light off reflective ceilings, side walls, back walls, or the floor. Bounced light is diffuse and nearly shadow free, but is tricky to work with.

For fast work in typical residential and office interiors, with white ceilings and light walls from which you will bounce the flash, provide two stops more exposure than for direct flash.

To pinpoint exposure, particularly for color photography, first figure the total distance the flash must

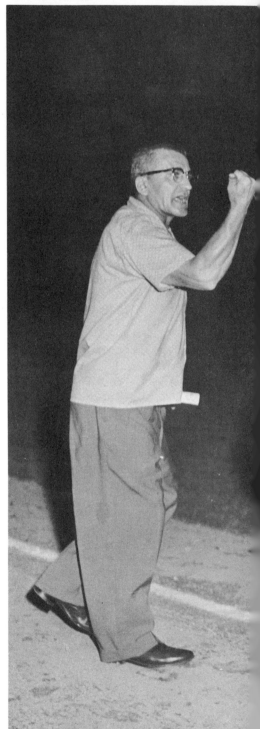

travel from its position to the ceiling surface and back to the subject. Second, divide the exposure guide number by this distance to get the basic *f*-number. Third, open up a full stop more to allow for the light absorbed by the ceiling surface. This is for a bounce flash directed halfway between camera and subject, as well as for flash aimed just above the subject. If the flash is aimed directly overhead, open up another stop.

If the flash is bounced off a vertical surface, such as the back wall or the floor, the calculation is the same—add up the distance from

Flash at night makes possible shots which otherwise would be lost. The umpire and irate baseball fan are sharply delineated by the flash, but the background is blacked out, a typical result when flash is used outside at night. (Photo: Ray Matjas / Cleveland Plain Dealer)

flash to wall to subject and allow an extra opening according to the reflectivity of the surface.

In bounce flash the light takes on the color of the surface from which it is bounced. This is of little importance in black-and-white photography, but with color, it is a problem. Only neutral bounce surfaces, white or gray, should be used unless the effect of tinted light is wanted.

The nearer the flash is to the bounce surface, the smaller the area it will illuminate. If a relatively strong directional effect is wanted, the flash is used only a few feet from the bounce surface. If aimed to illuminate the entire wall behind the camera, the wall becomes a giant, soft-light source.

FLASH FILL WITH SUNSHINE

Subjects outdoors in the sunshine may have very dark shadows, too much contrast, or may be lighted from the wrong direction. Exposure control alone cannot correct this. Synchronized flash can put extra light into the shadows while adding proportionately very little light to the sunlit areas and none to the general scene behind a foreground subject.

For most daylight pictures in the range of seven to fifteen feet, set exposure for the over-all daylight scene and simply shoot the synchronized flash from the camera at this exposure, particularly if the sun is to one side or behind the subject.

For more accurate control of the amount of flash fill, determine the proper exposure for the daylight scene alone, using an exposure meter or reference guide, and set the camera for this exposure. Then divide the exposure guide number by the aperture for which the camera is set to get the distance at which the flash must be used for normal fill.

The flash should be used as close

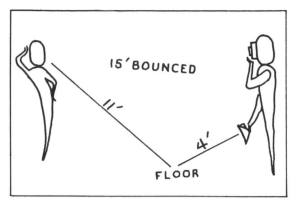

Flash bounced off the floor.

to the camera-to-subject axis as possible, preferably right at the camera. When placed at the camera position, if the flash is not close to the calculated proper flash-to-subject distance, a long connecting cord, 20 to 30 feet, allows it to be positioned near or far without moving the camera.

If the shooting distance is too close for flash at the camera, the light can be cut one stop in effectiveness by draping one thickness of a clean white handkerchief across the face of the reflector, and cut two stops by using two thicknesses.

The long connecting cord has a multitude of uses in extending elementary flash technique. On dull days flash used very high and to one side can act as a substitute for sunshine. Care must be taken to arrange the subject in front of a background, such as a wall or foliage, so that it too will be lighted by the flash. An open scene behind the flash-lighted subject on a dull day will print dull and flat, and the sunshine effect on the subject will appear unnatural.

THE FLASH CORD

The three-foot extension cord gives control over the angle, direction, and aiming of the flash. A longer extension cord allows even more shooting variety. The greater the camera-to-subject distance, the greater the need for getting flash far from the camera.

For routine subject matter it is generally desirable to have the extension flash as high above the camera as one half the camera-to-subject distance. To photograph a subject about 15 feet away, put the flash about seven and one half feet above the camera lens. To get this sort of elevation, an assistant may hold the light, or it may be fixed on a portable stand, or it may be held overhead on an extended tripod with the legs folded.

The unipod is one method of getting the flash far from the camera when assistance is not available. A tripod usually will be needed for

camera support. A six-foot unipod at the end of the photographer's three-foot arm allows him to get the flash nine feet or more from the camera.

BIG BULBS

Where large areas must be covered, as an entire stage at an indoor ceremony or an accident scene outdoors at night, the large, medium-screw base flashbulbs provide maximum light. Reference to

the exposure guide numbers will indicate how much coverage they will provide.

In lighting maximum distances, a considerable amount of foreground may be included in the scene. The flash must be elevated and aimed to the far part of the scene to prevent gross overlighting of the foreground. Or flash and camera both can be used, as from the front edge of a balcony, to photograph an entire stage 100 feet away.

To get more light for large areas, two or more bulbs may be used side by side or, if the subject is

A single flashbulb was used to make visible the myriad details of the blacksmith's shop, which was partially illuminated by sunlight streaming in the door. (Photo: Arthur Rothstein / Farm Security Administration)

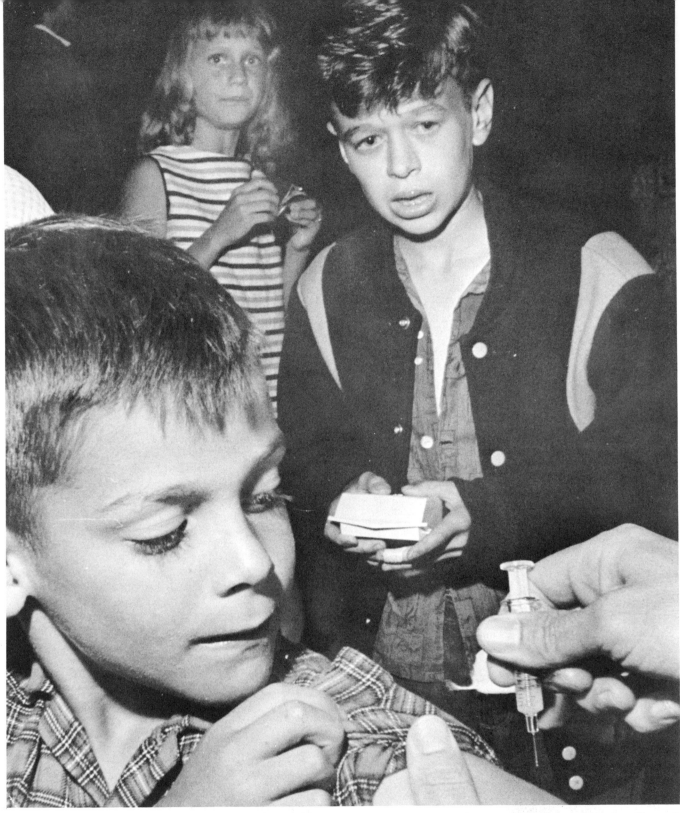

The blacking out of background when flash is used can strengthen the effect of a photo. The boy in the foreground, with the needle about to penetrate his arm, vies with the fearful faces in the background for the viewer's attention. The photo would be weakened if the background characters were sharply seen. (Photo: Thane McIntosh / San Diego Union)

static, two or more may be flashed in succession from the same position using open-flash technique. The exposure guide number for two bulbs is obtained by multiplying the one-bulb guide number by 1.4. Other factors are: three bulbs, 1.7; four bulbs, 2.0; five bulbs, 2.2; six bulbs, 2.45; seven bulbs, 2.65; eight bulbs, 2.8.

For maximum light on the subject, and to avoid any errors due to malfunction of synchronization, open flash is often used. The camera is placed on a solid support and the shutter is set for time or bulb. The shutter is opened and held open while the lamp or lamps are flashed.

WALK-AROUND FLASH

For vast interiors, caverns, architectural views, or shots outdoors

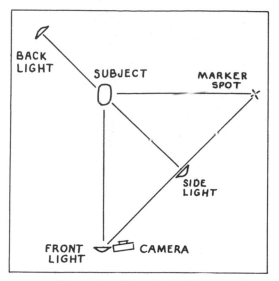

Figure 1. *Triangle lighting, a basic system for multiflash photography.*

at night, each part of the scene may be lighted separately by open-flash techniques. A basic flash-to-area-lighted distance is first established. Take this to be 20 feet, for instance. With a guide number of 160, the indicated aperture would be

$$\frac{160}{20} = 8, \ (f/8).$$

With the camera aperture at $f/8$ and the shutter open, the photographer walks into and around the scene and flashes each part of it in succession from twenty feet away until all important areas have been flashed. He returns to the camera and closes the shutter. Care must be taken with each flash to avoid standing between the camera and the area to be lighted, or the photographer will appear in silhouette in the picture.

TRIANGLE LIGHTING

Triangle lighting can give the photographer a variety of effects. Use two or three identical lamps in identical reflectors and wire all lamps together on one line from the camera-shutter synch by means of multiple-outlet connectors.

The frontlight is placed as close to the lens as possible. The distance from this lamp to the subject is measured. Then, at right angles, an equal distance is measured out to a marker spot. The sidelight is placed halfway along a line between marker spot and camera and raised somewhat.

If a backlight is used, place it diagonally opposite the sidelight and an equal distance away, also high. Be sure to shield the camera lens from backlight illumination. The set-up is shown in Figure 1.

In triangle lighting various effects are possible from the basic lamp positions: frontlight with sidelight; frontlight with backlight; sidelight with backlight. Manipulation of the sidelight from a floor-level position up to camera level, above camera, and far above camera level further increases the variety of effects. Exposure is usually based on the lamp-to-subject distance of the closest frontlight.

In multiflash photography the photographer may use the photocell-operated slave unit, which flashes its lamp with no wired connection between it and the camera lamp. It is triggered when the flash on the camera goes off.

When the lighting effect must be carefully seen and measured before photographing, particularly where a lot of light is needed for coverage, effect, contrast and control, and great depth of field, the picture is planned for large flashbulbs to be used in reflectors designed for photoflood lamps.

The scene is lighted with number 2 photoflood lamps in the reflectors. When the lighting is set, make an exposure-meter reading. The correct *f*-setting, substituting number 22 flashbulbs for the photofloods, will be found on the meter at the indicated photoflood exposure for four seconds; using 22B blue flashbulbs, the *f*-setting will be found at the photoflood exposure for two seconds; for number 50 flashbulbs, six seconds; for 50B blue flash, 2.5 seconds. Set the aperture, turn off the floods, take them out of the sockets, substitute the flashbulbs, open the camera shutter, switch on the current to the flashes, switch it off, and close the shutter.

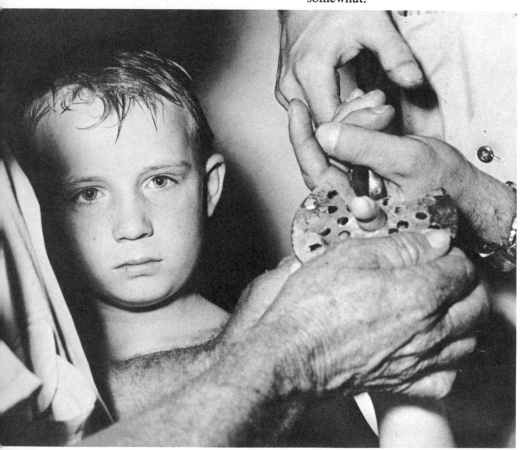

Flash used close to or attached to the camera provides a fast, easy means of operation often used by newspaper photographers. The lighting gives a flat appearance in the finished print. G. E. Arnold of The Times Picayune, *New Orleans, used electronic flash on a* Speed Graphic *with Tri-X film, 1/200 of a second at f/16.*

FLIGHT PHOTOGRAPHY

PHILIP E. DOUGLAS
Aerial Photographer, Writer
[This article explains the specialized field of aerial photography. Oblique views, air-to-air close-ups, cloud photography, and related ground photography are discussed.]
• *Also see: Aerial Photography.*

THERE ARE TWO TYPES OF AERIAL photography. The first is aerial photogrammetry, the technique of making photographs from which maps can be plotted. The second is largely pictorial, and involves taking pictures from the air of buildings, landmarks, farms, and factories, as well as photographing airplanes in flight.

EQUIPMENT

Many different cameras can be used in aerial photography. The 35 mm camera makes beautiful color slides for projection and reproduction, while larger cameras produce the bigger negatives often preferred for commercial use. Specifically, aerial cameras range from the hand-held K-20 using roll film five inches wide and making 50 pictures on a roll, to the huge mapping cameras using 200-foot rolls of film and making 9×9-inch or 9×18-inch negatives with as many as 250 on a roll.

A few cameras especially valuable to the average photographer who wishes to do aerial photography are:

The Kodak Medalist: Now obsolete, it can still be found in used-

Walter L. Richardson made the first aerial photograph for the Navy in 1914, using an early model Graflex camera. Many improvements in cameras, emulsions, and airplanes have transpired during the last 50 years since this photograph was made. (Official U.S. Navy photograph)

camera stores. The Medalist makes excellent $2\frac{1}{4} \times 3\frac{1}{4}$ negatives on standard 120 roll film. The 100mm Ektar lens originally made for this camera was of unusually high quality. Make sure the camera you buy still has this lens, as some turn up on the second-hand market with odd lenses of dubious quality.

The Aerial Camera K-20: A hand-held Air Force camera, available at reasonable cost on the surplus market. Its $6^3/_8$-inch $f/4.5$ lens was made by various manufacturers; some are excellent, others

Strong back- and sidelighting, good composition, and correct exposure combine to make this unusual photo of a plane in flight. The Boeing 720 jetliner was photographed as it passed over Puget Sound, Washington. Pictures of this type are often used for ads, travel brochures, etc. (Photo: Paul Wagner)

Press 23, the special Wide-Angle 65 camera, and the Aero Technika. All three will handle sheet-film, film-pack, roll-film and 70 mm-film cartridges. The Press 23 and Aero Technika have interchangeable lenses from 75mm to 270mm; the Wide-Angle 65 is a fixed-lens camera with a 65mm f/8 lens. None of these cameras have bellows, and all are safe to use even in the aircraft's slipstream. The Press 23 has a built-in coupled rangefinder, useful for low-level work with long lenses.

The Hasselblad: A single-lens reflex camera offering through-the-lens viewing and focusing, helical (nonbellows) lens mounts, and rapidly interchangeable magazine backs that permit changing film types in mid-roll and speedy camera reloading. Lenses available for the standard Hasselblad range from 60mm to 600mm.

The Hasselblad Superwide: A single-lens reflex camera with an angle of view of 90 degrees. It is superbly sharp and accepts the same film magazines as the standard Hasselblad. The Superwide has a 38mm lens.

The Bronica: A Japanese camera quite similar to the standard Hasselblad. There is no superwide Bronica, but a 50mm wide-angle Nikkor lens is available.

The Mamiya Press 23: A Japanese camera similar to the Linhof Press 23. It has lenses from 65mm to 150mm, a coupled range- and viewfinder, and takes sheet film, film packs, and 120 roll film in three formats: $2\frac{1}{4} \times 3\frac{1}{4}$; $2\frac{1}{4}$ square; or $2\frac{1}{4} \times 1\frac{5}{8}$ inches.

The Speed Graphic: (Figure 1). This camera works well, but can be used only in the cabin of the plane; the airplane's slipstream at 100 miles an hour will remove the bellows completely. A special version which has no bellows, the Combat Graphic, can occasionally be found on the surplus market.

SHUTTERS

The two basic shutters, the between-the-lens shutter and the focal-plane shutter, are both used on aerial cameras.

The between-the-lens shutter has

only fair. If stopped down and used with fast film, almost any of these lenses will produce good negatives.

The K-20 uses 5-inch roll film, available in 20-exposure and 50-exposure rolls, producing 4×5-inch negatives. This film is currently available from Kodak, and can also be picked up at surplus dealers. If you buy it from the latter, be sure to check one roll of each batch before accepting. A motorized processing device, available from Morse Equipment (and also from the surplus market), is practically essential to handle these long rolls of film,

though an occasional burst of six or seven pictures can be cut from the roll and developed by hand.

The F-8 Aerial Camera is hand-held, like the K-20, for high altitudes. It has interchangeable backs for sheet films in the 5×7 size, and also for rolls of 7-inch aerial film. The lens is a 15-inch, which is approximately a $2\times$ telephoto on 5×7 film.

The Linhof firm of West Germany, famous for precision large-format cameras, makes several cameras ideally suited to aerial photography. These are the Linhof speeds, usually, from one second to $1/500$ of a second, with some newer models on smaller cameras ranging to $1/800$ and $1/1200$ of a second. The larger shutters used on aerial cameras seldom go beyond $1/250$ of a second. The between-the-lens shutter exposes almost the whole negative at once, which is important in high-altitude mapping work.

But when using this comparatively slow shutter for ordinary photography, especially at low altitudes, motion vibration will blur or "smear" the negative as a whole. Here the use of the highest shutter speed available, with the lens at the required aperture for proper exposure, is necessary. Such use presupposes a good lens; a poor one may have to be stopped down a good deal demanding a slower shutter speed and resulting in blurred negatives due to motion.

With the focal-plane shutter, you can "have your cake and eat it too." Since the negative is exposed a portion at a time, vibration smear is greatly reduced. If a focal-plane shutter is set at $1/200$ of a second, the vibration smear will be less than that produced when $1/400$ of a second is used with a between-the-lens shutter. Remember this when using your Speed Graphic.

The main fault in the movable-slit focal-plane shutter is displacement of the image as the shutter cuts the focal-plane field, resulting in chimneys on opposite sides of the negative having large tilt angles. As the focal-plane slit cuts the field, the camera describes an arc in the air about the subject, the image is displaced in the focal plane proportionately, and, as the slit advances, the portion of the view now being exposed is displaced from its original position. This effect can be lessened by flying at a minimum angle to the desired view. In most cases this problem is more theoretical than actual. The focal-plane shutter of a small camera completes its travel in about $1/40$ of a second, and the aircraft won't move very far during this time. Focal-plane shutters actuated longitudinally in mapping cause a slight stretch of the actual view; a parallelogram distortion results if the shutter operates at right angles to the path of flight. For this reason mapping cameras always have between-the-lens shutters.

LENSES

The need for a high-quality lens cannot be overstressed since it contributes most to the quality of the finished picture. A camera with a fuzzy lens torments the beginning aerial photographer as he tries various apertures, shutter speeds, and film combinations in a vain effort to obtain a sharp picture.

Some of the inexpensive lenses for the Speed Graphic that may be obtained from the "used" counter are poor for aerial work. This is especially true since their aperture is opened to enable the use of a high shutter speed with fine-grain film. It is best to take any used equipment on a trial basis and accept it only after making field tests.

A common lens aberration is *coma*. Under high magnification a point on the periphery of the field is rendered as an arrow pointing toward the center. This same lens may have an area of fairly good sharpness in the center.

Another aberration is a full exposure in the center of the film with a gradual or rapid fall-off in the extreme corners of the negatives; this is called vignetting. Too small a lens hood or even filter holders on wide-angle lenses may cause vignetting. In some cases, the lens itself may be at fault.

For most work, a focal length equal to the diagonal of the negative, i.e., a normal lens, will give the best results. However, a wide-angle lens is excellent for panoramic views of the countryside or of "cloudscapes," especially with 35 mm cameras.

On the other hand, telephoto lenses are a "must" when photos of small business concerns, gas stations, marinas, and the like are needed. Because of the CAA regulations you cannot fly at altitudes low enough to fill the negative with the normal lens.

A word of caution may be inserted here. The back focus of a lens is the distance between the rear-

Figure 1. *Photographer Philip E. Douglas demonstrates how to hold a Speed Graphic camera within the cabin of a plane to avoid any damage to the bellows from the propellor's slipstream.*

lens element and the focal plane. This distance is almost equal to the focal length of the lens focused on infinity. The depth of field of the scene at various apertures is familiar to all, but the less familiar depth of *back focus* is critical; buckling of the film inside the camera can result in fuzzy zones, especially with long-focus lenses.

It is imperative to check the infinity setting of every lens and to mark it accurately. Using a magnifier to view the groundglass and focusing on a target at least 2000 feet away will give an optimum adjustment.

FILTERS

Generally, it is good practice to use the K2 yellow filter over the lens in black-and-white photography.

This filter cuts the light haze usually present on the average good day and improves contrast. Open the lens about one stop when using this filter.

The red filter (A, No. 25) cuts even more haze, but its use is limited to fast films because of its 6 to 8 X filter factor. This filter renders blue subjects and green foliage darker than the eye sees them.

In color photography, the skylight filter should always be used, even on the clearest days, to cut the excess blue always present in the atmosphere. On slightly hazy days, the Haze 1 and Haze 2 filters may be required. It is best, however, to shoot color on only the finest days, when visibility is over 15 miles. Close-ups of small subjects can be

taken with visibility down to five miles, but some experience is needed in judging when to stop.

Be careful that the use of filters does not seriously degrade the sharpness of the taking lens. Poor filters may cut the resolving power of a good lens in half. Tests should be made to determine that the filter does not degrade the lens. Focus on a test chart and view the image on the groundglass with a high power loupe or microscope.

FILM

Many excellent films are available today and the choice depends primarily on the photographer. Generally, fine-grain film, although slower, will be preferred for 35 mm cameras because of the large blow-ups required. As the camera size is increased, more grain can be tolerated and faster film used.

The drama and excitement of a mid-flight fueling are caught in this excellent photo. The aerial photographer has many opportunities to shoot extraordinary pictures from the unique vantage point of the sky. (Photo: Bill Sanders)

This ground-to air shot of a jet fighter taking off from a carrier was shot from the carrier itself. A fast shutter speed was used to freeze the action and a low angle to emphasize the upward thrust of the plane.

For color slides, Kodachrome II and Kodachrome X are excellent for small-format cameras. Ektachrome roll film or sheet film, Ektacolor sheet film, or Kodacolor roll film yield excellent pictures in the larger cameras. Check to see if your processor can double the ASA rating of Ektachrome in developing. The added speed and slightly greater contrast can be very useful.

EXPOSURE

A photoelectric exposure meter may be used fairly accurately if it is pointed away from the sun at a steep angle to the ground. For back-lighted subjects, open up one stop. A representative setting of $f/8$ at $^1/_{400}$ of a second with the yellow filter on Super XX film might always be indicated for general low-altitude work. After you have standardized your film, the settings will be the same for most front-lighted subjects.

In the winter, open up one stop, for as the sun goes south, the light value will be found to decrease. The hours during which a good photograph may be made will also diminish as the sun dips to its southernmost position.

As the altitude is increased above 5000 feet, the effective contrast of the earth decreases and the exposure may be decreased proportionately. High-altitude oblique shots, in general, are not too interesting to anyone except the photographer, and are difficult to sell.

If you want cloud pictures in color, use the settings recommended in film data sheets for sand or snow —generally a one to one and one half stop decrease from a normal ground shot in the bright sun.

DEVELOPMENT

There are as many developers available as there are films. Each has advantages and disadvantages, and it is once again up to the photographer to choose his developer on the basis of his own requirements. The following list of prepared developers may help in selecting the best for you.

Acufine combines fairly fine grain with freedom from blocking up. It lasts well in tanks and when replenished maintains its activity for up to three months of occasional processing. Develop about seven minutes at 73 F for good contrast.

Diafine developer gives twice the effective film speeds of Acufine. It is a two-solution chemical, requiring only two minutes' development in each bath. Diafine handles all films at the same developing time, and lasts indefinitely.

Microdol-X is perhaps the finest-grain developer available, but loses strength rapidly when processing

long reels of film or when stored. For aerial roll film, it may be considered a one-shot developer undiluted; it allows one stop less film speed than Acufine. However, if the lens is of excellent quality and may be opened up without loss of sharpness, Microdol-X will produce negatives capable of the largest blow-ups. Develop about 20 minutes at 75 F for optimum density and contrast.

DK-50 is a medium-grain developer of good activity and will make excellent negatives when the need for enlargement is not too great.

DK-50 is also recommended for shots taken in the winter months when more "developing power" is needed.

The larger aerial films of five to nine inches in width and up to 200 feet long may be developed on special reels manufactured by Arriflex or on the Morse B-5 motor-driven machine. A Kodak handbook entitled *Kodak Materials for Aerial Photography* contains detailed information on films and development.

AIRPLANES

The Piper Cub, virtually unchanged for years, is inexpensive to operate and its fold-down side door facilitates oblique shots. The relatively slow flying speed makes it easy to get into position and shoot just as the best view appears in the viewfinder. The vibration component is, however, high. For this reason, the photographer must be careful that no part of his body above the waist touches any part of the plane. Also the highest shutter speed possible should be used regardless of the flight altitude.

The Piper Tri-Pacer makes a good photoship. After removing its rear door, the photographer has all the room he needs for action. Once again, vibration is fairly high.

Perhaps the most stable and smoothest ships are the Cessnas. The window of these ships can be opened and the pin removed from the closing lock; with the plane slowed down and a positive angle of attack, the window will stay up against the wing without being tied.

Perhaps the best way to take pictures from the four-place Cessna is to remove the right door, turn the front seat around, and shoot through a wide angle behind the wing strut. Communication with the pilot also is easily accomplished from this position.

Helicopters make the best shooting platforms; they can be maneuvered easily in any direction until they are in exactly the right position, and can hover there almost indefinitely if it's necessary to wait for a particular bit of action, cloud placement, etc. There is, however, more vibration when hovering, and the best solution may be to "crab" slowly toward the subject. Now vibration is much less, and air speed (horizontal) may be as low as 20mph. If there is a 20-mile wind, ground speed may be brought to zero, allowing ample time for smooth photography. If possible, avoid shooting through Plexiglas. With a good safety belt, you can almost walk around on helicopters; they are a pure joy to shoot from. The newer gas-turbine aircraft have less vibration than conventional helicopters, and may prove to be *the* photoaircraft of the future.

Other airplanes may be adapted to aerial photography, but the above can be rented and used with a minimum of effort and without modifications.

Of course, if you own your own airplane you may cut holes in the bottom fabric or skin, providing this does not impair the structural integrity of the plane. Before making any modifications of this type for vertical pictures, check with your mechanic. Certain papers must be drawn up and signed before the airplane may be considered airworthy.

FLYING TECHNIQUE

A word of caution to those who are not familiar with airplanes: Never enter or alight from a plane with the propeller turning. Always fasten your seat belt before taxiing out to take-off position. You need not fear an open door if your belt is firmly locked.

When you hire the plane and pilot, you need not worry about regulations; if you direct the pilot to fly lower than minimum altitudes, he will refuse. Please understand that the pilot can lose his license because you are attempting to fill the negative with a small two-pump gas station.

In case you are going up with a friend who is a private pilot, make sure he knows the minimums—500 feet over sparsely settled land and 1000 feet above the highest obstruction in a city area. These are only the basic rules which are fully explained in copies of the *Civil Air Regulations,* available from the airport office.

The airplane should be operated in a rectangular flight pattern over the site to be photographed. The site should be approached at a 45-degree angle to the front of your subject. When the subject is best framed in the viewfinder, the shot is made. After some practice, either flying or directing the flying, you will learn to anticipate and direct the airplane to the proper point in space which allows taking the desired view. This process of planning the flight path, compensating for wind drift, angle of approach, and angle of the camera in respect to the site will come with practice; it is aided by the rectangular flight pattern.

PHOTOGRAPHIC TECHNIQUE

Frontlighting, with the sun shining directly on the subject, might at first seem the best way to shoot all

Good low-level photographs can be made with cameras using 120 film as in this photo by Franz Thorbecke. Rolleiflex camera, f/5.6, 1/500 of a second. Agfa Isopan FF.

Figure 2. *When using frontlighting for a large industrial plant good detail may be lost. Here the picture lacks a three-dimensional effect.*

air views. Real estate, where fields and wooded areas are included, will be rendered best when shot in this way. To shoot this subject backlighted would so darken the trees that the picture would be difficult to print. However, a large manufacturing plant, if shot frontlighted, will render so that it has no form at all. (Figure 2.) The same plant viewed with three fourths backlight and a one half stop increase in exposure has good separation and dramatic impact. (Figure 3.)

The truth of the old adage, "Expose for the shadows and develop for the highlights," has often been debated. It has some merit when applied to aerial photography. Take a picture of a light-colored building against a background of trees. Ex-

posing for the trees will overexpose the building so that it is poorly defined. On the other hand, exposing for the bright building will underexpose the trees and destroy shadow detail. "Pushing" the development only aggravates the condition. In this case, a compromise must be effected by stopping down one half stop from the usual full exposure and giving normal development, or exposing for the shadows and cutting development time 20 to 30 percent.

In general, use the light meter at low altitudes, pointing it down and away from the airplane. Open up one stop for backlighted subjects when dramatic results are desired. Open up one half stop for sidelighted subjects. For bright subjects stop down one half to one full stop from the general light meter reading.

AIRPLANES IN FLIGHT

Photography of airplanes in flight is one of the most fascinating facets of aerial photography. Much of what has been said already applies also to this type of photography. Cloud pictures are naturally more impressive if an airplane or even a group of airplanes is silhouetted against their background. With ever-increasing air traffic, the opportunity to catch a passing ship on its path through the air should present itself more and more often to the flight photographer. Close proximity to the ship does not matter in taking such a picture. In fact, quite often a small distant plane will enhance the effect of a gigantic cloud and the immense space of the sky.

The amateur photographer intent

on obtaining pictorial views will find this type of picture much more impressive than the detailed and somewhat dangerous close-up shot. Take care that the color of the plane does not merge with the background of the sky. Backlighted shots with the plane silhouetted against a cloud background will always produce impressive pictorial effects.

Composition should be watched carefully and an alert hand at the shutter is necessary to catch the moment when the relative positions of plane and background appear pleasing to the eye.

On prearranged flights, both ships should be flown side-by-side after approaching cautiously in parallel flight. This will afford the photographer the double advantage of being able to use a reasonable shutter speed and to take his time in placing the almost "stationary" airplane against the moving panorama of the sky background.

Naturally, there will be variations in the relative speed of the two ships. Moreover, there may be horizontal as well as vertical accelerations due to turbulence in the air. For these reasons it is advisable, in taking pictures of airplanes in flight, to use a comparatively fast shutter speed of, say, $1/200$ of a second.

Light-colored planes will always look best if pictured against a strongly filtered dark ground or sky, and dark-colored ships will stand out best against the bright background of clouds. When flying above clouds, the light reflected from the top of the cloudbank will show strongly on the lower surface of the wings, and a plane photographed from below against the deep blue

Figure 3. *The same plant as in Figure 2 is shown here with ¾ backlighting and a ½ stop increase in exposure. Note the increased detail and better separation of the buildings.* (Photo: Philip E. Douglas)

dome above will stand out in brightly lighted contrast. Similar effects can be obtained in winter at much lower altitudes when the blanket of white snow on the ground serves as a reflector illuminating the shaded undersurface of a plane's wings.

EQUIPMENT FOR AIRPLANE CLOSE-UPS

Close-up photography of airplanes in flight requires some special equipment and thorough advance planning and coordination on the part of the pilots; it may be dangerous unless practiced by well prepared and experienced cameramen and pilots. As mentioned previously, the long shot showing a relatively small image of a plane against a sky or cloud background is usually satisfactory or even desirable for all pictorial purposes. The real close-up has its value mainly in commercial use where details of the airplane itself are required.

Cameras. Any camera of the type previously suggested for flight work will also serve its purpose well in close-up flight photography. However, a direct focusing device, preferably a lens-coupled rangefinder, is essential because quick and accurate focusing is one of the most vital requirements in obtaining crisp and sharp images of the swiftly moving ships. Under ordinary circumstances, the usual shutter speed of $1/200$ of a second is adequate in this work. However, if any sort of maneuvering is necessary, such as banking the ship which is to be photographed, or if the air is turbulent, faster shutter speeds should be employed. Hence, the camera should preferably be equipped with a fast focal-plane shutter.

Again, only two types of filters, the medium-yellow and orange or light-red, are needed. In fact, the medium-yellow is usually the most satisfactory. When making pictures of this sort it is usually desirable to retain as much detail as possible

Flight photography can be attempted by anyone who flies in a plane. This shot was made by a 12-year-old passenger. Ansco All Weather Pan film in a simple camera. (Photo: Robert W. Pearson / Scholastic-Ansco Photography Awards)

in the plane's surface, haze correction in the background is secondary. A dense filter may result in loss of detail due to overcorrection.

Telephoto lens. No mention has yet been made of the use of long-focus lenses in flight photography because there is rarely a need for anything except the regular focal-length lens in photographing skyscapes. A long-focus lens would contract space unrealistically; it is usually more desirable and of greater pictorial effect when the photograph covers the greatest possible field.

However, different considerations enter into the making of close-up flight photographs of planes, where the background is only of secondary importance. Because of the aircraft's speed and the constant turbulence present in the air, it is difficult, if not impossible sometimes, for the pilots to fly close enough together to afford the cameraman a large enough image within the confines of his regular lens. Because of the lack of perspective in the air, a plane 200 or 300 feet away may look quite large to the photographer's eye. However, one brief glance through the viewfinder of his camera will convince him that it is much too small within the wide frame of his regular lens. With the help of the telephoto, he can bring his object into range without risk.

The 35 mm camera, with its interchangeable lenses, its compactness, even with telephoto attached, and its lens-coupled rangefinder, seems to be ideal for this type of work if one is willing to accept the slight disadvantage of small film size. A 35 mm with telephoto lens can be used to great advantage on occasions when flying conditions, the limited space available in the plane, the small open-window space, or the speed of action required would not have permitted the use of larger equipment.

A medium-sized telephoto should be sufficient for most practical purposes. Very long focal-length lenses, especially in conjunction with large cameras, are not only extremely difficult to handle in a plane, but present an additional difficulty in focusing the image, because the depth of field decreases with focal length and adjustments in distance settings would be necessary each time there was a slight variation in position. The longer the focal length of a lens, the faster the shutter speeds required; hence a telephoto lens used in air work should have a fairly large aperture. However, with fast panchromatic emulsions, this is not of paramount importance, and maximum apertures of $f/5.6$ or $f/6.3$ are sufficient.

It must be remembered, when using the telephoto lens, that the

background of the photograph will usually be thrown out of focus. To retain some of the detail of the background in addition to obtaining a clear picture of the foreground object, the regular camera lens is used whenever circumstances permit.

CLOSE-UP PLANNING AND PROCEDURE

Making close-up photographs of airplanes in flight begins on the ground prior to the take-off. Most of the conventional types of cabin ships are satisfactory for this work, provided the wing struts do not obstruct vision. In many instances it will be of advantage to remove the cabin door.

Background. Before taking off, the photographer should have a clear idea of the exact background for his photographs and he should discuss the flight path thoroughly with the pilots of both ships. Choice of location depends on the type of photograph desired, on weather, and on the terrain near the airport. If it is to be a real close-up, background does not matter so much because it will show merely as a washed-out blur. The more satisfactory and more impressive shot, however, is the one showing a large image of the plane as well as some striking, well-defined background, such as a bank of clouds, the skyline, a mountain range, or seashore.

The color of the ship should be considered in making a choice of background. Whenever possible, the shading of the background should be in contrast with that of the airplane. If there are broken or scattered clouds in the sky, it is generally advisable to choose these for the background. There is nothing more impressive in flight photography than the picture of a plane against its natural element—the sky. The skillful worker will place the light-colored ship so it will be superimposed on the dark background of blue sky, and he will wait until a bright cloud fills the space behind a dark plane.

The choice of background when shooting toward the ground will depend principally on the location. Almost any terrain will furnish a suitable background if properly handled, but it is best to keep away

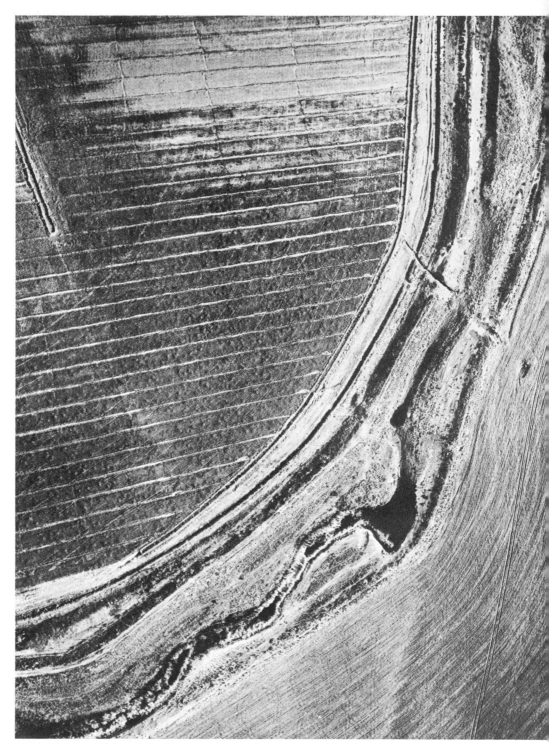

An infinite number of earth patterns can be photographed by those who are interested in getting something of special pictorial value. (Photo: Ralph Samuels)

from places that are broken up into many small patches of black, white, and gray, such as the dwellings of a town or small fields. Instead, be on the lookout for large dark or light patches of woods, farmland, or water which will detract the least from your principal object, the plane. Perhaps you can manage to include a well-known landmark, such as a bridge, a mountain peak, or the skyline of a city—perhaps a river, a lake, the seashore, or the criss-cross runways of an airport. As long as they are not dominating and their outlines do not occupy the space immediately behind the plane, these will all be good.

DIRECTION OF FLIGHT

When background has been chosen and the necessary altitude determined, the cameraman should thoroughly discuss the course of the flight with both pilots. To save time and trouble in getting both ships together over the chosen location, both ships should fly in formation from the take-off, if possible. The pilot of the camera ship should be instructed to fly a straight and steady course. All further maneuvering should be left to the ship which is to be photographed, and should be directed by prearranged hand signals given by the cameraman. In this manner there will be the least chance of both ships coming accidentally too close together. If the planes are flown by competent pilots, the ship to be photographed can, by means of hand signals, be directed to almost any desired spot in the sky and "held" there while the picture or even a number of pictures are taken.

Whenever it is necessary to fly over the same course two or three times, the other ship should follow the camera ship on the entire circuit. Not only will much time be saved, but also additional opportunities for striking shots may offer themselves when the other ship is coming around in a bank and is flying with the sun lighting it from the back. In the late afternoon when the sun is low, it may even be possible to direct the other plane into a position where it will cover the direct rays of the sun and where the picture will show the outline of the plane silhouetted against the sun.

There is no rule determining whether pictures of airplanes in flight should be taken from the front or the rear, or from above or below. Often the design of the plane will determine the angle. The best rule to follow is: Make the first shot while the ship is still behind and below at about a ¾ angle. Follow by another picture when both ships are side-by-side, and then signal the ship being photographed to fly slightly ahead for a three-quarter rear view. A similar series should then be taken in the same positions, but from below.

Problems of exposure. Exposure should be determined by the color and light-reflecting characteristics of the plane. An exposure meter would be of little help because it would react to the light of the background rather than to the ship. However, for general guidance and if judiciously applied, a meter reading may be taken on the ground before the take-off. Use a part of the fuselage exposed to bright sunlight.

Light-colored planes will look best in the air and will show most detail. Metal-surfaced ships are often difficult to photograph. While they may appear bright to the eye, their surface reflects a great amount of blue coming from the sky above. The blue will appear dark in the picture, due to the use of a blue-absorbing filter. The shade of the plane may blend with the grayish shade of the background of sky or blue haze.

When photographing metal ships, the cameraman should be on the lookout for those strong highlights often reflected from the round surfaces of wing or fuselage. Back-lighting will often produce such highlights around the contour of the ship. When planning to photograph a metal airplane, it may be advisable to wait for a sunless day with a bright overcast and to photograph the ship against darkened ground. This is one of the few instances in flight photography where sunlight is not preferred. By taking the picture without a filter, one will be able to retain the original bright metal surface of the plane in the final print.

PHOTOGRAPHING AIRPLANES ON THE GROUND

When photographing a plane on the ground, try to avoid the common mistake of shooting it from eye level. The wings will show little or not at all if photographed at eye level from the side. Get down on your stomach and try a low-angle shot. The result will be a dramatic picture of wings reaching up into their natural environment.

Photographs of planes on the ground without background or activity usually look like pages taken from a catalog. A plane is a symbol of power, of fast action, of adven-ture and excitement. Try to incorporate some of this feeling in your picture when photographing a plane, even if it is stationary. Get people climbing in or out, or sitting in the cockpit. Show them spinning the prop, checking the engine, or pushing the ship.

Try to get the powerful sweep of the nose of the fuselage pointing up against the sky, and catch the play of reflected light on the fast-moving disk of a metal prop. To do this, use a slow exposure. A fast shutter speed will practically stop the propeller in its tracks. A slow speed, however, will permit it to whirl around once, twice, or several times in the interval, and the whole disk of bright light will record on the picture.

PHOTOGRAPHING AIRPLANES FROM THE GROUND

Catching the picture of an airplane in flight from the ground is often quite difficult. First of all, fast shutter speeds are always required because of the high relative speed of the plane compared with the stationary camera on the ground. Furthermore, the plane will usually be too far away to show up in the picture.

A cameraman will seldom be permitted to operate from the airport runway where he could get close to the planes on their take-offs and landings. His activities will practically always be restricted to the field boundaries. His only remedy is to ascertain wind direction from the windsock. Since planes will always make their landings and take-offs into the wind, he can then take up a position at either end of the runway in use and catch them while they are flying comparatively low, either coming in or going out.

A telephoto lens, of course, will be very helpful in obtaining flight pictures from the ground. However, remember that a very fast shutter speed should be used with the long-focus lens. Swinging the camera along with a fast-moving plane is good practice even at the risk of completely blurring the background. Often the blurred background will enhance the effect of fast motion in the picture.